PSYCHOLOGICAL ISSUES

VOL. X, No. 3   MONOGRAPH 39

A HISTORY OF AGGRESSION IN FREUD

by

PAUL E. STEPANSKY

INTERNATIONAL UNIVERSITIES PRESS, INC.
315 Fifth Avenue   •   New York, N.Y. 10016

Library of Congress Cataloging in Publication Data

Stepansky, Paul E
    A history of aggression in Freud.

    (Psychological issues ; v. 10, no. 3 : Monograph ; 39)
    Bibliography: p.
    Includes index.

    1. Aggressiveness (Psychology) 2. Psychoanalysis.
3. Freud, Sigmund, 1856-1939. I. Title. II. Series.
[DNLM: 1. Aggression. 2. Psychoanalysis—History.
W1 PS572 v. 10 no. 3 / [WZ100 F889SU]
BF575.A3S76   152.5'2   76-53907
ISBN 0-8236-2326-2
ISBN 0-8236-2325-4 pbk.

Manufactured in the United States of America

PSYCHOLOGICAL ISSUES

HERBERT J. SCHLESINGER, *Editor*

Editorial Board

To my parents and Deane

CONTENTS

ACKNOWLEDGMENTS

Grateful acknowledgment is made to the following publishers for permission to use material from:

The Standard Edition of the Complete Psychological Works of Sigmund Freud, revised and edited by James Strachey, Sigmund Freud Copyrights Ltd., The Institute of Psycho-Analysis, and The Hogarth Press.

The Life and Work of Sigmund Freud, Volumes 1, 2, and 3, by Ernest Jones, M.D., © 1953 by Ernest Jones, Basic Books, Inc., Publishers, New York.

The Interpretation of Dreams by Sigmund Freud, translated from the German and edited by James Strachey, published in the United States by Basic Books, Inc., by arrangement with George Allen & Unwin Ltd. and The Hogarth Press, Ltd.

Studies on Hysteria, by Joseph Breuer and Sigmund Freud, translated and edited by James Strachey in collaboration with Anna Freud, assisted by Alix Strachey and Alan Tyson, published in the United States by Basic Books, Inc., by arrangement with The Hogarth Press, Ltd.

Three Essays on the Theory of Sexuality, by Sigmund Freud, translated and revised by James Strachey, © 1962 Sigmund Freud Copyrights Ltd., Basic Books, Inc., Publishers, New York.

Collected Papers, by Sigmund Freud, Volumes 1, 3, and 4, edited by Ernest Jones, M.D., authorized translation under the supervision of Joan Riviere, published by Basic Books, Inc., by arrangement with The Hogarth Press Ltd. and The Institute of Psycho-Analysis, London.

Beyond the Pleasure Principle, by Sigmund Freud, published by W. W. Norton, Inc.

FOREWORD

For analysts and analysands alike, the threat of the return to repression hangs over primitive aggression at least as much as it does over primitive sexuality, for the proposition that each of us is unconsciously and inevitably murderer and murdered has emerged as one of Freud's greatest and most disturbing guides to psychoanalytic interpretation. Freud also showed how primitive destructiveness takes abiding oral, anal, and phallic forms, and how defensive measures of various sorts are used both to cope with this destructiveness and, through distortion of every kind, to evolve individual accounts of aggression in the world that are consciously tolerable.

Taking into consideration the common lack of clarity about just who we are and just who those around us are—a lack that expresses all the uses and consequences of incorporative and projective fantasies—analysts must deal continuously with bewildering mergings of villain and victim in the experience of one and the same person. To understand oneself and to change, one must come to grips with this realm of horror and confusion.

For theoretical purposes, it is perhaps less important (it may even be meaningless) to try to establish whether aggression is primary or secondary, endogenous or reactive, and more important to recognize that once a person may be regarded as an agent, once he or she is old enough to be regarded as psychologically born, that person cannot be adequately understood psychoanalytically unless aggression occupies a central place in the interpretations that are put forward. The danger is of underestimating, rather than overestimating, the importance of the aggressive factor.

1

The analyst's conception and estimation of aggression, which surely influence his or her work profoundly, have an intertwined life history only part of which is represented by the period of professional training, practice, and institutional role definition. Much of that history is bound to lie in the analyst's early formative years and to be only partly modified by later education and experience. One does not theorize about aggression—or sex—altogether disinterestedly, and one has every reason to expect this generalization to apply to Freud as much as it does to anyone else. But just how does it apply to Freud? In the interest of securing our hold on aggression as one of the majestic life themes, the question of Freud's troubled relations with the theory of aggression is well worth pursuing, and its being pursued in this number of *Psychological Issues* is therefore to be welcomed.

In this monograph, Mr. Stepansky sets for himself two challenging (and interrelated) goals, and in the attempt he adds something valuable to the critical history of psychoanalytic ideas. One goal is to present the evolution of Freud's metapsychology of aggression and to do so with an eye to the systematic and logical problems of the several developmental phases of this theory. The other goal is to establish a psychohistorical interpretation of this theory's evolution, which is to say, a psychoanalytically conceived account of the role of historical, professional, and personal factors in shaping the problematic way Freud dealt with aggression metapsychologically.

On the side of the history and interpretation of theory, Mr. Stepansky works within the tradition represented by, among others, Edward Bibring, Heinz Hartmann, Ernst Kris, David Rapaport, and more recently, Paul Ricouer. On the side of Freud's psychobiography, the present work falls within the tradition represented by Ernest Jones, Erik Erikson, Max Schur, and others. In addition to his close reading of Freud, the author draws on a wide range of expository and critical sources, one byproduct of which is that his extensive, even if incomplete, bibliography has a value of its own. Deserving of special mention are the treatment of aggression in Freud's theory of jokes and the account of the controversy with Alfred

Adler over the place of an aggressive drive in psychoanalytic theory.

It is to be expected that so ambitious a project will arouse controversy with respect to both the sifting of evidence and the conclusions drawn. But we live now in a productive era of interpretations of Freud's system, of Freud the man, and of the relation between the two, and controversy being the life force of interpretation, we must be indebted to the author for his thoughtful and scholarly execution of the project.

To mention in this connection two reservations of this reader: (1) The author develops a complex case for attributing to Freud a persistent, personally, and professionally defensive need to avoid postulating a primary aggressive drive, and he presents as the final manifestation of Freud's defensiveness Freud's poorly argued, logically inconsistent introduction of the "death instinct"—the vitalist conception of an urge inherent in organic matter to return to an original inorganic state. One may question, however, whether the theoretical analysis and the historical-biographical analysis on which this conclusion is based are sufficiently comprehensive to warrant the author's insistent emphasis on this one factor. In view of Freud's continuing and central emphasis on destructiveness toward the self and others, acknowledged by Mr. Stepansky, can it be correct to conclude that Freud was *that* defensive in this regard or that it was exactly *that*—primitive, if not primary, aggression—that he was being defensive about? (2) The author attributes to the postulation of the death instinct a dominant influence on all of Freud's subsequent theorizing about aggression, e.g., in *The Ego and the Id*. That this postulation was consequential cannot be doubted, but that Freud gave up that much theoretical freedom while he developed his structural theory is open to question, his Thana-tos-laden essays on culture notwithstanding. Although one might therefore consider Mr. Stepansky overzealous at times in developing his theses, one may apply the correctives of further reading, rereading, and reflection, and end up with an enhanced comprehension of Freud, the theory of aggression, and the enduring problems of metapsychology.

A final word of praise is due the author. This impressive monograph is the result of his labors as an undergraduate at Princeton University! It is to be hoped that Mr. Stepansky will continue his searching study of Freud and psychoanalysis, for psychoanalytic psychology will surely be the better for it.

Roy Schafer, Ph.D.

PREFACE

Three years after Freud's death, the distinguished American analyst Karl Menninger forcefully summarized what he perceived to be the emergent direction of psychoanalytic thought. "There is everything to make us believe," he wrote in *Love Against Hate*, "that man's chief fears are not of the immensity of the universe but of the malignity of his own aggressive instincts" (Menninger, 1942, p. 190). The "dynamic processes in psychoanalytic therapy," on the other hand, sought to ensure that the individual's aggressions were "well invested," and in this respect pointed toward "the establishment of a situation in which the aggressions which have failed of sublimation are redirected" (Menninger, 1942, p. 131). Eight years later, Frieda Fromm-Reichmann echoed Menninger's clinical priorities in the advice she offered to a new generation of psychotherapists. In her influential *Principles of Intensive Psychotherapy* (1950), she observed that

> At the turn of the century, when Freud discovered and began to teach the concept of repression, it appeared that sexual fantasies and experiences were the main entities and phenomena which had to be barred from awareness and to be resolved by interpretation. At the present time feelings of hostility, antagonism, and malevolence between any two individuals seem to be more subject to disapproval in our Western culture, therefore to more repression, than any other unacceptable brand of human experience and behavior. Could this perhaps be due to an attempt to counterbalance the generally accepted manifestations of hostility between cultured peoples of our time, as manifested in the growing extent and cruelty of waging war? [p. 83].

Had Freud been alive, his response to these suggestive generalizations would have been interesting. Juxtaposed with his enduring commitment to sexual etiology as the sole motive power in pathogenesis would have been the devastating finality of his last cultural critique, one premised on man's constitutional inability to defuse the deflected legacy of a biological death instinct: aggression, hostility, self-destruction.

Unfortunately, historians of psychoanalysis have generally failed to explore systematically the theoretical and clinical presuppositions from which Freud's reply would have issued. Despite the overriding concern with the aggressive ramifications of a death instinct to which he ultimately had recourse, Freud has not been systematically treated as an aggression theorist, and his ultimate inference of a biological death instinct has not been organically linked to the historical development of aggression in his thought. Indeed, though Freud dwells on the etiological significance of "sexual aggression" as early as 1896 and postulates a non-phase-specific cruelty impulse by 1905, the mistaken contention that it was only the impetus of World War I which forcefully "turned" his attention to the importance of repressed aggression remains common (Thompson, 1950, pp. 46-47; Fromm, 1973, p. 439). It is this basic misperception that this work seeks to dispel.

This study was originally formulated and drafted during 1972-1973 as a Senior Thesis for the Department of History at Princeton University and was the recipient in June, 1973, of Princeton University's Walter Phelps Hall Prize in European History. I wish to acknowledge gratefully the initial encouragement and support provided by my advisor, Professor Jerrold Seigel. A versatile and broad-minded historian of ideas, Professor Seigel saw fit to let me formulate a problem area in the internal history of psychoanalysis as a topic in European intellectual history, monitored the evolution of the thesis, and provided helpful critical advice all along the way. Dr. Peter Hesbacher, Department of Psychiatry, University of Pennsylvania, was another initial source of supportive interest for the study, and I remain appreciative for our many discussions on the significance and scope of the project as a whole.

In revising the manuscript for publication, I have had the benefit of the valuable methodological criticisms of Dr. Roy Schafer, Department of Mental Hygiene, Yale University. Lastly, I would like to thank my wife for her considerable editorial assistance in revising the manuscript, and my very able and conscientious typist, Mrs. Judith Augusta, for producing a clean final draft.

For intellectual support during the drafting and redrafting of this study, I am grateful for the indulgent ears and steadying words of two special friends—Todd Sitomer and Jeffrey Merrick. My greatest intellectual and personal debt, in this project as in so many other things, however, belongs to my father, William Stepansky, whose own search for excellence in medical theory and practice remains my foremost model and source of inspiration. My wife Deane knows how deep and inexpressible my gratitude is to her. Her involvement in this work is as great as mine, and I am confident that without the heartfelt conviction and indomitable spirit she imparted to my efforts, I would not have been able to return to the study after an interval of three years and revise it for inclusion in this distinguished monograph series.

Paul E. Stepansky

1

THANATOS AND AGGRESSION: THE STRAINED LINKAGE

More than 50 years after the publication of *Beyond the Pleasure Principle,* the death instinct has assumed a position of deathlike repose. Despite the provocative, indeed heroic, efforts of the meta-Freudians to rescue Thanatos from therapeutic oblivion and make of it the living embodiment of religious and social aspirations (Marcuse, 1955; Brown, 1959), Pratt's (1958) "Epilegomena" to Freudian instinct theory has been written—and its verdict is convincing. Norman Brown notwithstanding, the technical arguments which propelled Freud from successive dualities to his final hypothesis of life and death instincts are neither "logically coherent" nor "strongly based on empirical data" (Brown, 1959, p. 81). Instead, as John Pratt (1958) has brilliantly argued, Freud's specious construction of the Eros-Thanatos duality in 1919 involved recourse to a dated theoretical biology dominated by the now obsolete vitalist-mechanist controversy. *Beyond the Pleasure Principle* is clearly dominated by the then current vitalist conception, and the Eros-Thanatos theory which emerges is consequently nonempirical and vitalist, i.e., metaphysical-transcendental.

Freud's supposition in this work is that life cannot be explained by any mere summation of mechanical elements, and in view of its directive and purposive character, necessitates the postulation of a special factor, entelechy, or vital force. This position, Pratt observes, "is nowadays regarded as contrary to the accepted nature and function of scientific concepts and theory, insofar as anthropomorphic concepts such as 'force' or 'power' or 'purpose' are useful only as operational concepts within a theoretical system ... and are not to be taken as primary 'explanations.' " The implication of this development on the scientific status of psychoanalytic instinct theory becomes immediately apparent. Pratt (1958) continues,

> Now in the earlier phases of instinct theory the Freudian enlargement of the conception of sexuality was made on the basis of clinical observations relating to both neuroses and perversions, as well as to normal states, and the genetic hypotheses could be verified by the study of child development. But having made such an enlargement once, it was perhaps very tempting to go still further, to equate the libido with the 'life instinct' of the vitalists. Now the postulation of such a quantitatively variable force, the libido, is entirely justified on the basis of operational empiricism. But the equation of this hypothetical sexual force with the life instinct of the vitalists unfortunately means that, at this point, the Freudian instinct theory removes itself from the field of scientific explanations, as these are at present understood [p. 19].

Even far more sympathetic explicators like Bernfeld and Feitelberg (1931) have been anxious to divorce any coincidental convergences between *Beyond the Pleasure Principle* and modern theoretical biology from Freud's deductions for a psychoanalytic instinct theory. Even if Freud's death instinct were a special case of the entropy principle for the organic system, they submit, and even if the pleasure principle could be understood as a special psychological case of entropy, the life and death instincts tied to entropy would not be "instincts" in the narrow sense of the word, but principles or natural forces that describe the general behavior of systems. These in turn would characterize not the forces within the personality but the general condition of living substance, and the "death instinct" denoting this condition could not meaningfully be characterized as an "instinct" (pp. 61, 78). Thus, even while contending that narcissistic-destructive and object-libidinal behavior in fact represent two different routes by which the individual can reach equilibrium, the authors explicitly dissociate the sexual and destructive instincts from entropy from the standpoint of psychoanalytic explanation:

> Though the instincts may be characterized generally as being directed towards gratification, and this may in fact mean the

restoration of a state of repose or equilibrium, and though we may even identify this equilibrium of 'release from tension' with a physical equilibrium—nevertheless, all this is merely a quite general proposition inadequate for the characterization of an instinct or its differentiation from other instincts. The gratification aimed at (even if it were in the physicist's view an increase in the entropy of the system) is in every instance a qualitatively determined situation, which has become historic and has certain conditioning factors which are extradynamic. From the point of view of dynamics there is no sense in considering it except in its *quantitative* aspect. The qualitative and historic factors must be considered from other points of view [p. 77].

In fact, this lonesome attempt of Bernfeld and Feitelberg to equate the death instinct with the entropy principle in even general systemic terms was convincingly discredited from the standpoint of physical theory as soon as it was written (Kapp, 1931; Penrose, 1931). By now, it has become quite clear that Freud's effort to recognize in the attempt of the psychic apparatus to keep the quantity of excitations as low as possible "a special case under Fechner's principle of the 'tendency towards stability'" (Freud, 1920, p. 9) mistakenly appropriated the physics of closed systems to explain a phenomenon of life which could occur only in open systems. Here von Bertalanffy's (1950) theoretical work on open systems remains conclusive, and Freud's fundamental scientific error has been restated and elucidated by several commentators (Szasz, 1952, pp. 26-28; Holt, 1965, p. 144; Fromm, 1973, pp. 476-478). In a comparable way, modern theoretical biology has dismissed Haeckel's biogenetic law which Freud appropriated to illustrate the repetition compulsion as an "outworn theory"— speculative, logically inconsistent, and misleading; in pointing to the theory of migration as a dramatic demonstration of the repetition compulsion of species, Freud indulged in a naïve anthropomorphizing that erroneously treats the species as though it were a single individual. Scientifically, this ranks with such dated anachronisms as "racial memory" and "collective unconscious" (Pratt, 1958).

The properly psychoanalytic reasons for adducing a repetition compulsion have proved to be no more impressive. For most analysts, the contention that certain repetitive features of behavior involve unpleasurable states of mind which cannot be subsumed by the pleasure principle was satisfactorily refuted by the counterarguments Freud offered at the time: "unpleasure" for one system invariably corresponds to "pleasure" for another (Pratt, 1958).[1] This is immediately clear with reference to the posttraumatic dreams Freud considered the most valid psychological contradiction to the pleasure-unpleasure principle. As Schur (1972) has argued, clinical observations that contradict those available to Freud indicate that the repetition of traumatic events in dreams does indeed represent the ego's unconscious wish to undo the traumatic situation: "The resulting anxiety is an ego response to danger, no different from the outcome of other anxiety-producing dreams, in which the wish represents a forbidden instinctual (sexual and/or aggressive) demand. The other examples Freud cited to support his hypotheses can be explained along similar lines" (p. 326).

Clinically, Kubie (1939) long ago effectively questioned the ability to distinguish the repetitiveness of the repetition compulsion from those repetitions that are common to all neurotic phenomena:

> The mere fact that a certain pattern recurs repeatedly is no evidence that this is a result of a *compulsion to repeat* as distinguished from the compulsion which leads to the act itself. *A priori* one has a right to say only that the cravings which motivate this behaviour have not been satiated and that, therefore, they continue to make demands; and furthermore, that the conscious and unconscious forces which determine the form in which gratification is sought are inflexible. This, however, is of the very essence of all neurotic manifestation— whereas, on the contrary, it is one of the essential characteristics of normal behaviour that it should be flexible and variable [p. 397].

For Kubie, also, the fact that all instinctual demands are recurrent, together with the observation that neurotic substi-

<hr/>

[1] Cf. Ricoeur (1970, p. 283): "By skirting the reader's resistances and prudently laying siege, Freud lines up facts that could indeed be explained by the pleasure principle but which could also be explained in some other way. Strangely enough, Freud decisively undermines the dominance of the pleasure principle at the very moment he says it might adequately explain the facts."

tutive gratifications never really gratify, clearly puts the repetitiveness of all neurotic phenomena within the jurisdiction of the pleasure principle. Neurotic patterns which are characterized as manifestations of the repetition compulsion invariably prove "to have been one[s] that served the largest amount of neurotic demands, or which gave the patient the greatest temporary relief from tension" (1939, p. 400).

Even those psychoanalysts in general sympathy with the repetition compulsion see it only as a delimited clinical phenomenon significant apart from any alleged relation to "primal instincts." Repetition compulsion can be viewed simply as a special case of the general phenomenon of the repetition of unconscious desires, repetition "with decreased intervals and decreased variability of intervals" (Toman, 1956, p. 350). Indeed, Freud's own link between repetition compulsion and the death instinct and his designation of repetition compulsion as a regulative principle of the mental apparatus "beyond the pleasure principle" has been taken as a great "stumbling block" to understanding adequately the repetitive "passive instinctive behaviour patterns" subsumed under this concept (Schur, 1960, p. 285). On the other hand, following Loewald (1971), psychoanalytic repetition can be taken to subsume not only such passive reproductive forms, but active "recreative" potentials that earmark the very process of therapeutic change.

Even Bibring, who seizes the repetition compulsion as an important articulation of "fixation" to unpleasant experiences, acknowledges the blatant incongruities that characterized Freud's initial formulation of the concept. In adducing support for his life and death instincts, Freud used the concept only as a restitutive, tension-discharging ego function, not as "the expression of the 'inertia' of living matter, of the conservative trend to maintain and repeat intensive experiences" (Bibring, 1943, p. 487). The life instincts, for example, are characterized by the tendency to bring together the "dispersed fragments of living substance." If the repetition compulsion is taken literally as a tendency seeking to undo the traumatic impression through repeated reproduction of the traumatic event, the life instincts should try to undo the splitting of living substance into particles by reproducing this traumatic event. Similarly, instead of positing an assumed tendency of the death instinct to effect a return to a prior inorganic condition, an instinctual repetition compulsion should compel them to repeat the creation of life—the traumatic loss of inorganic existence (Bibring, 1943, pp. 487-488).

I.

Although the deduction of a death instinct is problematic, the clinical concerns which prompted this metabiological speculation are real enough. "The clinical basis of the new Freudian theory," Fenichel wrote in 1945, "is the existence of aggression" (p. 58), and although the death instinct itself has been largely reduced to a philosophical problem "based on Freud's original commitment to a mythology of primeval instincts" (Erikson, 1950, p. 68), the "aggressive drives" that Thanatos seeks to rationalize continue to grow in clinical and theoretical importance.[2] As Bibring (1934) has convincingly argued, it was research into the clinical nature of sadomasochistic phenomena that initially compelled Freud to consider the possibility of a "primary destructiveness." Between 1915 and 1920, it became increasingly clear that "aggressive trends" were present that lacked any sexual characteristics and operated outside the field of all self-preservative functions. In particular, the presence of masochistic manifestations, self-destructive melancholic depressions, and superego-generated self-punishment proved resistant to interpretation as a biologically warranted "aggressiveness" of the ego instincts. Insofar as the ego could be routinely observed defending itself *against* aggressive trends, Freud was forced to consider the possibility of an instinctual trend with a directively self-destructive effect. It was in this clinical setting that Freud

---

[2] See, for example, the valuable essay of Karpman (1950). Among recent literature, the most noteworthy contributions include the books by Fromm (1973) and Rochlin (1973), and the whole series of papers contributed to the 27th International Psycho-Analytical Congress, Vienna, 1971, and published in Volume 52 of *The International Journal of Psycho-Analysis.*

formulated the theory of primal instincts. Unable from the standpoint of his far-reaching biological presuppositions to comply fully with the classificatory criteria set forth in the new instinct theory, Freud was able to fall back on his clinical material on sadism as the primary derived material that illustrated the basis of the new classificatory procedure (Bernfeld, 1935, p. 132).

Thus, once Thanatos had been biologically inferred, Freud could refer to sadomasochistic phenomena as the central piece of clinical evidence verifying his hypothetical construction. In its capacity to "make itself independent" as a perversion, sadism emerged as the primary external manifestation of Thanatos:

> But how can the sadistic instinct, whose aim it is to injure the object, be derived from Eros, the preserver of life? Is it not plausible to suppose that this sadism is in fact a death instinct which, under the influence of the narcissistic libido, has been forced away from the ego and has consequently only emerged in relation to the object? It now enters the service of the sexual function [1920, p. 54].

In *The Ego and the Id,* Freud grants the facility with which instinctual impulses can be traced back to Eros and contends that "ultimately" it is only these "sadistic constituents which have attached themselves to Eros," that point to the necessity of retaining the "fundamental dualistic point of view" (1923a, p. 46).

Serious problems remain, however. Even if the speculative biological construct presented in *Beyond the Pleasure Principle* is accepted at face value, it is not clear that the death instinct actually provides a theoretical basis for the clinical problems of "primary destructiveness." Indeed, it is highly questionable that any clinical implications at all can be posited from a biological death instinct.

II.

Despite the careless reductionism that has long equated "death" with "destruction," Freud himself clearly perceived the persistent tension between the hypothetically deduced death instinct and the daughter "aggressive" instinct, which he came to consider its "derivative" and "main representative" (1930, p. 122). In several important later works, however, Freud actively sought to blur this distinction by borrowing the intuitive appeal of "aggressive" instincts to *justify* the existence of the death instinct. In the thirty-second New Introductory Lecture, he did not even wish to bore his audience with his newly discovered "novelty" in the theory of instincts: ". . . it too is based essentially on biological considerations." Rather, he presented his hypothesis as a "ready-made product" consisting of "two essentially different classes of instincts: the sexual instincts, understood in the widest sense—Eros, if you prefer that name—and the aggressive instincts, whose aim is destruction" (1933a, p. 103). Presented in this intuitive light, Freud contended that his hypothesis could "scarcely" be regarded as a novelty; that it paralleled the commonplace opposition between loving and hating; and that to consider the formulation of the death instinct as innovative was, in itself, "remarkable." Only after he had presented such an appealing and comprehensible sketch of the "aggressive" instinct could Freud proceed to outline the theoretical groundwork lying behind Thanatos.

Again, in *Civilization and Its Discontents,* Freud hurriedly sketched the theoretical conclusions reached in *Beyond the Pleasure Principle,* but proceeded to justify his allegiance to the resulting death instinct by maintaining that "the inclination to aggression is an original, self-subsisting instinctual disposition in man. . ." (1930, p. 122).

Freud's important theoretical work, *The Ego and the Id,* though somewhat more problematic and ambivalent on the relationship of death to aggression, still retained the basic commitment to tie Thanatos to the aggressive impulses of everyday life. Freud hedged only in guaranteeing the *total* expression of the death instinct through externally directed destruction. That all destructive behavior must emanate from Thanatos, however, is left unchallenged:

> It appears that, as a result of the combination of unicellular organisms into multicellular forms of life, the death instinct of

the single cell can successfully be neutralized and the destructive impulses be diverted on to the external world through the instrumentality of a special organ. This special organ would seem to be the muscular apparatus; and the death instinct would thus seem to express itself—though probably only in part—as an instinct of destruction directed against the external world and other organisms [1923a, p. 41].

Indeed, in this work Freud took an additional step in confirming the instinctual primacy of "destructive behavior." Noting that the polarity between love and hate paralleled the opposition between his two classes of instincts, and noting the facile interchangeability of love and hate in human relationships, Freud derived from the pool of desexualized libido "a displaceable energy, which, neutral in itself, can be added to a qualitatively differentiated erotic or destructive impulse, and augment its total cathexis" (1923a, p. 44). In this way, Freud was able to veer away from the supposition of a direct transformation of hate into love, which would have been incompatible with his qualitative distinction between the two classes of instincts. For our purposes, the formulation becomes important because it skirts the biological derivation of aggression and treats externally directed destruction as a primary impulse to which desexualized libido can in fact become attached. As such, destruction becomes more than the imperfect displacement of an internal death instinct. Rather than being viewed as a mere manifestation of Thanatos, destructive behavior has become identified with it *in toto,* and thus becomes a primary impulse in its own right.

By the time of his concluding résumé, *An Outline of Psycho-Analysis,* Freud had inconsistently reversed the causal chain. Thus, in 1938, his "two basic instincts" had formally become *"Eros* and *the destructive instinct,"* with Thanatos itself introduced as a mere derivative: "In the case of the destructive instincts, we may suppose that its final aim is to lead what is living into an inorganic state. For this reason we also call it the *death instinct"* (1940, p. 148).

In all of these works, Freud's semantic pragmatism obscures the metabiological basis of the death instinct: in his attempt to communicate convincingly the "reasonableness" of his final instinct theory, he interchangeably uses the terms "death" and "aggression/destruction," contending that the "energy of the death instinct" and the clinically observable "aggressive instincts" are functionally identical. In terms of the biological analysis in *Beyond the Pleasure Principle,* however, it remains clear that aggressive behavior lacks any theoretical claim to "primary impulse" status. Recognizing Freud's semantic inconsistency as such, it is only through identification that externally displaced aggression can borrow the primal impetus of Thanatos. It is the success of this identification that requires further examination within the framework of Freud's own internal persuppositions.

III.

To Freud, the death instinct is ultimately forced to serve the purposes of Eros (1933a, p. 107). Thus, in being diverted towards the external world, Thanatos "comes to light" as an instinct of aggressiveness and destructiveness. In this way, Freud (1930) wrote, "the instinct itself could be pressed into the service of Eros, in that the organism was destroying some other thing, whether animate or inanimate, instead of destroying its own self" (p. 119).

The crucial problem rests in the supposition that Thanatos can be turned outwards *as* aggressiveness. Simply put, the theoretical rationale behind the death instinct does not elevate "aggression" to the status of primal mover. Aggression can at best describe, and only in a highly metaphorical sense, the means employed to achieve the goal of the death instinct: the total elimination of tension (Freud, 1920, pp. 34-43).

In the theoretical exposé of *Beyond the Pleasure Principle* (1920), the organic impetus underlying a death instinct or death impulse must be distinguished from an actual death "wish." The actual instinct, to Freud, consists of *"an urge inherent in organic life to restore an earlier state of things"* which the living entity has been obliged to abandon under the pressure of external disturbing forces" (p. 36). Thanatos, then, is really nothing more than the urge to eliminate tension through the restoration of an abandoned, tensionless past. Death, as such, merely represents one link in the chain of regression toward the consummate removal of stimulation. Insofar as it is the final "stage," death comes to represent an end point, the logical culmination of an organic process. There can be no desire to die apart from the desire to eliminate tension and "The death instinct is destructiveness not for its own sake, but for the relief of tension" (Marcuse, 1955, p. 27).

In freely translating Thanatos into an impulse to destroy, Freud failed to perceive it as an instinct whose motive power is a function of the organic end point to which it is attached. "Death" represents a goal-directed end point, not a directionless release of aggressive energies. Freud never intimates that the *process* of death (dying) is in itself "instinctual." Indeed, at the time of *Beyond the Pleasure Principle,* this directional requisite implicit in the death instinct embodied an "essentially new concept of instinct." Instead of being defined in terms of "origin" or "organic function," the life and death instincts contained in the last metapsychology evolve "in terms of a determining force which gives the life processes a definite 'direction' [*Richtung*], in terms of 'life-principles' " (Marcuse, 1955, p. 25). To attribute an instinctual rationale to a displaced process of destroying, i.e., the display of aggression, consequently becomes incongruous. In *Beyond the Pleasure Principle,* man does not destroy for the sake of destruction. He wishes only to return.

Given the directional requisite of the death instinct, cannot the aggressive instincts function to relieve the same "tension" that Thanatos is concerned with eliminating? The answer is no, and revolves around another unresolvable dichotomy between the tension "relieved" by external aggression and the tension that Thanatos seeks to undo. By defining the tension to be eliminated by Thanatos as a phylogenetic, developmental, and — before all else — organic, phenomenon, Freud actually made it oblivious to externally displaced aggression.

External aggression functions momentarily to relieve recurrent accumulations of tension, not organically to undo tension. It hence derives from the premetaphysical and empirically justifiable 1915 notion of instinct in which the somatic source of an instinct is susceptible to an aim of satisfaction "which can only be obtained by removing the state of stimulation at the source of the instinct" (Freud, 1915a, p. 122). With Thanatos, however, the "state of stimulation" cannot be momentarily "abolished," but must be organically undone. The external *displacement* of this kind of internally generated biological tension thus appears to be a psychological impossibility. Freud (1920) realized that the complete satisfaction of the repressed Thanatos would have to consist of "the repetition of a primary experience of satisfaction," and that consequently, "No substitutive or reactive formations and no sublimations will suffice to remove the repressed instinct's persisting tension . . ." (p. 42).

Indeed, Freud must be given full credit for having theoretically deduced that "The backward path that leads to complete satisfaction" of Thanatos "is as a rule obstructed by the resistances which maintain the repressions" (1920, p. 42). Unable to achieve the final "regressive" satisfaction, the individual organism was forced to advance in the only direction in which growth was free—forward. In conceptualizing Thanatos as an inverted growth process, we recognize it once more as a basically *directional* impetus.

By translating the death instinct into external aggression, contemporary analysts subtly betray the fundamental directional mandate of Freud, for insofar as an aggressive instinct is "inherent," it is devoid of inherent direction; it would be the act, not the consequence, of aggressive behavior that constitutes release. This clearly runs counter to the inner logic of *Beyond the Pleasure Principle*. Tension is eliminated not through an *act* of aggression/destruction, but through organic regression. Insofar as the tension is organic, it cannot permit momentary external displacement. Because a directionless act of aggression cannot appease a biological tension, Thanatos is not served by aggressive behavior. Rather, Thanatos strives only to regress beyond life and attain a prior mode of nonexistence. The fact that such an inconceivable transformation would seem to us to necessitate a "destruction" of the existing organic mode is merely literary extrapolation.

"Destruction" can still exist only as an inductive and hypothetical "means" apart from an instinctual impulse of regression to quiescence. It is this presumption that paves the way for Freud's important conclusion that "no substitutive or reactive formations and no sublimations" can remove Thanatos' "persisting tension." The death instinct can be appeased only by some *permanent* dissolution of tension, inasmuch as its end point involves a permanent and irreversible regression. The "removal" of tension must consequently be distinguished from the momentary "relief" of tension. Insofar as externally directed aggression "relieves" tension, it can only pertain to the narrower psychophysiological tension generated by the intermittent pressure of "somatic demands upon the mental apparatus." Once Freud begins talking about a vitalist "instinct" with transcendent, nonempirical goals, this mode of "relief" becomes an impossibility. Thanatos does not seek to "relieve" biological pressures of periodic intensity; it seeks to undo a piece of irreversible biological development. This verdict, recently restated by Fromm (1973, p. 453), was first spelled out with sufficient clarity by Bernfeld and Feitelberg (1931) in the one important study that actually sought to make a case for the death instinct from the standpoint of the status of the entropy principle in theoretical biology:

> But in psycho-analytical discussion it is just the instinct of destruction which constitutes the real difficulty. In *Beyond the Pleasure Principle* Freud recognizes as the pleasure principle within the ego the death instinct of biological speculation . . . Since then, however, it has become increasingly clear that he is seeking to identify the death instinct with the instinct of destruction, and in his terminology the two are interchangeable. The question is whether it is justifiable so to identify them even from the dynamic-economic standpoint. We shall show that this is not so unless the death instinct which Freud identifies with the instinct of destruction has already acquired a meaning other than that attaching to the term in *Beyond the Pleasure Principle*, where it is regarded as a special case of the stability principle. His writings of recent years do not lead to any final decision on the point. But it is noteworthy that he accepts the death instinct (or instinct of destruction) as a psychological fact — a dynamic, and no longer an economic, fact. He does not

attempt to describe it in terms of biological theory, nor does he link it up with the stability principle. He views it as a counterpart to the sexual instinct, but not in relation to the pleasure principle [pp. 74-75].

IV.

Clinicians have generally remained unbothered by the problematic mechanics by which an "out-turned death instinct" becomes therapeutically accessible "aggression."[3] Charles Brenner is right: most analysts accept the theory of drives formulated in *Beyond the Pleasure Principle* simply by accepting the clinical *utility* of viewing instinctual manifestations as admixtures of sexual and aggressive drives (1957, pp. 22-23).

Within the last two decades only the meta-Freudians, it seems, have been at least sensitive to the inherent questions of internal logic involved in deriving "aggression" from Thanatos. Convinced that in his final instinct theory Freud actually infers some sort of dialectical unity between life and death at the organic level which separates into conflicting opposites only at the "neurotic" human level, Norman Brown (1959) sees the hypothesis of the death instinct, "which has been received with horror as the acme of pessimism," as "the only way out of the really pessimistic hypothesis of an innate aggressive instinct": "Freud never saw that the hypothesis that aggression is extroverted death opened up the possibility of a solution to the problem of aggression. To the end of his life he continued to speak of innate aggressiveness and the destructive instinct as if these were the same as a death instinct" (p. 99).

---

[3] "We feel that at least a part of the considerations, on which Freud bases his speculation in his monograph 'Beyond the Pleasure Principle' refer to questions to be discussed and probably to be decided within biology proper, possibly with the help of experimental biologists.... Assumptions concerning the existence of drives toward life or death at present facilitate neither the 'fitting together' of existent propositions, nor the formulation of new ones, at least if one limits oneself, as we do, to hypotheses that can now or in the foreseeable future be checked against empirical evidence, against data of clinical observation, developmental studies, or experimentation in normal or abnormal psychology" (Hartmann, Kris, and Loewenstein, 1949, pp. 10-11).

Instead of reducing aggression to a fusion of life and death instincts (as Freud himself did), the final instinctual hypothesis actually suggests that it is only man's repressed flight from death that necessitates the extroversion of the death instinct into an aggressive principle of negativity. For Brown, once man passes beyond repression, accepting the fact of dying as the final ascent to individuality which embodies "the nature of the species," the death instinct will no longer operate malignantly (1959, pp. 106-107). Analogously, Marcuse (1955) submits that under nonrepressive social conditions, sexuality will grow into Eros, and pleasure principle and Nirvana principle will converge. Moreover, since the Nirvana principle tends toward that state of "constant gratification" where all tension is absent, "This trend of the instinct implies that its *destructive* manifestations would be minimized as it approached such a state" (p. 214). However, while Brown sees the elimination of aggression in a nonrepressive acceptance of biological death, Marcuse (1955) sees the nonrepressive order as one in which a strengthened Eros will absorb the objective of the death instinct itself:

> As suffering and want recede, the Nirvana principle may become reconciled with the reality principle. The unconscious attraction that draws the instincts back to an 'earlier state' would be effectively counteracted by the desirability of the attained state of life. The 'conservative nature' of the instincts would come to rest in a fulfilled present. Death would cease to be an instinctual goal. It remains a fact, perhaps even an ultimate necessity—but a necessity against which the unrepressed energy of mankind will protest, against which it will wage its greatest struggle [p. 215].

Such constructions, however provocative, seem to miss the basic point that the biological death instinct really provides no basis for instinctual destructiveness, and consequently tell us less about Thanatos and aggression than the individual *Weltanschauung* which presupposes the viability of a death instinct and then proceeds to reconcile it with the utopian vision.

In the present study, we take the strained linkage between Thanatos and aggression as a more delimited problem in the history of psychoanalysis which must be probed in terms of Freud's own *Weltanschauung.* "Psychoanalysis," he wrote in 1932, "is incapable of creating a *Weltanschauung* of its own. It does not need one; it is part of science and can adhere to the scientific *Weltanschauung*" (1933a, p. 181). Given this fact, why did Freud ultimately choose to organize an accumulating body of empirical data about clinically observable aggressive impulses within the speculative, vitalist garb of a death instinct? Why, in other words, was the Eros-Thanatos theory needed to establish the idea of aggression/destruction as second partner in the pragmatically successful dual drive theory? As Fenichel (1935) has pointed out, the clinical facts correctly perceived by Freud around this time merely denoted

> that primitive instinctual life has a powerful destructive coloring; that this coloring is maintained throughout the "vicissitude of turning against the ego," and is reinforced in every libidinal regression. The clinical facts do not, however, posit anything concerning the genesis of this coloring. They say nothing about this destructiveness having been originally directed against the own ego, nor about its being of a different quality from a second, also-existing, contrary instinct [p. 369].

Pratt (1958) has actually argued that if only Freud had anticipated himself by even a year or two and introduced the structural hypothesis, the libido-aggression dual drive theory "could well have been established without the obscure and devious bypath of *Beyond the Pleasure Principle.*" "Increased clinical knowledge," he adds, "would, in any case, have led to the same result in empirical theory, and ... prior to Eros-Thanatos, the natural prospective development of instinct theory was pointed in this direction anyway" (pp. 17, 22).

The issue involves more than the scientific and clinical *necessity* of the Eros-Thanatos construction, however. Even if the faulty biological premise is uncritically accepted, there appear to be insurmountable problems to the contention that an organic death instinct can satisfactorily account for innately *gratifying* "aggressive tendencies." The impulse to regress biologically as formulated through the repetition compulsion cannot be served by the kind of momentary release entailed in aggressive behavior.

The dubious scientific status of the death instinct and the problematic nature of its transmutation into an aggressive instinct earmark it as a significant problem area in the development of Freud's thought. In what way is the death instinct organically connected to Freud's previous comprehension of aggressive and destructive drives? To what extent does the biological speculation in *Beyond the Pleasure Principle* represent a clean break from the development of instinct theory, one generated by both the social and psychological situation in which Freud found himself in 1919? These are the important questions to which a history of aggression in Freud's thought may rightly address itself.

2

ON PASSIVE SEDUCTIONS
AND PRECOCIOUS DESIRE:
THE ETIOLOGY OF OBSESSIONAL
NEUROSIS AND FREUD'S EARLIEST
THEORY OF "AGGRESSION"

Bristling with indignation over the allegedly Viennese character of sexual repression, Freud's truant protégé C. G. Jung would offer in 1932 an early attempt to assess the Master "in his historical setting." The problematic nature of this enterprise was immediately apparent. "It is always a delicate and dangerous task," he wrote, "to place a living man in historical perspective" (1932, p. 33). Analogously, there are real difficulties involved in tracing a "living" therapeutic concept to the distant and delimited clinical conditions which marked its earliest usage. This is particularly true of a heuristic concept like aggression, whose limited meaning within a historically determined system of psychopathology is thoroughly intertwined with the ethical and sociological ramifications of its expression in the present social environment. Within the body of Freud's early work, moreover, aggression is hardly perceived as a self-contained clinical problem area. It functions, instead, as a descriptive and socially intuitive presupposition involved in the explication of different categories of mental phenomena. The "history of aggression" is consequently a history of different conceptual layers of usage corresponding to the independent clinical contexts in which it becomes operative as an explanatory tool.

Unlike the relatively late incorporation of aggression within a formulated theory of the instincts, the first "explanatory" layer of aggression in Freud's works is deceptively remote, antedating both the discovery of "death wishes" in dream life and the isolation of an "aggressive" sexual impulse. Indeed, the organic history of aggression actually begins precisely where the very possibility of a "psychoanalysis" is therapeutically conceived: in the clinical facts of hysteria and obsessional neurosis. In his attempt to locate the causes of these two prototypical psychoanalytic disorders, Freud was operating on the basis of certain implicit assumptions about "aggression." This chapter will reveal those assumptions. Because the earliest role of aggression evolves clinically, the historical significance and interpretive ramifications of this "role" become apparent only after reviewing the course of Freud's confrontation with the two categories of disturbance which initially occupied him.

I.

It was the perplexing treatment of Frl. Anna O., Breuer's "classical case of hysteria," that provoked Freud's clinical interest as early as the fall of 1882. During his 1885 stay in Paris it was Charcot's "revolutionary views on the subject of hysteria" that most significantly impressed him and generated the conflict with his senior colleagues, notably with his former teacher Theodor Meynert, that ensued upon his return to Vienna (Jones, 1953, pp. 226-232). Most essentially, however, it was with reference solely to "hysterical phenomena" that Freud first located a "psychical mechanism" entailing "defense," a discovery that was initially little more than clinical supposition.

Freud had opened his private practice in the summer of 1886 and by December, 1887, had turned to the therapeutic use of hypnotic suggestion, a technique with which he had gained ample experience in Charcot's clinic. By the spring of 1889, hypnosis was used not simply to offer therapeutic suggestions, but, more importantly, to employ Breuer's "cathartic method" by which patients were induced to trace each hysterical symptom back to its inception (Jones, 1953, pp. 235-240). Freud quickly discovered, however, that not all hysterics were either amenable or susceptible to hypnosis. In an attempt to bypass this therapeutic roadblock, he urged patients to trace their symptom history in a fully conscious state; he met an initial inability to do so, but found that with repeated insistence and powerful persuasion, the desired recollections would eventually appear. Freud proceeded to correlate his own "effort" to evoke the memory with the "resistance" offered by the patient, and postulated that by means of *"psychical work,"* he *"had to overcome a psychical force in the patients which was opposed to the pathogenic ideas becoming conscious"* (1895a, p. 268). In its most fundamental sense, "repression" simply represents the theoretical formulation of this clinical manifestation; repression is called "resistance" when it operates in the therapeutic situation (Madison, 1961, pp. 43-44, 68). The attempt to direct the patient's attention to symptom origin always met with resistance, Freud discovered, because hysterical symptoms were always traceable to "psychic trauma" generated by an "exciting cause," a precipitating "idea" against which an analogous "defense" had been initially exerted to force the "incompatible idea" out of consciousness and out of memory.

To be sure, the French neurologist Charcot had already postulated a psychic mechanism operative in one particular type of hysteria, the traumatic (Andersson, 1962, p. 103). Charcot's belief that traumatic phenomena and sexual function could in some way be relevant to hysteria remained unsystematic, however. The "sociology of his work habits" as a neurologist obliged him to base his assessment of hysteria on the premise that it was an organic neurological illness (Szasz, 1961, pp. 30-31), and he relied heavily on the concept of an inherited neuropathic tendency to explain its genesis (Miller et al., 1969, pp. 608-615).

The Preliminary Communication "On the Psychical Mechanism of Hysterical Phenomena," which Freud published with Josef Breuer in 1893, extended the existing rationale for traumatic hysteria to the entire realm of common hysterias (Breuer and Freud, 1893). Thus, if the outbreak of traumatic hysteria was occasioned by the memory of "a single major trauma," their investigations seemed to justify a pathogenic analogy by which "a series of interconnected part-traumas" underlie common hysteria (Breuer and Freud, 1893, p. 14).[1]

At this early date, Freud was content with the assumption that only one group of hysterics had willfully exercised defense against the precipitating idea. A patient in this group, he maintained, "wished to forget and therefore deliberately repressed and excluded from his conscious thoughts" the original trauma. In a second group, however, abreaction was not forestalled because the original idea was intrinsically traumatic and worthy of repression, but because it had been introduced to the subject during "abnormal psychical states" which made "a reaction to the event impossible" and prevented its assimilation into consciousness (Breuer and Freud, 1893, p. 11). The contention here was that the patient's perceptual distortions could be adequately explained on the basis of postulated alterations in the receptor apparatus (Schlessinger et al., 1967, p. 415).

The belief that such states of mental abstraction were crucial in the introduction of hysterical ideas emanated solely from Breuer, and it was he who coined the generic term

---

[1] In extending the concept of traumatic hysteria to all the common forms of hysteria, Freud and Breuer were actually breaking with Charcot, who had maintained that *only* traumatic hysteria involved a psychic mechanism, while all common forms were to be accounted for by other, primarily hereditary, conditions. They were also taking issue with his conception of *how* psychic factors associated with hysteria. Charcot held that an initial fright affect produced a mental state resembling hypnosis and later ideas involving the meaning of the traumatic experience that arose during the hypnosislike state were subsequently able to function as autosuggestions. Breuer and Freud reversed this order of events when they postulated that the hypnoid state did not originate in the traumatic situation but, conversely, that traumatic events got their character of traumata because they occurred in hypnoid states. Moreover, their postulation of the abreactive mechanism as a therapeutic tool was clearly intended to take precedence over Charcot's autosuggestion hypothesis.

Despite the limited usefulness which Charcot's conceptual framework had for Freud, however, his personal experience with him in Paris in 1885 had a profound impact on him. To a significant degree, Freud identified with this powerful and charismatic figure and utilized Charcot's strength and sanction to justify his own psychological investigations. Indeed, the very fact that Breuer and Freud used traumatic hysteria as the model for explaining the common forms, and their belief

"hypnoid" to describe them.[2] While Freud was willing to "half-heartedly subscribe" to this notion at the publication of their joint paper, he considered it increasingly questionable and eventually rejected it completely.

A year earlier, in "The Neuro-Psychoses of Defence" (1894), Freud had distinguished both hypnoid and retention hysteria[3] from defense hysteria, but made it quite clear that his clinical concern was only with the mechanism of the latter which, he then announced, could be applied to cases of phobias and obsessions as well. In defense hysteria the ego protected itself against the intruding "idea" by utilizing hysterical conversion to transform a strong idea into a weak one; that is, to deprive it of the quantity of excitation that rendered it affectively charged.

For some unspecified reason, however, not all persons predisposed to hysteria possessed this capacity for conversion by which large quantities of psychical excitation could be

---

that mental states resembling hypnosis played a causally significant role, is evidence of the over-all influence Charcot exerted on them. See Andersson (1962, pp. 103-106) and Miller et al. (1969, pp. 615-622).

[2] Schlessinger et al. argue that Breuer's total reliance on a level of speculative psychological explanation in the "theoretical" section of *Studies on Hysteria* in general, and in the "hypnoid hypothesis" in particular, is "defensive" and stems from the unresolved internal conflict that his transference-countertransference embroilment with Anna O. had generated (1967, pp. 410-415).

[3] Freud first referred to "retention hysteria" in connection with the case history of Elisabeth von R. in *Studies on Hysteria* where he mentioned the significant part played by sick-nursing in the prehistory of the hysteric: "Anyone whose mind is taken up by the hundred and one tasks of sick-nursing which follow one another in endless succession over a period of weeks and months will, on the one hand, adopt a habit of suppressing every sign of his own emotion, and on the other, will soon divert his attention away from his own impressions, since he has neither time nor strength to do justice to them. Thus he will accumulate a mass of impressions which are capable of affect, which are hardly sufficiently perceived, and which, in any case, have not been weakened by abreaction. He is creating material for a 'retention hysteria' " (1895b, pp. 161-162). The retention hypothesis thus became an alternative explanation for the "splitting of consciousness" that occurred in hysteria. It maintained that the precipitating hysterical impulse was not intrinsically conflictual, but merely occurred in social settings which precluded its expression. It is an environmental explanation in which the "splitting of consciousness" in itself played an insignificant part, or perhaps none at all: "They are those cases in which what has happened is only that the reaction to traumatic stimuli has failed to occur" and was compelled to be "retained" psychically (Freud, 1894, p. 47). Cf. Freud (1895b, pp. 169-173) and Stewart (1967, p. 83).

transmuted into somatic innervation. In such situations, however, the ego possessed an alternative mode of defense against the dreaded idea: even if affect was condemned to persist in the psychical sphere, it still was considered to possess a certain degree of mobility, and the affect associated with an initially incompatible idea might still be separated from it and reattached to some less offensive content. In this way, the pathogenic idea

> is still left in consciousness, separated from all association. *But its affect, which has become free, attaches itself to other ideas which are not in themselves incompatible; and thanks to this 'false connection', those ideas turn into obsessional ideas.* This, in a few words, is the psychological theory of obsessions and phobias [Freud, 1894, p. 52].

By this analysis, the obsessional neurosis became a functional counterpart of hysteria. Each was instituted to defend the ego against equally "incompatible" ideas, although each accomplished this defense by a different route. With hysteria, the affect adhering to the idea was transmuted somatically; with obsessions, on the other hand, it was simply transposed to a different idea.[4] Jointly, these two neuroses were the principal clinical forms which, along with the "hallucinatory confusion" that ensued when the ego simply rejected the unbearable idea and its associated affect altogether (Freud, 1894, pp. 58-61), and later paranoia,[5] constituted Freud's neuropsychoses of defense. These he placed in juxtaposition with the "actual" neuroses, neurasthenia and anxiety neurosis, which lacked a remote psychic core,

---

[4] While both hysteria and obsessional neurosis were similarly motivated "defense" neuropsychoses, Freud did not at this time believe that they functioned with equal effectiveness. With obsessional neurosis, he thought, "The ego gains much less advantage from choosing *transposition* of affect as a method of defense than from choosing the hysterical *conversion* of psychical excitation into somatic innervation. The affect from which the ego has suffered remains as it was before, unaltered and undiminished, the only difference being that the incompatible idea is kept down and shut out from recollection" (1894, p. 54).

[5] For the analysis of paranoia as a pathological mode of defense analogous to hysteria and obsessional neurosis, see Freud's preliminary Drafts H and K to Fliess (Freud, 1887-1902, pp. 109-115, 152-154) and his "Further Remarks on the Neuro-Psychoses of Defence" (1896a, pp. 174-185).

emanating instead from current deleterious sexual practices.[6] If hysteria and the obsessional neuroses were initially bound through parallel operative "mechanisms," the more vital nosological linkage emerged when Freud attempted to find the developmental causes of his two defense neuropsychoses. In "The Neuro-Psychoses of Defence" (1894), he had already perceived that the "incompatible" ideas possessed by his female hysterics developed "chiefly on the soil of sexual experience and sensation" (p. 47) and similarly, that obsessions represented substitutes or surrogates for an "incompatible sexual idea" (p. 53). By the end of 1895, however, he believed that "ideas" were themselves generated by actual sexual experiences, and equally important, that these experiences were qualitatively different for patients suffering from hysteria and obsessional neuroses. Thus, in an early draft which would form the basis of his "Further Remarks on the Neuro-Psychoses of Defence" (1896a), he informed his friend Fliess that at the core of all the "defensive neuroses" one would invariably locate "a sexual experience (or series of experiences) which is premature and traumatic and has to be repressed" (Freud, 1887-1902, p. 148).

If the cause of the persistent "psychical excitation" was to be found in real experience, and specifically sexual experience at that, the task confronting Freud involved isolating the intrinsic characteristics which could make such experiences conflictual to the extent of ultimately evoking defense. The more apparent rationale emerged in relation to hysteria; here the original sexual experience was an actual seduction inflicted on the potential hysteric which the victim was impelled to experience "passively." It was because the ego's posture had been a wholly "passive" one that it was "overwhelmed" and obliged to respond with manifestations of fright, the primary hysterical symptom (Stewart, 1967, p. 89). Freud published this finding in "Heredity and the Aetiology of

---

[6] For the original presentation of Freud's views on the actual neuroses see especially the preliminary Drafts B and E (Freud, 1887-1902, pp. 66-72, 88-94) and Freud (1895c, 1895d). For interpretive discussions see Stewart (1967) and Sadow et al. (1968, pp. 259-267).

the Neuroses" (1896c) and definitively restated it that same year in his second paper on the defense neuropsychoses. Here he reiterated that

> the symptoms of hysteria can only be understood if they are traced back to experiences which have a 'traumatic' effect, and that these psychical traumas refer to the patient's sexual life.... In order to cause hysteria, it is not enough that there should occur at some period of the subject's life an event which touches his sexual existence and becomes pathogenic through the release and suppression of a distressing affect. On the contrary, *these sexual traumas must have occurred in early childhood (before puberty), and their content must consist of an actual irritation of the genitals (of processes resembling copulating)* [1896a, p. 163].

With the obsessional neuroses, however, the linkage between the primary sexual experience and resultant symptoms became slightly more problematical, simply because the "primary experience" Freud's obsessional neurotics purportedly revealed was one accompanied by pleasure. As early as October 8, 1895, he had written Fliess that while "hysteria is conditioned by a primary sexual experience (before puberty) accompanied by revulsion and fright," the obsessional neurosis "is conditioned by the same accompanied by pleasure" (1887-1902, p. 126). In his very next letter of October 15, he again communicated to Fliess "the great clinical secret" by which hysteria was tied to "presexual *sexual shock*" and the obsessional neurosis to "presexual *sexual pleasure* later transformed into guilt" (1887-1902, p. 127).

Freud thus resolved an apparent paradox through the mediating concept of guilt and solved the etiological puzzle of the obsessional neuroses by postulating that an originally pleasurable sexual experience could precipitate obsessional symptoms by giving rise to a distinctly "unpleasurable" recollection generated by "self-reproach." This self-reproach was initially conscious, but with the onset of repression became translated into the *antithetic symptom* of conscientiousness. Freud considered this "the primary defensive symptom" deriving from the unwanted "idea." Shortly thereafter, probably in early adolescence, the repressed experience and the self-reproaches attached to it returned and emerged in consciousness as "a pure sense of guilt" which quickly became attached to some definite content. It was to this latter content that "obsessive" self-reproaches became directed. The new-found content of the obsession, Freud noted, did not point toward the primal experience but away from it; it usually pertained to a contemporary or future action and involved fictitious subject matter unrelated to real experience. Owing to distortion, in other words, the conscious obsession became "a product of compromise, correct as regards affect and category, but falsified by chronological displacement and the substitution of something analogous" (Freud, 1887-1902, p. 150). Thus, Freud termed obsessions or obsessive affects such as anxiety (involving the consequences of the action to which the self-reproach applied) or shame (the fear of other which Freud labeled "the secondary defensive symptoms" of the illness."

The final stage of the obsessional neurosis occurred because the conscious ego, perceiving the obsession as alien, was obliged to launch its own defensive struggle against it. The problem, however, was that the ego's own struggle could, itself, gain expression only through fresh obsessive symptoms which Freud labelled "the secondary defensive symptoms" of the neurosis. Thus, in this final development,

> The obsession, like any other idea, is subjected to logical criticism, though its compulsive force is unshakable; the secondary symptoms consist in an intensification of conscientiousness, and a compulsion to examine things and to hoard them. Other secondary symptoms arise when the compulsion is transferred to motor impulses directed against the obsession: e.g., to brooding, drinking (dipsomania), protective ceremonials, etc. (folie de doute) [Freud, 1887-1902, p. 150].

This analysis, which was extracted from the Draft K submitted to Fliess, became the basis for the discussion of obsessional neuroses in "Further Remarks on the Neuro-Psychoses of Defence" (1896a). This was the paper in which Freud boiled down his findings to the simple formula by which "Obsessional ideas are invariably transformed self-reproaches which have re-emerged from repression and which always relate to some *sexual* act that was performed with pleasure *in childhood"* (1896a, p. 169). Here, Freud proceeded to amplify and systematize his earlier remarks, and further distinguished cases in which the presenting symptoms were obsessional "ideas" from cases manifesting obsessive "affects."

Despite the harmonious embellishment which Draft K received in the "Further Remarks on the Neuro-Psychoses of Defence," however, a cursory comparison is apt to overlook a fundamental shift which occurred when Freud's earliest sketches were translated into published clinical findings. In the letters sent to Fliess in the fall of 1895, the precipitating obsessional experience was simply one characterized by pleasure (Freud, 1887-1902, pp. 126-127). The polar relationship between "activity" and "passivity" was not initially perceived as the causal dimension separating those experiences which would generate hysteria from those which gave rise to obsessional features. In the Draft K we have previously cited, Freud intuitively assumed that this "primary pleasurable experience" would be "active" in boys and "passive" in girls without delineating any further (1887-1902, p. 149). However, when the analysis of obsessional neurosis was formally promulgated in the three important papers all written in that same year (1896), the "pleasure" attached to the "primary pleasurable experience" was conceptually linked to the fact that the experience had been an "active" one. Indeed, Freud decisively went beyond a vague assumption that "pleasurable" experiences were simply "active" (relative to the "passivity" causing the unpleasurable experience behind hysteria) and specifically related the "pleasure" behind the obsessional experience to its quality of masculine aggressiveness. The obsessional neurosis was now conceived as a masculine counterpart to a distinctly "feminine" hysteria; and even in those infrequent cases in which women did develop obsessive symptoms, analysis would reveal that their "primary experience" had been tinged with maleness, involving an "active" participation in rudimentary sexual acts. In published form the underlying obsessional experience was presented not simply as a "pleasurable" event, but as a pleasurable "sexual aggression" in males and a pleasurable "active" sexual participation in females. Thus, in "Heredity and the Aetiology of the Neuroses," Freud wrote:

At the basis of the aetiology of hysteria we found an event of passive sexuality [*de passivité sexuelle*], an experience submitted to with indifference or with a small degree of annoyance or fright. In obsessional neurosis it is a question on the other hand, of an event which has given *pleasure*, of an act of aggression inspired by desire [*d'une agression sexuelle inspirée par le desir*] (in the case of a boy) or of a participation in sexual relations accompanied by enjoyment (in the case of a little girl) [1896c, p. 155; 1896d, p. 420].

In the "Further Remarks on the Neuro-Psychoses of Defence," Freud maintained that in the obsessional neurosis it was

no longer a question of sexual *passivity* [*sexuelle Passivität*], but of acts of aggression carried out with pleasure [*um Lust ausgeführte Aggressionen*] and of pleasurable participation in sexual acts—that is to say, of sexual *activity*. This difference in the aetiological circumstances is bound up with the fact that obsessional neurosis shows a visible preference for the male sex [1896a, p. 168; 1896b, p. 386].

And in "The Aetiology of Hysteria," he confidently asserted that

obsessional ideas can be regularly shown by analysis to be disguised and transformed *self-reproaches* [*Vorwürfe*] *about acts of sexual aggression* [*sexueller Aggressionen*] *in childhood,* and are therefore more often met with in men than in women, and that men develop obsessions more often than hysteria [1896e, p. 220; 1896f, p. 457].

By asserting that "sexual aggression" was at the etiological core of the obsessional neuroses, Freud had provided an answer at the expense of a second and more apparent question. That is, in postulating a retroactively traumatic experience in which a child actor might function as an initiator, an "aggressor" as it were, in the sexual realm, Freud had provided an etiology which was logically incomplete. After all, this formulation was made while Freud was still in the clutches of a literal "seduction theory," before the discovery that his patients' purported memories were only fantasies led him to postulate the ideational and affective existence of an "infantile" sexuality. At this time, preadolescent sexual experience was conceptualized only as a reaction to an external event, apart from the constitutional "drive endowment" of the child (Stewart, 1967, p. 98; Jones, 1953, p. 321). The existence of childhood "sexual aggression," which could not be justified as an etiological end point, came to make sense only when Freud discovered that "In *all* my cases of obsessional neurosis there had been, at a very early age, years before the pleasurable experience, a *purely passive* experience; and this can scarcely be an accidental fact" (1887-1902, p. 149).

In its earliest formulation (Draft K), Freud utilized this observation to construct an alternate explanation that could account for the fact that an initially pleasurable experience was later recalled in a negative, reproachful light. In addition to the possibility that the pleasurable memory could, in its own right, release unpleasure when later reproduced, Freud additionally speculated that it might well be

> the later convergence of this passive experience with the pleasurable one that adds the unpleasure to the pleasurable memory and makes repression possible. Thus it would be a necessary clinical condition of obsessional neurosis that the passive experience should occur early enough not to interfere with the spontaneous development of the pleasurable experience [1887-1902, p. 149].

However, the discovery of a passive seduction behind every early "sexual aggression" could be employed even more profitably to explain how presumably presexual children could be incited to perform such actions: a previous seduction, Freud announced, would result in "precocity of sexual desire" (*la précocité du desir sexuel*) (1896c, p. 155; 1896d, p. 421). Thus, sexual misdeeds by "innocent" childish assailants could be logically accepted only if the following course of events could be conceptualized:

> the boy, that is to say, had been abused by someone of the female sex, so that his libido was prematurely aroused [*vorzeitig die Libido geweckt wurde*], and then, a few years later, he had committed an act of sexual aggression [*sexueller Aggression*] against his sister, in which he repeated precisely the same

procedures to which he himself had been subjected [1896a, pp. 164-165; 1896b, p. 382].

In "The Aetiology of Hysteria" (1896e), Freud wrote that

Where there had been a relation between two children I was sometimes able to prove that the boy—who, here too, played the part of the aggressor—had previously been seduced by an adult of the female sex, and that afterwards, under the pressure of his prematurely awakened libido and compelled by his memory, he tried to repeat with the little girl exactly the same practices that he had learned from the adult woman, without making any modification of his own in the character of the sexual activity.

In view of this, I am inclined to suppose that children cannot find their way to acts of sexual aggression unless they have been seduced previously [p. 208].

With this piece of analytic deduction, then, childhood "sexual aggressions" became reasonable within the theoretical confines of the pre-1900 seduction hypothesis. The child's own alleged "seductions" were not acts of spontaneous degeneracy, but "reactive" misadventures caused by denegerate adults. For the time being, theoretical cogency and scientific respectability appeared to be precariously maintained.

II.

Despite its intuitively logical character, the explanation of childhood "sexual aggressions" in terms of a doctrine of "precocious sexual desire" contains a hidden incongruity. The spoiler in this case is Freud's pre-1900 theoretical comprehension of repression: for all its attractive simplicity, the doctrine of "precocious sexual desire" does not at all accord with the "delayed-reaction" hypothesis through which Freud constructed his first metapsychological explanation of repression at this time.

For a short period, in acknowledgment of Binet and Janet, and in obvious deference to Breuer, Freud was willing to understand repression in the limited descriptive sense provided by the notion of a "split consciousness." A repressed idea could be understood in terms of the dreamy "hypnoid" state in which it first appeared, a state which originated during "positively abnormal psychical states, such as the semi-hypnotic twilight state of day-dreaming, auto-hypnoses, and so on" (Breuer and Freud, 1893, p. 11). Ideas which were introduced in such hypnoid states were descriptively "repressed" insofar as they were "cut off from associative communication with the rest of the content of consciousness" (Breuer and Freud, 1893, p. 12).

Freud soon abandoned this explanation and replaced it with the dynamic rationale that analyzed repression as a defense employed against ideas entailing painful memories, and that understood "pain" as the release of a chemically endogenous "unpleasure" (Stewart, 1967, p. 97). Yet, Freud could not really explain repression by simply postulating a mechanism by which it might occur; it was necessary to understand why repression occurred when it did. Given the nature of his own clinical evidence, Freud felt compelled to determine why repressed childhood memories were always sexual while nonsexual memories, though they might be painful and cause the release of unpleasure, were not subject to repression. The question was answered by positing the concept of a delayed reaction to preadolescent sexual experiences.[7]

Nonsexual memories, however painful, could ultimately be tamed by the ego precisely because the memory could be subject to "attention" and the power of consciousness. Even if a nonsexual memory was initially distressing, Freud believed that an alerted ego would progressively learn to master the unpleasurable release because

---

[7] The delayed-reaction hypothesis was initially delineated in Part II of the *Project for a Scientific Psychology* on "Psychopathology" (Freud, 1895e, pp. 405-416). The first clinical application of this model occurred in the brief case history of Katharina in *Studies on Hysteria* (Freud, 1895b, pp. 131-133). Amacher (1965, pp. 79-82) has done the essential work of linking Freud's clinical inference of a delayed reaction to the scheme of neurological functioning he employed at this time. In this context, the delayed-reaction hypothesis can be approached as a perfectly consistent application of Meynert's model of the adjoining cortical associations that mirror all psychic processes: the delayed reaction was explained as the transmission of a large impingement of excitation to a cortical pathway which has not been initially tied to motor discharge at the time of the initial trauma, and over which the inhibiting ego was subsequently unable to control the increased inflow of excitation that followed puberty.

If an event A, when it was a current one, aroused a certain amount of unpleasure, then the mnemic registration of it, AI or AII, possesses a means of inhibiting the release of unpleasure when the memory is reawakened. The more often the memory recurs, the more inhibited does the release finally become [Freud, 1887-1902, p. 176; cf. Freud, 1895e, pp. 414-415].

Thus, Freud felt that the trend towards defense, i.e., "an aversion to directing psychical energy in such a way that unpleasure results," was actually normal and innocuous when directed against nonsexual memories, because here it only dealt with ideas "to which unpleasure was at one time attached but which are unable to acquire any contemporary unpleasure (other than remembered unpleasure)" (1887-1902, p. 146). This could not be the case with memories of "sexual ideas," however, because such ideas represented the

one possibility of a memory subsequently producing a more powerful release than that produced in the first instance by the corresponding experience itself. Only one further condition must be fulfilled, namely, that puberty should have occurred between the experience and its repetition—an event which very greatly intensifies the effect of the revival [Freud, 1887-1902, p. 147].

The impact of Freud's analysis rests on two critical assumptions. The first is that the "premature sexual experience" itself could not be contemporaneously traumatic, and the second is that, even apart from the consideration of trauma, the experience could become sexually "meaningful" only from the vantage point of sexual maturity and the onset of realistic sexual intuition in adolescence; only, that is, as a "memory." Such a memory, Freud noted, "behaves as though it were some current event ... because the magnitude of the excitations which these release increases of itself as time passes (i.e., as sexual development takes place)" (1887-1902, p. 176). Pathological defense indicated that the ego had been "taken by surprise": since the premature sexual experience itself had not been accompanied by release of affect, the ego's attention had not been directed towards the possible threat of danger associated with it. When, in connection with puberty, the memory of the event became emotionally charged and capable

40   PAUL E. STEPANSKY

of releasing strong affects, the "surprised" ego was unable to master them consciously, and thus repressed the memory (Freud, 1895e, pp. 415-416; Andersson, 1962, p. 184). When applied to the clinical data, this "delayed-reaction" theory of repression totally harmonized with the "psychical mechanism" Freud had posited for hysteria. "It is precisely because the subject is in his infancy," he had written,

> that precocious sexual excitation [*l'irritation sexuelle précoce*] produces little or no effect at that time ... Later, when at puberty the reactions of the sexual organs have developed to a level incommensurable with their infantile condition, it comes about in one way or another that this unconscious psychical trace is awakened. Thanks to the change due to puberty, the memory will display a power which was completely lacking from the event itself [1896c, p. 154; 1896d, p. 419].

He reiterated this supposition again in "Further Remarks on the Neuro-Psychoses of Defence," maintaining "that it is not the experiences themselves which act traumatically but their revival as a *memory* after the subject has entered on sexual maturity" (1896a, p. 164). Indeed, this retroactive traumatization of experience was considered a viable explanatory mechanism even when Freud's belief in literal sexual seductions had been shaken and the most he could posit were "childhood impressions" relating to sexual matters. Thus, in "Sexuality in the Aetiology of the Neuroses" (1898) he restated that the pathogenic effect of childhood sexual experiences was produced

> only to a very slight degree at the time at which they occur; what is far more important is their deferred effect, which can only take place at later periods of growth. This deferred effect originates—as it can do in no other way—in the psychical traces which have been left behind by infantile sexual experiences. During the interval between the experiences of those impressions and their reproduction (or rather, the reinforcement of the libidinal impulses which proceed from them), not only the somatic sexual apparatus but the psychical apparatus as well has undergone an important development; and thus it is that the influence of these earlier sexual experiences now leads to an abnormal psychical reaction, and psychopathological structures come into existence [p. 281].

This very concept of delayed reaction, however, is at complete odds with the causal chain of events that Freud had posited to explain the obsessional neuroses. It was in these cases, he insisted, that infantile seductions actually succeeded in provoking a "prematurely aroused libido," indeed, one aroused to such an extent that it would generate preadolescent "sexual aggressions." The incongruity in Freud's scheme is apparent: both the hysteric and the obsessional neurotic endure equivalent sexual seductions in early childhood. Both are in an initial state of sexual immaturity and are equally incapable of conceptualizing the sexual dimension of the assault. However, while the hysteric experiences the event with contemporary indifference and only retrospectively endows it with the quality of trauma, the obsessional neurotic is prematurely "aroused" and consequently incited to perpetuate a "sexual aggression" of his own.

Initially, it would appear that these two conflicting strands can be synthesized only at the expense of the actual clinical material. It might be suggested, for example, that the delayed-reaction hypothesis of repression be discarded while it is posited that hysterics *should* (hypothetically) experience immediate trauma with an adequate contemporary realization of the sexual component of their seduction. Even such a hypothetical integration, however, would not completely resolve all the problems generated by the contradiction. With obsessional neurotics, for example, why would retrospective trauma attach to the memory of a sexual aggression but *not* to the passive seduction that preceded it?[8] Moreover, what was actually preventing hysterics from undergoing the same "precocious sexual stimulation" that obsessional neurotics did? Admittedly, "The differentiation of the various psycho-

---

[8] This question somewhat unjustly simplifies the material at hand. Insofar as sexual aggressions were preceded by an earlier seduction, Freud did in fact observe in obsessional cases "the regular way in which the clinical picture is complicated by a certain number of purely hysterical symptoms." He still, of course, could not explain why, in the total symptom picture, the sexual aggressions proved *more* traumatic, retrospectively, than the previous seduction, and to that extent I believe my point is still well taken. See Freud (1896a, p. 162; 1896c, p. 153; 1926, p. 113) and also Freud's admission in Nunberg and Federn (1967, pp. 267-268).

neurotic affectations, and the distinguishing factors in their causation, was a problem that greatly occupied Freud in these years" (Jones, 1953, p. 282), and it must certainly be conceded that he did make early efforts at resolving the problem involved in the "choice of the neurosis." Without exception, however, these early efforts consisted only of rudimentary speculations communicated to Fliess and were concerned only with explaining why the two psychoneuroses gained expression through different operative "mechanisms." In two extended letters written to Fliess in 1896, Freud was convinced that it was the timing of the childhood "sexual scenes" that was the decisive determinant. In a communication dated May 30, he postulated that hysteria resulted when the "scenes" occurred during the first period of childhood (up to age four), a "preconscious"[9] stage in which the memory traces of experiences could not yet be translated into "verbal images." Lacking contemporary verbal representation, the later arousal of the exciting memory (which could not retroactively "verbalize" the experience due to the current "defense" precluding recall of it) could, of necessity, only gain expression somatically through hysterical conversion.

With obsessional neuroses, on the other hand, Freud submitted that the precipitating "sexual scenes" occurred between the ages of four and eight, a period during which they could be "translated" into words and consequently achieve later expression as "psychical obsessional symptoms," as ideas, that is, derived through verbal associations. Sexual experiences undergone between the ages of 10 and 14 could only generate a defense consisting of disbelief and projection which would manifest itself as paranoia. Beyond this age, sexual experiences would not result in "pathological consequences" and would only incur "normal repression" (Freud, 1887-1902, pp. 163-165; also Stewart, 1967, pp. 92-94).

Freud restated this formula in his letter of December 6, but here gave it a firm technical base by assuming that "our

---

[9] The German reads *praeconsc,* a term that Freud never used elsewhere, and which is not to be confused with his later conventional use of preconsciousness (*vorbewusst*). (See Freud, 1887-1902, p. 163n.)

psychical mechanism has come about by a process of stratification: the material present in the shape of memory-traces is from time to time subjected to a rearrangement in accordance with fresh circumstances—is, as it were, transcribed" (1887-1902, p. 173).

Hysteria resulted from repressed memories relating to scenes that were "actively current" between the ages of one-and-a-half and four, a time when the memory could only have been transcribed at the first primitive level of memory registration, one consisting only of causally unrelated and verbally unattached percept signs. Given this rudimentary registration of the sexual scenes, somatic conversion was, again, conceived as the only possible means of future discharge. By the time that "current" obsessional scenes occurred between the ages of four and eight, memory was being deposited at the second level of registration, one involving "association" and "causal relations." This was considered sufficient for "obsessional" symptoms to arise. Paranoia, entailing sexual scenes that were "current" between the ages of 8 and 14, presupposed that the memory in question had advanced to a third level of transcription (Freud, 1887-1902, pp. 174-178; also Stewart, 1967, pp. 94-96).

While certainly a model of speculative creativity, these letters clearly leave unresolved the basic problems we have posed. In the first place, they are in no sense offered as conclusive findings; Freud presented his May 5 letter as "the fruit of some tormenting reflections" (1887-1902, p. 163), while the one of December 6 was merely "the latest bit of speculation" (1887-1902, p. 173). By January 24, 1897, he was already doubtful that the choice of neurosis depended on either "the time of origin or the time of repression," but was at that point inclined to favor the latter (Freud, 1887-1902, p. 190). In his next letter of February 8, he simply confessed that "the time relationships have begun to seem uncertain" (1887-1902, p. 192).[10] Secondly, as we have indicated, these explanatory

[10] Freud's speculative interest in the problem of the "choice of neurosis," first broached in these early letters to Fliess, would be a recurring theme in the later discussions of the Wednesday evening group that became the Vienna Psycho-Analytic Society. Between 1907 and 1910, the problem of the choice of neurosis was discussed with reference to the specific etiologies of dementia praecox (Nunberg

attempts were clearly mechanistic and were not intended to explain the choice of neurosis in terms of the susceptibility to differential etiology. This problem was never really confronted: although Freud posited that hysteria resulted from a passively experienced seduction and obsessional neurosis involved pleasurable "sexual aggressions" preceded by a passive "exciting" seduction, there was no attempt to explain what caused some individuals to experience their seductions with relative indifference and others to undergo a "premature arousal" that stimulated them to commit their own seductions. Although Freud never explicitly confronted this problem, we would suggest that an explanation for this differentiation can *implicitly* be derived from these very early writings, and that the entire dilemma can be fruitfully resolved if we retain Freud's carefully devised "delayed-reaction" hypothesis while

---

and Federn, 1962, p. 104), psychic impotence (Nunberg and Federn, 1962, pp. 395-396), hysterical pseudoepilepsy (Nunberg and Federn, 1967, pp. 20-21), and in relation to masturbation (Nunberg and Federn, 1974, pp. 343, 346). There were, moreover, relatively systematic theoretical discussions on the problem of the choice of neurosis stimulated by the presentations of Adler (Nunberg and Federn, 1967, pp. 262-274) and Reitler (Nunberg and Federn, 1967, pp. 435-444).

Freud's contribution to these discussions mimics the pattern established in the early letters to Fliess: he fluctuates from a confessed inability to make concrete headway in solving the problem to an anticipatory excitement that a solution is near at hand. In January, 1907, Freud referred to the choice of neurosis as "what we know least about," while submitting that the problem was related to "A combination of the psychosexual constitution with other constitutions" (i.e., specific motor endowments) and to the locus of regression (Nunberg and Federn, 1962, pp. 100-101). A year later (January, 1908), Freud reported he had "come close to the solution of this problem" (Nunberg and Federn, 1962, p. 294). In June, 1909, he again emphasized the differing vicissitudes of the libido as constituting the "disposition for the choice," especially inasmuch as specific vicissitudes at least partially corresponded to inhibitions occurring at specific stages of psychic development (Nunberg and Federn, 1967, pp. 267-268). By March, 1910, however, Freud was content merely to enumerate the many factors that would ultimately have to be incorporated in any theoretical attempt to account for the choice of neurosis: "... the predisposition to neuroses, an hypertrophy of an instinct, the age at which the fixation occurs, the stage of development at which the child finds himself, and finally the mechanisms of repression by which the individual neuroses differ essentially from one another" (Nunberg and Federn, 1967, p. 442). In the fall of 1910 he once more attempted to be specific and singled out the developmental stage of the erotic instincts and the state of the ego (pleasure ego versus reality ego) when the developmental disturbance took place as the relevant factors (Nunberg and Federn, 1974, p. 30).

Freud's alternating optimism and frustration at these meetings find an interest-

carefully re-examining the "quality" of the distinctly obsessional experience he posited. Upon doing so, we discover that what Freud was actually describing were "aggressions" rather than actual "sexual" actions. At the time of these formulations, Freud's use of the term libido was only loosely descriptive; as a technical term in his theory of mental dynamics, it remained to be discovered. Moreover, it would be eight years before Freud would formally postulate "aggression" as simply one component impulse of an amorphous sexual instinct which, as sadism, could become "independent and exaggerated" through displacement (1905a, p. 158). In short, while Freud's causal chain of events could rely on the explicit "aggressive" elements of mature male sexuality and the explicit "passive" elements of mature female sexuality based on the physical reality of coitus, psychoanalysis was not at this time a psychology of the instincts, and thus could not rationalize *childhood* aggressions in terms of sexual component impulses. It consequently becomes deceptively retrospective to equate his notion of childhood "sexual aggressions" with experiences of genuine "aggressive sexuality."

If we take into account the fact that the obsessional neurosis was conceptualized as a male syndrome related to childhood

---

ing parallel in certain revelations contained in his correspondence to Jung during 1908. In January, 1908, for example, he wrote Jung that "a little while ago I thought I had my hands on something really worthwhile, the solution of the choice-of-neurosis problem, in which you too take such an interest, but it slipped through my fingers as it did once before, many years ago. But I shall catch it yet" (Freud, 1906-1923, p. 113). Two months later, Freud offered the concrete suggestion that the distinction between hysteria and obsessional neurosis related directly to the content of the sexual component instincts which were repressed: obsessional neurosis stemmed from disturbances in the nonautoerotic "object" components (i.e., the instincts to see and to know and the possessive sadistic instinct), while hysteria hinged on the repression of the erogenous components connected to the erogenous zones proper (Freud, 1906-1923, p. 128). By June, however, he had grown disenchanted with the inferential guesswork involved in this line of reasoning. In reply to Jung's suggestion that the precocity of the infantile fixation created the specific predisposition to dementia praecox, Freud observed, "But after all, have we the right to look for this predisposition and the conditions for the choice of neurosis in such developmental disturbances on the path taken by the libido? In my opinion there is nothing to be gained by speculation; we must wait for especially revealing cases that will show clearly what we can thus far only suspect" (1906-1923, p. 159).

acts that were gratifying not because they were sexual, but because they were aggressive, we are able to reconcile its etiology with that of hysteria within the framework provided by the "delayed-reaction" hypothesis. Moreover, through this reinterpretation, which firmly adheres to Freud's working clinical assumptions, we can discover rudimentary trends in Freud's thought which would blossom in future years, after the "seduction theory" itself had become little more than a historical relic.

Both females and males, Freud had argued, were subject to analogous sexual seductions in early childhood. In neither case could the sexual content of the seduction be appreciated by the preadolescent victim, and in neither case could it generate immediate trauma as a sexual experience. With females, the memory of the childhood seduction would ultimately come to constitute a "sexual" memory when, following adolescence, the "passive" role played in the seduction was identified with the "passivity" intrinsic to the normative female sexual role: an early seduction became sexual precisely because female participation in coitus always remained associated with the passive reception of a violent seduction. As Freud had written in Draft K, it was "The *natural* sexual passivity of women [which] accounts for their being more inclined to hysteria" (my emphasis), and he further noted that when hysteria *was* found in men, "I have been able to trace a large amount of sexual passivity in their anamnesis" (1887-1902, p. 154).

With males, however, the normal constitutional disposition was not towards "passivity." In being seduced, the male victim was able to identify vicariously with the aggressive posture of the seducer precisely because he was "male" and possessed an inclination towards aggression as an allegedly *masculine* instinctual strain. Thus, even before the role of aggression in adult "male sexuality" could be appreciated, Freud apparently suggested, the male child could be incited to "seduce" solely because gratification at this stage could be linked with aggressiveness. The "precocious stimulation" of the child, in other words, did not arouse immediate sexual feelings in the male child and thus could not predispose him to an immediate assault which was cognitively "sexual." Only after adolescence did the memory become associated with a sexual aggression because only then did aggressiveness become recognized as a normative component of the male sexual role. This interpretation is strongly buttressed by the impact of Freud's own phraseology. The obsessional neurosis was essentially a masculine syndrome in which the precipitating experiences were labeled "acts of aggression carried out with pleasure" (*um Lust ausgeführte Aggressionen*); only secondarily and in the unusual case of the obsessional female could it be "pleasurable participation in sexual acts" (*mit Lust empfundene Teilnahme an sexuellen Akten*) (1896a, p. 168; 1896b, p. 386; also see 1896c, pp. 155-156). With the male, it was invariably a question of playing "the part of the aggressor" (*die aggressive Rolle spielt*) (1896e, p. 208; 1896f, p. 445) in actions that could be characterized in certain cases by "a repetition of a brutal abuse" (*abus brutal réitéré*) (1896c, p. 152; 1896d, p. 418).

Consequently, like the hysteric, the obsessional neurotic attached sexual significance to his childhood experience only retrospectively. The following fundamental difference remained, however. Female hysterics originally perceived their seductions with relative indifference and attached sexual meaning to them later when they perceived passive resignation as the primordially "feminine" sexual pose. With male obsessional neurotics, on the other hand, sexualization did not spring from a childhood experience which was, at the time, affectively unimportant. Rather than simply "resigning" himself to the seduction, the male child identified with his aggressor, and consequently became an aggressor.[11] The secondary experience of aggressor acquired sexual meaning after adolescence, because aggression then became a sexually charged concept based on the physical nature of coitus. The passive role in the original seduction did not usually generate hysterical symptoms in male obsessional neurotics because passivity was antagonistic to active male sexuality and be-

---

[11] The identification with the aggressor was first examined as a particular ego defense strategy by Anna Freud (1936, pp. 117-131).

cause, even in being seduced, the male child's "aggressive" disposition allowed him to identify with the seducer.[12]

Even at the time of the seduction theory, this linkage of aggression with male sexuality could hardly be considered revolutionary. In the theoretical delineation of hysteria in the *Studies on Hysteria* (Breuer, 1895), which Freud increasingly viewed as invalid and for which he denied any responsibility (1887-1902, p. 95), Breuer had equated sexual excitation, "at least in males," with "an intensification of the aggressive instincts" (Breuer, 1895, p. 201), and in describing ideas with a "sexual content" as the most numerous and important "ideogenic phenomena" consequently converted to affective excitation, he had commented that "The tendency towards fending off what is sexual is further intensified by the fact that in young unmarried women sensual excitation has an admixture of anxiety, of fear of what is coming, what is unknown and half-suspected, whereas in normal and healthy young men it is an unmixed aggressive instinct" (Breuer, 1895, p. 246).

III.

If the seduction hypothesis itself is now of only historical interest, the explanation for the obsessional neuroses which this scheme provided remains noteworthy for two interrelated reasons. In its implicit assumption that before sexual aggressions could even be conceptualized or conatively desired,

---

[12] The only source I could locate that was sensitive to the "aggressive" dimension of the precipitating obsessional action was Peter Madison's *Freud's Concept of Repression and Defense* (1961). In his discussion of the motives of repression and defense, he refers to the seduction theory as "the earliest instance in which a systematic role was given to hostility." For him, however, the etiology of obsessional neurosis is based on "the primacy of sex and the associative status of hostility in repression" (p. 122). Aggression only becomes repressible, that is, through its associative connection with childhood sex (p. 128). This is clearly not the point I am making. Rather than arguing that the repressed event in obsessional neurosis was one of *sex-linked hostility* (p. 123), I am suggesting that the delayed-reaction theory of repression operative at this time makes it necessary to *translate* the "sexual" component of the alleged action to an independently gratifying "aggressive" one.

there were pleasurable aggressions, the explanation of the obsessional neuroses constitutes the starting point for Freud's clinical appreciation of aggression, and hints at the vital role it would come to assume in a formulated theory of the instincts. Moreover, it is in the early clinical "evidence" concerning hysteria and obsessional neurosis that we can detect the first inkling of the misogyny which would come to play such a "vital intellectual function" in Freud's entire system.[13] At a later evolutionary stage in Freud's work, women would come to "express what is primal and static as contrasted with masculine dynamism." Masculinity would come to represent what is "active and proper to the virtues of a person, while the feminine is passive and proper to the constraints a person may suffer through the persistence of certain primal forms" (Rieff, 1961, p. 201). Philip Rieff has argued that as early as *The Interpretation of Dreams* (1900), Freud's "special attitude" toward women was evident through a theory of dream symbolism which focused on the dichotomy of male power and feminine passivity (Rieff, 1961, p. 193).

We are suggesting that this analysis can be traced back one step further; that, in fact, Freud's misogyny does not only represent an important and irreducible intellectual substrate, but has very real roots in the earliest clinical materials on hysteria and obsessional neurosis. Freud's masculine "bias" does not emerge as a full-blown metapsychological given; it is clinically based and first manifests itself as an unintentional subreption of clinical evidence. It is in relation to the differ-

---

[13] See Philip Rieff (1961, p. 200): "His misogyny, like that of his predecessors, is more than prejudice; it has a vital intellectual function in his system. In the nineteenth century strong links, the origins of which have not yet been closely studied, existed between irrationalist philosophy and misogyny. Freud's views echo those of Schopenhauer (in the essay 'On Women') and Nietzsche. And just as sympathetic expositors of Schopenhauer and Nietzsche want to dismiss these philosophers' views on women as idiosyncratic and philosophically irrelevant, so the neo-Freudians (led by eminent women analysts like Karen Horney) would like to omit that part of Freud's work as mere culture-prejudice, maintaining that much of the remaining doctrine can be realigned without damage. But actually the pejorative image of woman serves as a measure of the general critical component in Western philosophies. That the great critical figures in modern philosophy, literature, psychology—Nietzsche, Lawrence, Freud—were misogynists is a fact the significance of which has not yet been properly assessed."

ential etiologies of the two neuropsychoses of defense and their differential frequency in male and female populations that the earliest "bias" emerges. The "unpleasurable" recollection of the obsessional neurotic is assertively masculine. Because female patients were initially believed to be the passive childhood victims of "brutal" assaults, "passivity" could be conveniently associated with "unpleasure" on the one hand, and with the entire empirical realm of "female sexuality" on the other. Finally, by a simple transitive identity, female sexuality itself became linked with "pain." Once detached from the constricting necessity for actual seductions, these earliest clinical associations would blossom into central psychological themes.

Once Freud had freed himself from the constricting intellectual straitjacket that literal belief in the seduction of his patients imposed upon him, and once he was no longer obsessed with the mission entailed in proclaiming to others the reality of these sexual seductions, his creative genius and his wealth of clinical insight would fully unravel in the wonderfully complex and overdetermined case history of Dora (Freud, 1905c). Written in the first two weeks of 1900, this extended exposition, while a "fragment" in itself, marks Freud's transition from fragmented clinical insight to total clinical competence.[14] Rather than searching for lonesome seductions, Freud now approached the causes of hysterical disorders "in the intimacies of the patients' psycho-sexual life." Hysterical symptoms, instead of simply being somatic innervations, were taken as an expression of the patient's "most secret and repressed wishes" and as a result, "the complete elucidation of a case of hysteria is bound to involve the revelation of those intimacies and the betrayal of those secrets" (1905c, pp. 7-8). Yet even here, after the "break" had been made, Freud occasionally revealed the residual influence of his earliest etiological formulations and gave faint glimmer-

---

[14] As Erik Erikson (1964, p. 168) has written, "The description of Freud's fragmentary work with Dora has become the classical analysis of the structure and the genesis of a hysteria." Erikson's insightful reinterpretation of Dora in the light of current ego psychology makes special reference to her preoccupation with "historical truth," which Freud misconstrued (Erikson, 1964, pp. 166-177).

ings of the metapsychological presuppositions that would gradually evolve from them. For example, before even analyzing the intense repugnance Dora felt upon being kissed by Herr K, Freud submitted as an a priori theorem his categorical belief that he "should without question consider a person hysterical in whom an occasion for sexual excitement elicited feelings that were preponderantly or exclusively unpleasurable; and I should do so whether or no the person were capable of producing somatic symptoms," even while confessing that the elucidation of this mechanism remained "one of the most difficult problems in the psychology of the neuroses" and one which he was "still some way from having achieved" (Freud, 1905c, p. 28).

In later years, Freud would return to the central triad of femininity-passivity-pain first located in the earliest work on hysteria, equating erotogenic and libidinally bound masochism with a distinctly "feminine" model in which male subjects placed themselves "in a characteristically female situation," embracing the "pain" entailed in castration, in playing the passive part in coitus and in the act of giving birth (Freud, 1924, pp. 162, 165).[15] And although Freud did eventually discover that little girls, too, could normatively pose as "little boys" in early childhood and did indeed entertain "active" preoedipal fantasies toward the mothering one, he persistently maintained that the biological threshold of true "femininity" could only be crossed when the "masculine" clitoris was renounced in favor of the receptive vagina—"the female organ proper" (Freud, 1931, p. 228)—and when "activity" itself became no more than a means employed in behalf of distinctly "passive" aims (Freud, 1933a, p. 115).[16]

---

[15] For the traditional analytic contentions concerning the constitutional relationship between feminine passivity and masochism, see Deutsch (1930), Rado (1933), and to a lesser extent, Bonaparte (1935). The standard revisionist rebuttal of these views can be found in Horney (1939, pp. 246-275) and Fried (1970, pp. 24-49).

[16] In "Some Psychical Consequences of the Anatomical Distinction between the Sexes" (1925a), Freud discussed the female "masculinity complex" in terms of ths long prehistory of the Oedipus complex that occurred in little girls. Before the discovery of their "organic inferiority" and the onset of penis envy, the sexual orientation of the female was "active" and "clitoridal." Once the recognition of the

Likewise, Freud's earliest equation of the obsessional neurosis with "activity," while unable to generate such a compellingly subjective mythology, was to outlive the usefulness of the seduction hypothesis in which it was initially framed. In "My Views on the Part Played by Sexuality in the Aetiology of the Neuroses" (1906), the very paper which rang the official death knell of the seduction hypothesis, Freud confessed that while he had been obliged to abandon entirely his previous

---

lack of a penis had occurred, however, any persisting hope of attaining one would "put great difficulties in the way of their regular development towards femininity" (p. 253). The abolition of this masculinity complex was associated with the intense current of feeling against masturbation which little girls purportedly experienced after the first signs of penis envy: "This impulse is clearly a forerunner of the wave of repression which at puberty will do away with a large amount of the girl's masculine sexuality in order to make room for the development of her femininity" (p. 256). The rejection of masculine sexuality, Freud maintained, was generated by the "narcissistic sense of humiliation" that recognition of the lack of a penis entailed. In rejecting masturbation that was in itself masculine (clitoridal), the little girl was guided by "the reminder that after all this is a point on which she cannot compete with boys and that it would therefore be best for her to give up the idea of doing so. Thus the little girl's recognition of the anatomical distinction between the sexes forces her away from masculinity and masculine masturbation on to lines which lead to the development of femininity" (p. 256). The elimination of clitoral sexuality was stated as the necessary precondition for the development of femininity.

These remarks were restated in the essay on "Female Sexuality" (1931), where Freud described at greater length both the "intensity" and the "active" male element in the little girl's earliest attitude towards her mother. Activity was here presented as the preferred male modality which figured in the aspiration of both sexes, but which the anatomical "organic inferiority" of little girls compelled them to renounce. Femininity, with its corresponding stress on passivity, was clearly second best, and was embraced unwillingly (if at all) only because little girls were not in an anatomical position to compete "actively" with their male counterparts: "The girl's sexual aims in regard to her mother are active as well as passive and are determined by the libidinal phases through which the child passes. Here the relation of the activity to passivity is especially interesting. It can be observed that in every field of mental experience, not merely that of sexuality, when a child receives a passive impression it has a tendency to produce an active reaction. It tries to do itself what has just been done to it. This is part of the work imposed on it of mastering the external world and can even lead to its endeavouring to repeat an impression which it would have reason to avoid on account of its distressing content.... Here we have an unmistakable revolt against passivity and a preference for the active role. This swingover from passivity to activity does not take place with the same regularity or vigour in all children; in some it may not occur at all. A child's behaviour in this respect may enable us to draw conclusions as to the relative strength of the masculinity and femininity that it will exhibit in its sexuality"

belief "that a passive attitude in these scenes produced a predisposition to hysteria and, on the other hand, an active one a predisposition to obsessional neurosis," there still remained some facts which demanded "that in some way or other the supposed correlation between passivity and hysteria and between activity and obsessional neurosis shall be maintained" (p. 175). Such facts withstood the clinical test of time, and in his "Notes upon a Case of Obsessional Neurosis" (1909a), he submitted that all his investigated obsessional neuroses, "unlike those of hysteria, invariably possess the characteristic of premature sexual activity" (Freud, 1909a, p. 165). Moreover, even in asserting that such premature activity was usually of an "onanistic character" and that it was only after maturity that the obsessional neurotic attempted to efface the recollection of autoerotic activities by exalting their memory traces to the level of object love (Freud, 1909a, p. 206n.), Freud still maintained in this case history that his 1896 definition of obsessional neurosis, if "open to criticism upon formal grounds," was still in its component elements "unobjectionable" (p. 221).

(p. 236). True femininity, in other words, entailed renouncing masculine "activity" even though such activity remained the intrinsically desirable and preferred modality from the female perspective.

Passive femininity was not initially embraced, but only bitterly endured. Indeed, it was the discovery that she lacked the principal badge of maleness that turned the little girl away from her mother, substituting for her formerly "masculine" attachment "the reproach that her mother did not give her a proper penis—that is to say, brought her into the world as a female" (p. 234). It was, according to Freud, only from this wellspring of bitter disappointment and resentment that "femininity" blossomed. In turning away from her mother, the little girl underwent more than a simple change of object: ". . . we may now add that hand in hand with it there is to be observed a marked lowering of the active sexual impulses and a rise of the passive ones . . . the active trends have been affected by frustration more strongly, they have proved totally unrealizable and are therefore abandoned by the libido more readily. . . . The transition to the father-object is accompanied with the help of the passive trends insofar as they have escaped the catastrophe. The path to the development of femininity now lies open to the girl to the extent to which it is not restricted by the remains of the pre-Oedipus attachment to her mother which she has surmounted [p. 239] . . . Biological factors subsequently deflect those libidinal forces [in the girl's case] from their original aims and conduct even active and in every sense masculine trends into feminine channels" (p. 240).

These insights were presented in somewhat less technical terms in the thirty-third new introductory lecture on "Femininity" (Freud, 1933a, pp. 112-135).

Certainly, by this late date, Freud could not let his earliest formulation go wholly uncriticized. It had been, he conceded, "aiming too much at unification," and had taken

> as its model the practice of obsessional neurotics themselves, when, with their characteristic liking for indeterminateness, they heap together under the name of 'obsessional ideas' the most heterogeneous psychical structures. In point of fact, it would be more correct to speak of 'obsessive thinking', and to make it clear that obsessional structures can correspond to every sort of psychical act. They can be classed as wishes, temptations, impulses, reflections, doubts, commands, or prohibitions [1909a, pp. 221-222].

In the case history in question, Freud once again dealt with a patient who had engaged in childhood sexual activities and who later experienced severe self-reproaches, but the relationship between these two variables had been considerably modified. The self-reproaches were no longer attached to the "pleasurable" nature of the premature experience itself, but were rather a response to the violent rage directed against the father who, in connection with "some sexual misdemeanor connected with masturbation" (Freud, 1909a, p. 205), had harshly castigated the patient, interfering with his infantile sexual enjoyment and incurring his "ineradicable grudge." The "Rat Man's" self-reproaches, that is, were generated by unconscious hatred harbored toward the father who *ended* his childhood sexual activity, and it was the repression of this infantile hatred, Freud surmised, which had "brought his whole subsequent career under the dominion of the neurosis" (p. 238). The resulting obsessive indecision and doubt which plagued him reflected the strained tension between love and hate within him, a paralyzing ambivalence that characterized not only his attitude toward his father, but all his interpersonal relations as well (*passim*, esp. pp. 237-249).

When he formally returned to the problem of "the choice of the neurosis" in 1913, Freud was at last compelled to admit that the assumption that hysteria and the obsessional neurosis were respectively conditioned by passivity and activity was "erroneous." The content of his new theoretical explanation, however, represented something less than a bold departure from the old one. If "activity" itself could no longer be correlated with obsessional neurosis, the implicit "aggressive" quality of this activity still retained its tight linkage with this syndrome: Freud had recognized the crucial part played by sadistic instinctual components in the genesis of obsessional neurosis in the "Rat Man" case history of 1909; now he theorized that the "disposition" to a particular neurosis was derived from a fixation at a specific stage of libido development, and the fixation generating obsessional neurosis was to that pregenital stage of sexual life dominated by anal-sadistic impulses (Freud, 1913a, pp. 320-321). This contention, which received theoretic restatement in the *Introductory Lectures* (Freud, 1916-1917, pp. 309, 343) and its most dramatic clinical illustration in the "Wolf Man" case history (Freud, 1918, pp. 61-71) would never be abandoned. Thus, if obsessive symptoms had previously been conceptualized as distorted self-reproaches for previously committed aggressions, symptoms such as compulsive washing and cleanliness, and the energetic protective measures against injuries one is liable to commit, could now be understood as reaction formations against anal-sadistic, i.e., aggressive, impulses (Freud, 1913a, p. 320).

While "premature sexual activity" retained, at least for a time, its close connection with the predisposing childhood fantasies that were believed to generate obsessional neuroses, the belief in the concept of literal "sexual aggressions" was naturally discarded as soon as the "prematurely arousing" seductions were discovered to exist only in the realm of fantasy. In accord with the abandonment of the seduction theory, it would be replaced with the more "fantasied" aggressions against the parent of the same sex which the postulation of an Oedipus complex made imminent. The earliest belief in the pleasurable nature of these "sexual aggressions" would later surface in close association with the purported "unpleasure" of the passive hysterical seduction to form the substrate from which Freud's understanding of the female sexual role could easily evolve. The fact that these "sexual aggressions" were originally believed to become sexualized only after repression, however, remains an insight of considerable historical significance: in considering the earliest formulations on the role of aggression, Freud's point of departure is not to be found in the dose of "aggression" he posited as derivative of the drive for sexual mastery (Hartmann, Kris, and Loewenstein, 1949, p. 9) nor in the nonlibidinal "aggressive" trends he ascribed to ego instincts (Bibring, 1934, pp. 103, 110-113) nor in the "aggressive" component of the Oedipus complex (Roazen, 1968, pp. 194-195). Before any of these uses, Freud possessed clinical evidence that led him to believe that pre-adolescent males could be stimulated to seduce their female counterparts as acts of "aggression" that offered intrinsic and presexual gratification.

3

THE INTRUDING INSIGHT
OF SELF-ANALYSIS: AGGRESSION
AND WISH FULFILLMENT
IN *THE INTERPRETATION*
OF DREAMS

While the discovery of seduction fantasies may well have heralded the transformation of psychoanalysis into "a psychology of the instincts," the fantasied oedipal "aggressions" that remained after the cumbersome seduction hypothesis had been abandoned were not sanctioned as "psychologically real" through a formulated theory of instincts. Instead, the new evidential medium would become the dream, and the now "fantasied" movers behind childhood reminiscences would be formulated in terms of the dream's own mediating source of meaning, the wish fulfillment. It was this new footing that emerged as the sole surviving remnant of Freud's discarded Neurotica. With the discovery that perverted acts against children were not "so general," the core of his therapeutic system had dissolved. In the wake of this veritable catastrophe, he wrote Fliess, "Only the psychology has retained its value. The dreams still stand secure, and my beginnings in metapsychology have gone up in my estimation" (Freud, 1887-1902, p. 218).

It was to the world of the dream that Freud would turn with renewed vigor and conviction, staking both the therapeutic efficacy of his own self-analysis and the theoretical framework on which a more mature appreciation of impulse life could emerge. Childhood aggressions would no longer represent real, if precociously induced, actions undertaken in waking life. Henceforth, the childhood *wish* to aggress would appear principally in sleep. Moreover, analytic reconstruction would testify that the content of such wishes would not merely focus on gratifying "destructive actions" per se, but ultimately on the very real desire that those near the dreamer, particularly siblings and the parent of the same sex, would die. With the emergence of oedipal conflict, the child's fantasied wish productions would become, perforce, symbiotically dualistic: sexual union with one parent would constitute a "wish" only to the extent that the child actively wished the elimination of its rival.

Several years later, Freud would preface his revelation of infantile sexuality by noting the paradoxical nature of the amnesia that shields us from remembering the earliest years of childhood. Freud found such amnesia truly surprising, since psychoanalysis informs us that it is during those very years that

> we reacted in a lively manner to impressions, that we were capable of expressing pain and joy in a human fashion, that we gave evidence of love, jealousy, and other passionate feelings by which we were strongly moved at the time, and even that we gave utterance to remarks which were regarded by adults as good evidence of our possessing insight and the beginnings of a capacity for judgement [1905a, pp. 174-175].

In *The Interpretation of Dreams* we discover a significant precursor to this observation. Here, we are no longer pre-occupied with the child's superficial and prematurely induced "aggressions" of the seduction hypothesis. Instead, we penetrate to a new level of clinical significance: children (and the adults who nightly become children) do not merely indulge in short-lived aggressive actions, but routinely formulate oneiric death wishes which indicate a sophisticated ability to grasp unconsciously and utilize egoistically one principal end point of aggression: death.

Freud does not, however, proceed to label the child (and the adult who in dreams relives the conflicts of childhood) instinc-tively "aggressive." Rather, he merely attributes to it the capacity to generate aggressive fantasies and to fulfill them *reflexively* in dream-life. The distinction is not semantic, but crucial. While willing to exchange the myth of actual seductions and precociously induced arousal for the colorful fantasy life of childhood, Freud was not immediately willing to reduce the child's fantasy productions to circumscribed instincts. Instead, in turning to dream-life, he was able to seize upon the wish fulfillment as an open-ended instrument which could encompass the rich diversity of childhood fantasy. Writing at the height of his crusade to convince the world of an exclusively sexual etiology of the psychoneuroses, it is obvious that Freud would attribute a large role to the sexual wishes prompting dream formation. However, in this chapter we are not concerned with the extent of sexual wishes in dream-life, but with the observation that, while coming close, Freud never chose to *define* wish fulfillment exclusively in terms of sexual wishes as he had defined the neuroses in terms of exclusively sexual etiology. Such cautious open-mindedness, we will argue, stems in large part from increasing recognition of "aggressive fantasies" revealed not only in the death wishes of patients, but in the recurrent aggressive motifs that appeared in the course of Freud's own self-analysis.

In the ensuing pages, then, we tackle the problem of aggression in dreams by re-examining the concept of wish fulfillment, that mediating crossroad which bridges Freud's transition from the belief in "actual" etiologies, to the positing of independently subsisting instincts. In doing so, we discover that even before his scrupulous preoccupation with the sexual instincts per se, Freud already possessed a more flexible kind of psychic mover which could hypothetically subsume the total reality of the oedipal situation; not only sexual impulses, that is, but murderously aggressive ones as well.

I.

Freud's most important attainment in *The Interpretation of Dreams* was not the clinical revelation that certain dreams embodied wish fulfillments, but the construction of a model of the psychic apparatus by which all dreams could be nothing *more* than the deferred fulfillment of infantile wishes. The reason the unconscious had "nothing else to offer during sleep but the motive force for the fulfillment of a *wish*,"that is to say, rested on "the psychical nature of wishes" and its relation to "our schematic picture of the psychical apparatus" (Freud, 1900, p. 565). Because both the motive force and starting point for dream formation resided in the unconscious (Freud, 1900, pp. 541-542), the dream became a wish fulfillment because the activity of the unconscious "knows no other aim than the fulfilment of wishes and has at its command no other forces than wishful impulses" (Freud, 1900, p. 568). Freud writes:

> nothing but a wish can set our mental apparatus at work. Dreams, which fulfil their wishes along the short path of regression, have merely preserved for us in that respect a sample of the psychical apparatus's primary method of working, a method which was abandoned as being inefficient. What once dominated waking life, while the mind was still young and incompetent, seems now to have been banished into the night—just as the primitive weapons, the bows and arrows, that have been abandoned by adult men, turn up once more in the nursery. *Dreaming is a piece of infantile mental life that has been superseded* [1900, p. 567].

In his attempt to assign a definite content to the wish fulfillment, Freud at once betrayed the more grandiose design that lay behind the writing of *The Interpretation of Dreams*. Freud never could be content with the role of astute clinical observer, and his intellectual fascination with the dream itself was never completely self-contained. Always lurking beneath the surface was the exciting, if presumptuous, hope that the psychology of dreaming, if diligently pursued, would illuminate and rationalize the psychology of the neuroses, and that if one penetrated far enough below the surface, a common denominator explaining both processes would emerge. Although he was perfectly willing to admit in the latter part of the study that his own line of approach to the comprehension of dreams "was determined by my previous work on the psychology of the neuroses," Freud still maintained that to work in the opposite direction, starting with the dream and proceeding to establish its junction with the psychology of the neuroses, constituted a different and far more challenging problem. Moreover, it was this attempt, he submitted, that would substantially "put a higher value on [his] efforts" (Freud, 1900, p. 588). The junction was first heralded by observing similar pathogenic processes operative in the expression of neuroses and dreams.

Freud believed that the dream-work proper, which ensued when a preconscious trace of thought acquired cathexes from the unconscious, and which transformed the dream thoughts through compression, condensation, and intermediary ideas, was in essence "a psychopathological structure" (1900, p. 595). To explain the derivation of this psychic process, he returned to his clinical observations on hysterics. There, too, he had initially found that "a series of perfectly rational thoughts, equal in validity to our conscious thoughts," could be reconstructed. In forcing their way to perception, however, these normal thoughts, like the precipitating dream thoughts, "have been submitted to abnormal treatment: *they have been transformed into the symptom by means of condensation and the formation of compromises, by way of superficial associations and in disregard of contradictions, and also, it may be, along the path of regression"* (1900, p. 597). It was in view of this "complete identity between the characteristic features of the dream-work and those of the psychical activity which issues in psychoneurotic symptoms" that Freud felt justified "in carrying over to dreams the conclusions we have been led to by hysteria" (1900, pp. 597-598). These ultimately reduced to the proposition that "*a normal train of thought is only submitted to abnormal psychical treatment of the sort we have been describing if an unconscious wish, derived from infancy and in a state of repression, has been transferred on to it"* (1900, p. 598). It had been in compliance with this proposition, he continued, that he had "constructed our theory of dreams on the assumption that the dream-wish which provides the motive power invariably originates from the unconscious —an assumption which, as I myself am ready to admit, cannot be proved to hold generally, though neither can it be disproved" (p. 598).

The entire chapter on "The Psychology of Dream-Processes," then, ultimately rings with another of Freud's brilliant "pathogenic analogies." Even more important than the simple clinical analogy between dream-work and neurotic symptom formation, however, was the common etiological mechanism revealed in both processes. The unconscious system Freud delineated in the dream book had not been initially discovered in relation to dreams, and thus could not posit "unconscious" dictums which were proper only to the dream. If there existed a system of the *Ucs.*, Freud wrote, "(or something analogous to it for the purposes of our discussion), dreams cannot be its only manifestation" (1900, p. 568). By consequence, if the dream was a wish fulfillment only because it was a function of the system *Ucs.*, there had to be other forms of wish fulfillment embracing other psychic phenomena. In fact, there were. Freud proposed that a different form of such unconscious expression resided in the "theory" governing psychoneurotic symptoms. Like dreams, such symptoms ultimately reduced to wish fulfillments of the unconscious (1900, p. 569).

Here then was the new meeting point Freud had been anticipating. The language of dream analysis could now be appropriated partly to recast and partly to elucidate the problem of symptom formation. While Freud had previously expressed some misgivings because the dream psychology had borrowed all its "themes" from the work on neurosis (1887-1902, p. 257), he had at this point confirmed his initial hunch and demonstrated the value of working in the opposite direction. Having learned from the study of hysteria the importance of an actuating "wish" and having transferred it to the study of dreams, he now derived from the dream the elemental necessity of the wish's "fulfillment" and reapplied it to the problem of symptoms. Thus, it had now become "the dream pattern," as he wrote Fliess in January, 1899, which "is capable of universal application, and . . . the key to hysteria really lies in dreams" (1887-1902, p. 271). Six weeks later he wrote:

> My last generalization holds good and seems inclined to spread to an unpredictable extent. It is not only dreams that are

fulfilments of wishes, but hysterical attacks as well. This is true of hysterical symptoms, but it probably applies to every product of neurosis—for I recognized it long ago in acute delusional insanity. Reality—wish-fulfilment: it is from this contrasting pair that our mental life springs [1887-1902, p. 277].[1]

If the concept of an actuating dream wish was borrowed from the theory of hysteria, it stood to reason that Freud would return to the theory of hysteria in defining the content of the dream wish. Certainly he had taken a large step in this direction when he transferred from the work with neuroses the qualifying proposition that the dream wish had to be in a state of repression (1900, p. 598). Yet, the analysis of hysterics and obsessional neurotics had surely been able to do more than simply pinpoint the developmental origins of wish impulses; it had been able to ascribe to them a definite nature:

> The theory of the psychoneuroses asserts as an indisputable and invariable fact that only sexual wishful impulses from infancy, which have undergone repression (i.e. a transformation of their affect) during the developmental period of childhood, are capable of being revived during *later* developmental periods (whether as a result of the subject's sexual constitution, which is derived from an initial bisexuality, or as a result of unfavourable influences acting upon the course of his sexual life) and are thus able to furnish the motive force for the formation of psychoneurotic symptoms of every kind [1900, pp. 605-606].

Surprisingly enough, however, Freud was unwilling to commit himself to this final and perhaps most important clinical analogy. For the time being, he would "leave it an open question whether these sexual and infantile factors are

---

[1] Freud had seen the relationship between dreams and neurosis earlier in the *Project for a Scientific Psychology*. In the nineteenth section on "Primary Processes —Sleep and Dreams," he noted that "the pathological mechanisms which are revealed by the most careful analysis in the psychoneuroses bear the greatest similarity to dream-processes" (Freud, 1895e, p. 398). The editors of his early letters and drafts suggest that he then lost sight of this discovery and did not rediscover it till the letter of February 19, 1899. In an intervening Draft N, dated May 31, 1897, however, Freud had again noted that "symptoms are *fulfilments of wishes*, just as dreams are" (Freud, 1887-1902, pp. 208-209).

equally required in the theory of dreams." "I will leave that theory incomplete at this point," he added, "since I have already gone a step beyond what can be demonstrated in assuming that dream wishes are invariably derived from the unconscious" (1900, p. 606). This abrupt and rather inadequate assertion was his final word on the matter. He added in a footnote on the same page that his refusal to treat exhaustively the part that psychosexual life plays in the dream was solely a function of his desire to avoid "the still unsolved problems of perversion and bisexuality" which the explanation of sexual dreams would entail (1900, pp. 606n.-607n.).

Earlier, in the massive chapter on "The Dream-Work," his refusal to reduce the latent dream thoughts to the sexual had been less tentative. While the obvious importance of the "sexual complexes" could never be forgotten, he warned, "we should also, of course, avoid the exaggeration of attributing exclusive importance to them" (1900, p. 396). Indeed, in an addition appended to the dream book in 1919, Freud went on to state: "The assertion that all dreams require a sexual interpretation, against which critics rage so incessantly, occurs nowhere in my *Interpretation of Dreams*. It is not to be found in any of the numerous editions of this book and is in obvious contradiction to other views expressed in it" (Freud, 1900, p. 397).

For our present purpose, this final refusal to attach the sexual label to dream wishes in the dream book after elaborately synthesizing the psychology of dreaming with the psychology of the neuroses is an important paradox worthy of further examination. Why was Freud unable to make the most crucial linkage of all between the two modes of unconscious psychic activity he had investigated? He had certainly been willing to *explore* the sexual element in dream life, particularly with reference to superficially innocent dreams (where the motive for the censorship was "obviously the sexual factor" [1900, p. 188]) and anxiety dreams (where "the sexual material present in their dream-thoughts" could be regularly demonstrated [1900, p. 583]). Moreover, if the assumption that the dream wish originated in the unconscious was "a step beyond" the demonstrable, it was equally a step beyond the demonstrable for the wishes generating hysterical symptoms. In the latter case, however, Freud had not hesitated to label these fantasies sexual. Similarly, the "still unsolved problems of perversion and bisexuality" had not prevented him from proclaiming, as a categorical generalization, the inevitable and irreducible sexual content of psychoneurotic symptoms (1898). Why, then, this final glimmering of uncertainty in *The Interpretation of Dreams?*

The answer to this question is overdetermined and can be delineated at several different levels. In previous clinical work, Freud could assert that "the most immediate and, for practical purposes, the most significant causes of every case of neurotic illness are to be found in factors arising from sexual life," largely because the "factors arising out of a sexual life must really be acknowledged to be causes of illness" (1898, pp. 263, 264). This could not be the case with the study of dream specimens. Despite the convincing argument that the process active in dream formation revealed the closest analogy with the processes operative in the formation of hysterical symptoms, the dream itself was not a pathological phenomenon and presupposed no pathogenic disturbance of psychic equilibrium. Indeed, one crucial outcome of the analysis of dreams was the very discovery that "the psychical mechanism employed by neuroses is not created by the impact of a pathological disturbance upon the mind but is present already in the normal structure of the mental apparatus" (Freud, 1900, p. 607). Despite its utility in exposing the conflict behind neurotic symptoms, the dream itself was not a "symptom" and produced no symptomatic residue in waking life which could interpretively testify to its intrinsic character.

Thus, despite the neurosislike psychic process operative in dream formation, the dream itself was "pathological" only in the most figurative sense (Freud, 1900, pp. 607-608), and there was consequently no *clinical* reason why wish fulfillment in dreams had to be sexual. And in fact, Freud's evidence never indicated that it was so. In the course of *The Interpretation of Dreams,* wish fulfillment emerges as a genuinely plastic concept. In both this work and the *Introductory*

Lectures that Freud would deliver some 16 years later, wish fulfillment was introduced not with reference to the great "tendencies" of psychic life, but according to the simple (and unique) model of children's dreams. Here, owing to the absence of prolonged dream-work and its ensuing distortion, the direct, undisguised fulfillment of the dream wish could be immediately seen. Such "fulfillment," however, rather than serving only the circumscribed needs of the sexual instinct, might be directed to any unsatisfied wish of the previous day, however impossible, silly, or trivial it might have been (1900, pp. 127-133; 1916-1917, pp. 126-131). Another kind of wish fulfillment, common to adults but still of a patently infantile cast, arose in response to "imperative physical needs" experienced by the dreamer. As reactions to "internal somatic stimuli" such "convenience dreams" might well be evoked by sexual arousal (1916-1917, p. 134), but even more apparent and frequent were those addressed to hunger, thirst, excremental discomfort, and other plainly nonlibidinal aims (1900, pp. 123-126; 1916-1917, pp. 132-135). Finally, individual dreams, as Freud repeatedly reiterated in the dream book, could actually be sustained by multiple wish fulfillments. In addition, not only could several wish fulfillments appear in simultaneous combination, but one might in fact be superimposed on the other (1900, pp. 219, 561-562).

Moreover, superimposed on the entire range of wish-fulfilling dreams was the problematic category of punishment dreams. Here the dream, "in the conflict between a *parvenu's* pride and his self-criticism," sided with the latter, and chose as its content "a sensible warning instead of an unlawful wish-fulfilment." While such dreams were still predicated on an "exaggeratedly ambitious phantasy," the alleged "masochistic impulses of the mind" impelled the ego to permit only the suppression and abasement of the wish to reach the dream content (1900, pp. 475-476). In 1923, Freud would label punishment dreams the only *"apparent"* exceptions to the theory of wish fulfillment, and would attribute them to the "critical agency" of an alerted ego that was "temporarily re-established even during the sleeping state" (Freud, 1923b, p. 118; cf. Freud, 1925b, pp. 132-133).

II.

The precise role of aggression in wish fulfillments is not immediately clear. Within the context of "The Psychology of the Dream Processes," aggression is certainly not posited as material for wish fulfillment. It is at best permitted, if only because Freud is unable to confirm the lowest sexual common denominator binding hysterical and dream processes. This fact alone, however, hardly provides a convincing argument for the importance of aggression in the work. Freud's interpretive method, as Rieff (1961, pp. 160-161) reasonably observes, is one of "conscientious indirection," relying on the interpretive distinction between latent and manifest, conscious and unconscious, distorted and authentic, without really positing the content of these categories. The injunction that all mental acts be stratified dictates only that meanings be concealed; it does not indicate what these meanings must be. Thus, if there is nothing in Freud's "method" guaranteeing that repressed sexuality be the root motive lurking behind the conscious, there is assuredly nothing suggesting it must unfailingly be a matter of repressed aggression.

It is only when we turn to the clinical groundwork from which the general propositions of Freud's Chapter 7 evolve, that the importance of "aggressive" dreams becomes apparent. Early in the book, in his analysis of "typical dreams" in the chapter on "The Material and Sources of Dreams," Freud explicitly cites the important role of aggression as enduring fantasy material in dream-life.

Typical dreams shared by many persons, Freud maintains, are the hardest to penetrate by interpretation. In them, the dreamer does not produce his own associations, but utilizes, in Paul Ricoeur's apt phrase, "symbolic fragments that have fallen to the sphere of the trodden commonplace" (1970, p. 101). Consequently, such dreams have the same significance to all dreamers and "presumably arise from the same sources in every case" (Freud, 1900, p. 241). Indeed, it is in the context of these "typical dreams" that Freud's growing appreciation of the role of symbolism in dreams received early expression (see Ricoeur, 1970, pp. 99-102).

As examples of "typical dreams," Freud first mentioned embarrassment dreams of nakedness. These dreams were actually exhibitionist dreams harking back to a childhood "paradise" when "we are seen in inadequate clothing both by members of our family and by strangers" and "feel no shame at our nakedness" (1900, p. 244). He also briefly investigated examination dreams in which the dreamer repeatedly failed in dream-life the very "tests" he had successfully passed in real life (1900, pp. 273-276). Freud reserved a more extensive analysis for a third category of "typical dreams," and it was here that he revealed the impact that the "aggressive tendencies" of his patients had made upon him.

The third category of "typical dreams" involved the "death of persons of whom the dreamer is fond." Here Freud became direct: typical dreams in which a beloved relative had died clearly indicated that the dreamer actively "wished" the person to die during his childhood, and proved perfectly consistent with the "vanished mental life of children" he proceeded to elucidate. The relation between siblings was not nearly as idyllic as it had been reported. Children are "completely egoistic," feel their wants acutely, and "strive ruthlessly to satisfy them" against all competitors, especially their siblings. Adult "love" between brothers and sisters is an emergent property, built on a foundation of unconscious evil wishes, and it was these latter wishes that gained expression in dream-life. To be sure, the child's "wish" that its sibling die was partly figurative. The child, Freud conceded, knew nothing of the "horrors of corruption" or the "terrors of eternal nothingness" associated with death. Rather, the child "wished" someone to "die" only in the sense that he "go away." The child's sentiments gained expression as a "death wish" only because it lacked the "adult" restraints which would preclude it from voicing its desire for the loved one's absence in such drastic terms. Once the different connotative implications of death are granted, however, the child's death wishes proved identical with the corresponding wish in an adult and denoted an intense hostility which was all too genuine (1900, pp. 248-255).

"Typical dreams" involving a death wish, however, occurred not only with reference to siblings, but with reference to parents as well, and it is in accounting for this latter expression of hostility that Freud introduced the Oedipus complex. If dreams involving the death of a parent normally refer to the parent of the same sex, it is because, even in the earliest years of childhood, a "sexual preference" had already emerged by which boys regarded their fathers and girls their mothers as "rivals in love" whose elimination was to be actively sought (1900, p. 256). Indeed, Freud had been receiving clinical hints that these two kinds of relationships involved "hostility" for some time, and had made his impressions explicit in the Fliess correspondence. As early as the spring of 1897, several months before the abandonment of the Neurotica compelled him even to consider the possibility that "sexual phantasy regularly makes use of the theme of the parents" (1887-1902, p. 216), he informed Fliess that "Hostile impulses against parents (a wish that they should die) are ... an integral part of neuroses," and further surmised that sons directed this death wish against the father and daughters against the mother (1887-1902, p. 207).

In *The Interpretation of Dreams* the insight is now made official; for the boy the father and for the girl the mother are actually "disturbing" rivals, and the fantasied aggressions that culminate in the actual "death-wish" receive recurring expression in dream-life. In his own self-analysis, Freud had recognized the love of mother and jealousy of father characterizing his own case. Now his thought had crystallized and his language hardened: the process of loving one parent and hating the other is not in itself "neurotic" and cannot be linked to any intruding precocious intervention. Rather, it is among "the essential constituents of the stock of psychical impulses" formed during childhood, and the psychoneurotic version of these emotions is, in all probability, a magnification of feelings of love and hatred "which occur less obviously and less intensely in the minds of most children" (1900, pp. 257-261).

These conclusions were consolidated and restated in the *Introductory Lectures* Freud delivered a decade and a half later (1916-1917, pp. 199-212). By that time, he was willing to generalize beyond the confines of intrafamilial strife. All censored dream wishes, he then observed, were above all manifestations of "an unbridled and ruthless egoism" which could take different forms. Consequently, dreams might be generated not only by the liberated sexual impulse, but by unrestrained feelings of hatred and revenge, in addition to the death wishes generated by both oedipal and sibling rivalry (pp. 142-143).

The omnipresent quality of intense hostility in dreams involving the death of close relations was probably an important factor in Freud's decision to leave the concept of wish fulfillment generically open-ended. Long embraced as the central experience of libidinal development, the Oedipus complex has only recently been appreciated as the nodal point from which aggressive impulses radiate as well (see, for example, Rangell, 1972). While heralded as the culmination of infantile *sexual* life, it is essential to note that the Oedipus myth is originally invoked not to explain infantile sexuality, but the fantasied aggressions, i.e., death wishes, occurring in dream-life. Indeed, the developmental pre-eminence of the oedipal situation serves to reduce sexuality itself to the aftermath of an "aggressive" overcoming: by tracing love back to the parental fact of domination, Freud makes "power" the father of love (Rieff, 1961, p. 168). Because love is initially authoritarian,

> sexuality—like liberty—is a later achievement, always in danger of being overwhelmed by our deeper inclinations toward submissiveness and domination. Indeed, sensuality becomes a mode of liberation and Freud may be seen, in this sense, as its champion. Tender love is a compliant and grateful response to parental dominance, and mature sexuality, which follows, signifies a freeing from the parents [Rieff, 1961, pp. 75-76, 184].

Through the investigation of typical dreams, Freud discovered the fantasied route which the "freeing from the parents" instinctively followed. The aggressive fantasies he located, even if conditioned by sexual rivalry, still reflect a new comprehension of "hostility," one which remained free of subsequent sexualization and thus distinct from the kind of "sexual aggressions" he had previously considered. Admittedly, the handling of the oedipal theme in *The Interpretation of Dreams* is severely circumscribed. Freud virtually ignored the cultural significance of the Oedipus complex and subordinated its institutionalization to its fantasy aspect in dream-life. Yet, even if oedipal aggressive impulses were reduced to dream fantasy, they still emanated from a universal fantasy from which none were exempt (see Ricoeur, 1970, pp. 192-193). No longer was the child's "aggressive" disposition believed to be prematurely aroused. It now became, instead, a phylogenetic inheritance, springing from "primeval dream material" over which, in dream-life at least, he exerted neither control nor direction. And while the Oedipus complex was initially the product of Freud's own self-analysis and thus cloaked in a secret character, the universality of the myth compelled the oedipal situation eventually to take its place in the etiology of the neuroses. Indeed, not only does the Oedipus complex signal the abandonment of the seduction hypothesis, it dictates that it be replaced with its very opposite. The Oedipus complex, as Ricoeur points out, is actually the seduction hypothesis in reverse. The seduction by the father thus becomes the distorted presentation of the true oedipal situation. It is not the father who seduces the child, but the child, in "wishing" to possess the mother, who desires the death of the father (Ricoeur, 1970, pp. 188-189).

III.

Even more important than oedipal aggressions in explaining Freud's refusal to sexualize wish fulfillment were the death wishes directed against siblings. Here, sexual rivalry was not even the precipitating factor; it was, instead, a childishly asocial "egoism" which consigned the sibling to the status of "rival" and made him the object of blatantly aggressive impulses. It was this kind of "aggressive" wish that Freud had never "failed to come upon" in all his female patients (1900, p. 253). More essentially, it is in relation to such non-oedipal "aggressive" impulses that we perhaps touch on the most critical phase of his own self-analysis.

Investigation of Freud's interpretations of his own dream specimens clearly reveals the seeds of an "aggressive" quest for professional vindication at the expense of recalcitrant patients and colleagues. Biographically, this quest for vindication can be understood in terms of the "wracking crisis" Freud experienced in the 1890's. By the writing of the dream book, the professional frustration which had plagued him from the outset of his career culminated in a "bitterness verging on despair." Prevented by poverty from becoming the research scientist he longed to be, he languished at the Vienna Children's Hospital from 1886 to 1896 with little opportunity for research. His failure to acquire scientific standing was crowned by the failure to receive the university professorship he ardently desired—a situation remedied shortly after the publication of the dream book. Superimposed on these private professional frustrations were the political frustrations Freud experienced as a Viennese liberal Jew confronted with the often anti-Semitic erosion of Austrian liberalism which was under full swing by this time (Schorske, 1973, pp. 330-332). Therapeutically, Freud's overcompensatory quest for professional vindication received further impetus from the very real therapeutic failures which characterized his early years of prepsychoanalytic clinical practice. Within this context, we have long been familiar with the deleterious consequences of Freud's outspoken advocacy of the clinical use of cocaine in the mid-1880's, with particular reference to the tragic cocaine addiction and subsequent death of his friend and laboratory colleague Ernst Fleischl von Marxow (Jones, 1953, pp. 78-97). Within the last decade, however, we have acquired new evidence of therapeutic mismanagement relating to Freud's uncritical reliance on Wilhelm Fliess as a medical and surgical consultant. In particular, Max Schur (1966) has provided a dramatic documented account of the "Emma" episode of 1895, where Fliess's surgical intervention and careless failure to remove a piece of iodoform gauze from the surgical site nearly resulted in the death of one of Freud's hysterical patients. In subsequent correspondence to Fliess, a traumatized, guilt-ridden Freud repeatedly wrestled with the overt fact of diagnostic failure and gross medical mismanagement associated with this case.

In short, then, if Freud's need for professional vindication had important antecedents in the institutional victimization that characterized his early career, the aggressive retaliatory features of this need probably partake of a projection fueled by self-knowledge of his own therapeutic inadequacies—what Leavitt (1956, p. 443) has termed his "repressed knowledge of his diagnostic deficits."

The "Irma" dream—the dream associated with the discovery of interpretability[2] and the first dream presented for analysis in the dream book—is the prototypical response to these anxieties.

The dream focuses on Freud's only partially successful treatment of "Irma" during the summer of 1895, and was triggered by the fact that a younger colleague, "Otto" (Dr. Oskar Rie) had recently visited her and reminded Freud that, while better, she was "not quite well." Freud was annoyed by this comment in which he detected a "reproach"—"such as to the effect that I had promised the patient too much" (Freud, 1900, p. 106). In addition, behind this reproach he thought he detected the stern authority of "Dr. M." (Breuer), a senior colleague who was "the leading personality in our circle." The ensuing dream was one of professional vindication in which Freud punished the three persons who had, in this instance, impugned his medical integrity. In the dream, Irma, who is reproached for not accepting Freud's "solution" to her problem, is found to have complicated organic pathology of which he had been previously unaware:

> —I at once called in Dr. M., and he repeated the examination and confirmed it.... Dr. M. looked quite different from usual; he was very pale, he walked with a limp and his chin was clean-shaven.... My friend Otto was now standing beside her as well,

[2] In a letter to Fliess dated June 12, 1900, Freud wrote: "Do you suppose that some day a marble tablet will be placed on the house, inscribed with the words: In this House on July 24th, 1895, the Secret of Dreams was revealed to Dr. Sigmund Freud" (Freud, 1887-1902, p. 322). This coincides with the date of the Irma dream (Freud, 1900, p. 107).

*and my friend Leopold was percussing her through her bodice
and saying: 'She has a dull area low down on the left.' He also
indicated that a portion of the skin on the left shoulder was
infiltrated. (I noticed this, just as he did, in spite of her dress.)
... M. said: 'There's no doubt it's an infection, but no matter;
dysentery will supervene and the toxin will be eliminated.' ...
We were directly aware, too, of the origin of the infection. Not
long before, when she was feeling unwell, my friend Otto had
given her an injection of a preparation of propyl, propyls ...
propionic acid ... trimethylamin (and I saw before me the
formula for this printed in heavy type).... Injections of that
sort ought not to be made so thoughtlessly.... And probably
the syringe had not been clean [p. 107].*

Interpretation reveals that the dream is clearly a vengeful
one. In it, Irma has actually been replaced by an intimate
friend of hers who is also hysterical and whom Freud has
anticipated treating. The "disobedient" patient who had
resisted his interpretive solution, that is, was exchanged for
one whom Freud visualized as "wiser and less recalcitrant."
Freud was additionally avenged upon Otto, who had annoyed
him by remarking about Irma's imperfect cure and who had
implicitly accused him of careless medical treatment. In the
dream, it is Otto himself who is to blame for her condition,
having "infected" her with an injection from an unclean
syringe. Lastly, Dr. M., whom Freud associated with Otto's
criticism and who has, like Irma, rejected Freud's solution, is
likewise punished. The consoling prognosis he offers in the
dream is designed to ridicule him and show that "he was an
ignoramus on the subject." In the process of acquitting
himself of the responsibility for Irma's continued suffering, all
three of these persons were compelled to feel the weight of
Freud's anger (1900, pp. 118-121). The latent "wish" was not
simply to be innocent of Irma's illness, but to punish aggressively those who would have it otherwise. To this end, Freud
enlists the support (and strength) of a "friend." In the "trimethylamin" which Otto has "rashly" injected into Irma,
Freud sees an allusion to Fliess (who believed trimethylamin to
be "one of the products of sexual metabolism") (Freud,
1900, p. 116). Freud subsequently sees the dream as a continual "turning from someone who annoyed me to someone

else who could be agreeably contrasted with him; point by point, I called up a friend against an opponent" (1900, pp. 294-295).[3]

The "deeply embittered and derisive dream-thoughts" (1900, p. 451) which Freud directed towards unreceptive colleagues are dramatically demonstrated in an "absurd dream" about his deceased father. Analysis reveals that the "father" who, to Freud, is made "the explicit object of ridicule" in the dream, is in reality "a senior colleague of mine, whose judgement was regarded as beyond criticism, [who] had given voice to disapproval and surprise at the fact that the psychoanalytic treatment of one of my patients had already entered its *fifth year*" (1900, p. 436). The instigating dream thoughts, Freud submits, "protested bitterly against the reproach that I was *not getting on faster*—a reproach which, applying first to my treatment of the patient, extended later to other things. Did he know anyone, I thought, who could get on more quickly?" (1900, p. 437). The allegation of once being drunk and "locked up for it," on the other hand, pointed to another professional "father" Freud sought to malign—the great Meynert—"in whose footsteps I had trodden with such deep veneration and whose behaviour towards me, after a short period of favour, had turned to undisguised hostility" (1900, p. 437).

In the aggressive response to professional censure in still

---

[3] Grinstein's (1968) more encompassing treatment of the "Irma" dream is generally compatible with mine, though he stresses the defensive and reactive aspects of Freud's quest for professional vindication in accord with the actual biographical basis for Freud's preoccupation with the theme of therapeutic self-reproach. In this connection, Grinstein also utilizes Schur's (1966) revelations concerning the therapeutic failure that followed Freud's use of Fliess as a surgical consultant in the "Emma" case, and incorporates material based on Freud's therapeutic misuse of cocaine as well. Leavitt (1956) also reviews the dream in terms of Freud's aggression, but he pushes this theme beyond the parameters of professional vindication established by Freud. He does this by equating Otto (the pediatrician of Freud's children) with Fliess (Freud's own personal physician at this time) at the level of Freud's dream thoughts, and consequently sees the dream "teleology" as an expression of the still latent conflict between Freud's adulation and unconscious hostility towards Fliess. Erikson's (1954) treatment of the "Irma" dream remains the most suggestive in terms of psychosexual and psychosocial dimensions wholly outside Freud's own narrow interpretation.

another "absurd" dream, Freud utilized as recent dream material the depreciative review of a book by Fliess which the editor of a medical periodical (and a friend of Freud's) had recently accepted for publication. Freud had intervened and called the editor to account. In the dream, Freud transmutes his previous defense of Fliess to an "egoistic" defense of his own theory of the psychoneuroses. Through supplementary material, Freud can make Fliess's cause his own and put himself in his place. For Freud, the dream consequently takes on significance in relation "to the opposition in which I found myself to most doctors on account of my belief in the sexual aetiology of the psychoneuroses. I could say to myself, 'The kind of criticism that has been applied to your friend will be applied to you—indeed, to some extent it already *has* been'" (1900, p. 441).

At the same time that Freud's dreams reveal an "aggressive-retaliatory" motif against a host of assaulting colleagues, they display a closely related strain of aggressive and often compensatory ambition with reference to his own social aspirations and professional "credibility." In the absurd dream involving his deceased father, for example, Freud believes the use of his real father to screen the illustrious Meynert is indicative of the following "conditional sentence": " 'If only I had been the second generation, the son of a professor or Hofrat, I should certainly have *got on faster.*' In the dream I made my father into a Hofrat and professor" (1900, p. 438). Similarly, in the same dream, Freud's observation that 1856 (his real birth date) seemed immediately after 1851 (the birth date attributed to him in a "dream" communication) and the implied conclusion that five years was "no time at all," is ultimately traced back to his inability to complete his medical studies in the normal five years, but his subsequent success in "getting through" in spite of the postponement. This, in turn, provides a "fresh reinforcement" of the dream thought with which he "defiantly" meets his critics: " 'Even though you won't believe it because I've taken my time, I *shall* get through; I *shall* bring my medical training to a *conclusion*. Things have often turned out like that before'" (1900, p. 451).

The "absurd" dream involving Count Thun stems from

Freud's recent meeting with the Count. Repulsed by the aristocratic pretense which characterized the Count's deportment, Freud attributes the dream's absurdity to the negative value judgment of the Count that is implicit in the dream thoughts: " 'It is absurd to be proud of one's ancestry; it is better to be an ancestor oneself.' This judgement, that something 'is absurd,' was what produced the absurdity in the dream" (1900, p. 434).

Analogously, in his Southern Railway dream, Freud takes revenge on the upper-class traveling companions who have snubbed him on a recent trip: "In my dream I took fearful vengeance on my disagreeable companions; no one could suspect what insults and humiliations lay concealed behind the broken fragments of the first half of the dream" (1900, p. 457).

IV.

The aggressive propensity to sacrifice intimate friends which underlies Freud's professional ambition ultimately coalesces — and receives its "infantile" rationale — in the Non Vixit dream which occurred in the fall of 1898.

I had gone to Brücke's laboratory at night, and, in response to a gentle knock on the door, I opened it to (the late) Professor Fleischl, who came in with a number of strangers and, after exchanging a few words, sat down at his table. This was followed by a second dream. *My friend Fl.* [Fliess] *had come to Vienna unobtrusively in July. I met him in the street in conversation with my* (deceased) *friend P., and went with them to some place where they sat opposite each other as though they were at a small table. I sat in front at its narrow end. Fl. spoke about his sister and said that in three-quarters of an hour she was dead, and added some such words as 'that was the threshold'. As P. failed to understand him, Fl. turned to me and asked me how much I had told P. about his affairs. Whereupon, overcome by strange emotions, I tried to explain to Fl. that P. (could not understand anything at all, of course, because he) was not alive. But what I actually said—and I myself noticed the mistake—was, 'Non vixit.' I then gave P. a piercing look. Under my gaze he turned pale, his form grew indistinct and his eyes a sickly blue—and finally he melted away. I was highly delighted at this and I now*

78   PAUL E. STEPANSKY

realized that Ernst Fleischl, too, had been no more than an apparition, a 'revenant' ['ghost'—literally, 'one who returns']; and it seemed to me quite possible that people of that kind only existed as long as one liked and could be got rid of if someone else wished it [1900, p. 421].

The manifest content of this dream occurs during Freud's early apprenticeship to the physiologist Brücke and focuses on the two men who forestalled his aspiration to receive an associate appointment in Brücke's laboratory. The two men whom Freud visually "annihilates" are Ernst Fleischl von Marxow, an associate of Brücke, and Josef Paneth, a close friend of Freud's and fellow "demonstrator" in Brücke's Institute who was next in line to succeed Fleischl.

Freud's relationship to both these "revenants" was deeply conflicted. Fleischl, a brilliant and rapidly advancing scientist, developed amputation neuromata (causalgia) from a laboratory wound necessitating the amputation of several fingers. At Freud's behest, he ingested large quantities of cocaine to cure a morphine addiction that had subsequently developed. Fleischl rapidly developed a cocaine addiction, however, with symptoms even more disastrous than those of morphinism. Freud was subsequently forced to witness the progressive physical and mental deterioration of an admired friend, tinged with the "guilt" associated with his initial recommendation of cocaine. His empathy remained admixed with hostility, however, for the number of associate appointments to Brücke's Institute was extremely limited and, in his own ambition, Freud had occasionally experienced death wishes toward Fleischl (Schur, 1972, pp. 155-157).

The second manifest revenant in the dream was Josef Paneth, an old friend toward whom Freud also felt concurrent hostility. Paneth, like Fleischl, came from a wealthy family and had made a generous loan to Freud. The subsequent sense of obligation and guilt that Freud felt was exacerbated by Paneth's own premature death. In the dream, it is Paneth who initially dissolves under Freud's gaze, a development explained by the hostile "train of thought" which existed beneath Freud's affectionate regard for his friend: "As he had deserved well of science I built him a memorial; but as he was guilty of an evil wish (which was expressed at the end of the dream) I annihilated him" (1900, p. 423). What was this "evil" wish? In his avidness to be promoted to associate in Brücke's laboratory, Paneth had impatiently "wished" that Fleischl would receive promotion. Given Fleischl's serious illness, Paneth's wish "might have an uglier meaning than the mere hope for the man's promotion" (1900, p. 484), i.e., that Fleischl die. Such apparent indignation on Freud's part was ultimately absorbed by aggressive egoism, however. Freud had himself "nourished a still livelier wish to fill a vacancy" (1900, p. 484) several years earlier, and such an ascension would have required the "annihilation" not only of Fleischl, but of Paneth as well. It was consequently Freud himself who expressed heartless ambition in the dream, and it was only through the distortion that "the dream punished my friend, and not me, for this callous wish" (1900, p. 484).

In the second part of the interpretation of the Non Vixit dream delivered later in the book, Freud unraveled the more immediate and more remote layers of expendable "revenants" who were masked by Fleischl and Paneth. The occasion of the dream, he now discovered, was news that Fliess had undergone an unsuccessful sinus operation and was seriously ill. While he planned to visit him in Berlin, Freud now contended that "a painful complaint which made movement of any kind a torture" prevented him from seeing him:

> The dream-thoughts now informed me that I feared for my friend's life. His only sister, whom I had never known, had, as I was aware, died in early youth after a very brief illness. (In the dream *Fl. spoke about his sister and said that in three-quarters of an hour she was dead.*) I must have imagined that his constitution was not much more resistant than his sister's and that, after getting some much worse news of him, I should make the journey after all—and arrive *too late,* for which I might never cease to reproach myself. This reproach for coming too late became the central point of the dream but was represented by a scene in which Brücke, the honoured teacher of my student years, levelled this reproach at me with a terrible look from his blue eyes. It will soon appear what it was that caused the situation [in regard to Fl.] to be switched on to these lines. The scene [with Brücke] itself could not be reproduced by the dream

in the form in which I experienced it. The other figure in the dream was allowed to keep the blue eyes, but the annihilating role was allotted to me—a reversal which was obviously the work of wish-fulfilment. My anxiety about my friend's recovery, my self-reproaches for not going to see him, the shame I felt about this—*he had come to Vienna* (to see me) *'unobtrusively'*—the need I felt to consider that I was excused by my illness—all of this combined to produce the emotional storm which was clearly perceived in my sleep and which raged in this region of the dream-thoughts [1900, p. 481].

Max Schur's incisive re-evaluation of the dream and the complicated biographical materials which surround it has made clear that Freud's manifest annihilation of his former rivals in Brücke's laboratory actually constituted "resistance downward" masking his increasing hostility towards Fliess during this period (Schur, 1972, p. 170). Indeed, the aftermath of Fliess's unsuccessful surgery augmented Freud's "aggressive reaction" and came to constitute another dimension of the occasion of the dream. Along with the unfavorable news after Fliess's operation, Freud writes, he received

a warning not to discuss the matter with anyone. I had felt offended by this because it implied an unnecessary distrust of my discretion. I was quite aware that these instructions had not emanated from my friend but were due to tactlessness or over-anxiety on the part of the intermediary, but I was very disagreeably affected by the veiled reproach because it was—not wholly without justification. As we all know, it is only reproaches which have something in them that 'stick'; it is only they that upset us. What I have in mind does not relate, it is true, to this friend, but to a much earlier period of my life. On that occasion I caused trouble between two friends (both of whom had chosen to honour me, too, with that name) by quite unnecessarily telling one of them, in the course of conversation, what the other had said about him. At that time, too, reproaches had been levelled at me, and they were still in my memory. One of the two friends concerned was Professor Fleischl; I may describe the other by his first name of 'Josef'—which was also that of P., my friend and opponent in the dream [1900, pp. 481-482].

Aside from establishing new links between the Fleischl-Paneth and Fliess themes previously uncovered, these new associations revealed a new "revenant" — Breuer, who shared with Paneth the first name "Josef."

These associations of petty resentment finally led Freud beyond the adult rivalries of the Brücke period and his conflicted misgivings regarding Fliess to his own early childhood and the memories recovered during the self-analysis. The dream thoughts coalesced around one knotty presupposition requiring further interpretation: Freud's slight anger at the warning not to divulge the secrets associated with Fliess's recent surgery (1900, p. 482). This emotional reaction, stemming from the trouble he had long ago created between Fleischl and Breuer, was not only apparent in his agitated response to Fliess's postoperative admonition, but was further indicated on the manifest level by his annihilatory vision towards Fleischl, who had inquired "how much of his affairs I have told P."

In a letter to Fliess dated October 3, 1897, Freud referred to his older nephew John who was his "companion in crime" between the ages of one and two and with whom he recalled occasionally treating his younger niece "shockingly" (1887-1902, p. 219). The relationship between Freud and John was highly ambivalent, however, composed of equal admixtures of hostility and affection. In his initial explication of the Non Vixit dream, Freud stated that his childish relations accounted for all his later feelings towards persons of his own age. While still dealing with the Fleischl-Paneth theme, he contended that the manifest hostility toward the latter could certainly be traced to his complicated relations with John during childhood. Having demonstrated the overdetermined nature of the revenant theme, Freud again returned to the John theme to explain his slight present-day anger "over the warning I had been given not to give anything away" in which his associations to Fleischl, Paneth, Breuer, and Fliess had coalesced. Such trivial annoyance, he announced,

> received reinforcements from sources in the depth of my mind and thus swelled into a current of hostile feelings against persons of whom I was in reality fond. The source of this reinforcement flowed from my childhood. I have already shown how my warm friendships as well as my enmities with contemporaries went

back to my relations in childhood with a nephew who was a year my senior; how he was my superior, how I early learned to defend myself against him, how we were inseparable friends, and how, according to the testimony of our elders, we sometimes fought with each other and—made complaints to them about each other. All my friends have in a certain sense been re-incarnations of this first figure who 'früh sich einst dem trüben Blick gezeigt': they have been *revenants*. My nephew himself re-appeared in my boyhood, and at that time we acted the parts of Caesar and Brutus together. My emotional life has always insisted that I should have an intimate friend and a hated enemy. I have always been able to provide myself afresh with both, and it has not infrequently happened that the ideal situation of childhood has been so completely reproduced that friend and enemy have come together in a single individual— though not, of course, both at once or with constant oscillations, as may have been the case in my early childhood [1900, pp. 482-483].

In submitting that adult colleagues simply constituted "a series of re-incarnations of the friend of my childhood" (1900, p. 485), Freud provided crucial developmental input which sheds light on the neurotic dimension of his own professional ambition and goes far in explaining why such a quest could be transmuted into an aggressive search for the "vindictive triumph."[4] The transferencelike reduction of competing peers to "revenant" status generated a neurotically induced "amorality" which, at the level of the dream thoughts, rationalized a policy of aggression towards rivals by claiming their inevitable expendability and replaceability. Just as his childhood companion John left Freud at age 3 only to return for a visit at age 14, Freud could afford to annihilate friends because they would inevitably return in new guises. Thus his final estimation of the dream thoughts of the Non Vixit dream:

'It's quite true that no one's irreplaceable. How many people I've followed to the grave already! But I'm still alive. I've survived them all; I'm left in possession of the field.' A thought of this kind, occurring to me at a moment at which I was afraid I might not find my friend [Fl.] alive if I made the journey to him, could only be construed as meaning that I was delighted because I had

---

[4] Here we follow Horney (1950, pp. 26-28).

once more survived someone, because it was *he* and not I who had died, because I was left in possession of the field, as I had been in the phantasied scene from my childhood. This satisfaction, infantile in origin, at being in possession of the field constituted the major part of the affect that appeared in the dream [1900, p. 485].

Freud's aggressive pursuit of glory at the expense of "intimate" friends drew support from a second infantile strain ignored in his own analysis of the Non Vixit dream. In the same letter in which he communicated to Fliess his ambivalent relation to his older nephew, Freud revealed that the birth of his younger brother Julius when he was one and a half years old had occasioned "ill wishes and real infantile jealousy," and that Julius's death several months later "left the germ of guilt in me." Together, Freud noted, "My nephew *and younger brother* determined not only the neurotic side of all my friendships, but also their depth" (1887-1902, p. 219, my emphasis). Grinstein (1968, p. 308) has gone one step beyond Freud's own chronological linkage of nephew and brother, and has plausibly suggested that, analytically, the hostile dream thoughts Freud directed toward his older nephew in tracing his associations back to an actual childhood fight between them actually mirror the identical aggressive wishes he had harbored toward the infant brother who died during the same period of his life.

To Schur, Freud's enduring problem of revenants is directly linked to the "guilt-of-the-survivor" motif stemming from these infantile experiences, and he examines the Non Vixit dream in this light. In the dream, he argues, Fliess is in reality a "revenant" not simply to Freud's nephew John, but to his younger brother whose death occurred in the year of Fliess's birth (Schur, 1972, p. 164). Furthermore, he submits that the omission of the dead brother Julius in the interpretation of the dream stems from Freud's "denial" of his own contemporary death wishes towards Fliess (p. 170).

For our purposes, a different theme emerges: it is clear that Freud's experience with his younger brother had a crucial "predisposing" effect on the kind of fantasies through which his adult aspirations would be formulated. Freud's earliest wish had been an "aggressive" one, and its immediate "fulfill-ment" provided enduring reinforcement for such infantile fantasies. The fact that Julius had actually died (in apparent obedience to Freud's aggressive wishes) seems to have trans-formed an infantile reflex into a permanent "coping" strategy. It was because Freud successfully "wished" his earliest rival away that he could so facilely reduce competing colleagues to expendable revenants vulnerable to his "searching gaze."

V.

While Freud's refusal to reduce dream wishes to the in-variably "sexual" impulses operative in neurosis can be technically rationalized on the level of the metapsychology in Chapter 7, examination of the "content" of the interpretation of dreams establishes the clinical and personal foundation from which this theoretical reticence evolves. In the analyses of his patients, Freud was impressed with the regular occur-rence of "aggressive" dreams involving hostile death wishes not only toward parents but toward rival siblings as well. Similar-ly, in his own dreams, Freud was undoubtedly struck by the "aggressive" redemptive motif operative against friends and colleagues. This, in turn, pointed to the crucial "aggressive" dimension in his own self-analysis.

The "love of the mother and jealousy of the father" that Freud discovered in his own case and believed to be "a general phenomenon of early childhood" were probably not indepen-dently sufficient to rekindle dormant infantile complexes in him. One good indication of this is the remarkably sterile language with which the discovery was communicated to Fliess: it was not an emotionally charged revelation, but simply "one idea of general value" which had occurred to him (Freud, 1887-1902, p. 223). Even Grinstein (1968), who shows great sensitivity to the latent parricidal associations which are also operative in the Non Vixit dream,[5] analyzes the under-

---

[5] Grinstein (1968, pp. 284-285) anchors this facet of his interpretation on Freud's relation to Ernst Brücke as an intimidating father figure. In the Non Vixit dream, Freud's visual annihilation of Josef Paneth actually represented an identification

lying "revenant" phenomena with almost exclusive reference to the fratricidal theme, and even suggests that "Freud's intense reaction of depression precipitated by the death of his father was not based solely on his guilty feelings over his unresolved Oedipus complex, but was also connected with the unresolved reaction to the death of his brother, for in both instances an aggressive wish had become fulfilled (pp. 315-316).

For Freud himself the analyzed priority of the aggressive fratricidal theme was clear enough: it was the need for a "hated" enemy—modeled on his relation to his nephew John—and the proclivity to dispose aggressively of that enemy —conditioned by his still earlier "wishful" success towards his brother Julius—that proved interpretively charged and contemporaneously relevant, determining the "neurotic side" of all his friendships.

In view of these insights, Freud's appeal to the "still unsolved problem" of bisexuality as a mitigating factor forestalling "the postulate of the sexual" for the theory of dreams takes on an added dimension. The "problem of bisexuality" had been theoretically explicated and introduced to Freud by Fliess, and it was Fliess with whom Freud forever identified the concept (Freud, 1887-1902, pp. 38-42, 242, 247-248, 289, 334-335, 337). We know that by the time he composed the concluding chapter of the dream book, Freud's positive transference relationship with Fliess was already in substantial jeopardy, and the unconscious hostility directed towards his friend and confidant mounted as Fliess's failure as an ego ideal in the clinical areas where Freud required help became more apparent (Schur, 1966, pp. 67-79; Leavitt, 1956, pp. 445-447). Indeed, Schur has argued that even in 1895, in the tortured correspondence to Fliess following the "Emma" affair, we can detect in Freud's associations "a highly aggressive wish against Fliess, *disguised as concern*" (Schur, 1966, p. 73). In attempting to justify his refusal to equate dream

---

with the "power" aspect of Brücke's omnipotence, as it had actually been Brücke who had "overwhelmed" Freud with his "terrible blue eyes" upon the latter's late arrival to his laboratory one morning (Freud, 1900, p. 422).

formation with an exclusively sexual motive power in the final chapter of *The Interpretation of Dreams*, then, Freud's recourse to the unsolved problem of bisexuality may actually have represented his troubled relationship with Fliess, and the unresolved aggressive "annihilatory" wishes he directed towards him.

In the immediate future, the explanation of such aggressive wishes would become tightly enmeshed with the study of the separate component impulses jointly comprising the sexual instinct. It is important to note that for purposes of the dream book, however, this reservoir of wishful aggressiveness—and its neurotic ramifications in adult life—was understood without recourse to a more elemental substratum of infantile sexuality.

4

THEORY CONFOUNDED: NEW STRAINS OF AGGRESSION AND THE EMERGENCE OF INSTITUTIONAL NEEDS

With the publication of two new Freudian texts in 1905, the explication of aggressive impulses becomes overdetermined. The more widely known and clinically significant half of the equation—articulated in the *Three Essays on the Theory of Sexuality* (1905a)—is the analysis that transmutes aggression into one "sadistic" component instinct which must formalistically yield to the heading "sexual." Less widely recognized and less seriously considered has been the precocious dualistic scheme initially presented in *Jokes and Their Relation to the Unconscious* (1905d). Here, in 1905, we already find "aggression"—with reference to the genesis of jokes—detached from the problem of sexuality and explicitly granted an independent instinctual rationale of its own.

In this chapter we approach the concurrent existence of these two strands of aggression as a significant problem area in Freud's own development. The coexistence of these competing analytic rationales is taken as neither incidental nor implicitly symbiotic; rather, the simultaneous existence of two perspectives on aggression by 1905 betokens a certain unresolved tension in Freud himself about the way in which his patient's aggressive propensities should be clinically construed. Should aggression be consigned to the status of a "component" derivative instinct relying on the explanatory strength of a "polymorphous perverse" infantile sexual disposition, or

87

should it be acknowledged as a "full" instinct, an independent motive power capable of *competing* with sexuality for a private store of psychic energy? Freud's initial equivocation between these two options, we hope to demonstrate, is indicative not only of the clinical knottiness of the problem he confronted, but of his personal stake in its resolution as well.

I.

We turn first to the *Three Essays on the Theory of Sexuality*. Clinically, the work is monumental, promulgating for the first time the developmental history of infantile sexual instincts, linking them to "adult" perversions on the one hand and the conflictual, symptom-generating fantasies of neurotics on the other. As an illustration of psychoanalytic epistemology it is equally crucial; by demonstrating the overriding weight of prehistory in man's sexual history, the work is a significant example of the genetic mode of interpretation (Ricoeur, 1970, pp. 193-198). Concerned with a disconnected bundle of infantile instincts, the work ostensibly sides with the "component" valuation of aggression as one of the *Partialtriebe*. To rest content with the logic of this simple deduction is misleading, however. While allegedly subsuming the issue of aggression within a developmental theory of sex, the book actually presents two distinct strands of aggression whose differing degrees of instinctual "independence" anticipate the larger tension between sexually and nonsexually based aggression which would emerge shortly thereafter.

The simultaneous existence of two parallel strands of aggression stems from the multiple origins of infantile sexuality itself. For Freud, the development of sexuality can never be elucidated as a linear — if highly vicissitudinous — progression. Indeed, the infant's sexual excitement has three distinct sources — the anaclitic imitation of gratification associated with organic processes, the peripheral stimulation of appropriate erogenous zones, and the expression of some partly inexplicable partial impulse, "of which the origin is not yet completely intelligible" (Freud, 1905a, p. 201)—each of which generates its own fixation and regression-prone gradient. The latter two sources of sexuality both posit separate analytic strands of aggression. In terms of erogenous zones, the source of aggressive impulses was believed to be anally situated. To be sure, the infant's first aggressive reaction is invariably an oral "spitting away" (Fenichel, 1945, p. 84), which antedates both true object consideration and true destructive intent. With the onset of anal pleasure in the second year, however, the potential for a more purposeful kind of aggressive reaction crystallizes. The physiological prerequisite for this development rests in the very nature of anal eroticism. Utilizing the erogenous sensitivity of the anal zone, children often hold back fecal masses until their passage through the anus produces "violent muscular contractions" of the mucous membrane, a pain which must also produce "highly pleasurable sensations" (Freud, 1905a, p. 186). Purposeful aggression coincides with the social valuation of the bowel movement that subsequently emerges. Conceptualized by the child as an additional part of the body, the bowel movement in effect becomes the first "gift" the child consciously elects to make. Thus, while its disposal expresses the "compliance" of the child, its retention can analogously express the child's hostile spite towards the environment (1905a, pp. 186-187). From this organic and social substrate emerges a pregenital sexual phase stamped with a *sadistic-anal* organization (1905a, p. 198). It would fall to Abraham, some years later, to amplify the physiologically "aggressive" dimensions of this stage, constructing an elaborate analogy between anal expulsion and the sadistic process of object destruction (Abraham, 1924, pp. 77-78). At the writing of this particular text, Freud was less sensitive to the "destructive" implications of anal expulsion than to the simple relationship between sexual excitement and muscular activity per se. It was through such activity, he believed, that we might recognize "one of the roots of the sadistic instinct" (*sadistischen Triebes*), and in the infantile connection between fighting and sexual excitement, he found a frequent determinant for the "direction subsequently taken by [their] sexual instinct" (1905a, p. 203; 1905b, p. 104).

The importance of this determinant was further reinforced by the child's own cognitive apparatus. The study of infantile sexual investigation convinced Freud that the childhood observance of the sexual act could be understood only as a kind of "ill-treatment or act of subjugation" (*Misshandlung oder Überwältigung*), and could consequently impress the child only "in a sadistic sense" (*sadistischen Sinne*) (1905a, p. 196; 1905b, p. 97). Freud would return to this insight several years later in a paper "On the Sexual Theories of Children" (1908). Here the sadistic conception of coitus would be appraised as a typical sexual theory entertained in childhood and as the expression of an inborn component of the sexual instinct. For the child, coitus was invariably seen as "something that the stronger participant is forcibly inflicting on the weaker" and that, especially for the boys, was comparable "to a romping familiar to them from their childish experience" (1908, p. 220; cf. Freud, 1909b, p. 134).

Moreover, in later life, the signal importance of aggression as a gratifying modality and its involvement in the sexual pleasure of most men would derive not only from such infantile precursors, but from an acquired biological reinforcement. Genitality, by definition, posited the necessity for overcoming the resistance of the sexual object by actions other than mere courting. Sadism, as a true perversion, would subsequently emerge only when this implicit aggressive component of the sexual instinct had "become independent and exaggerated and, by displacement, [had] usurped the leading position" (Freud, 1905a, p. 158). By another route, sadism could be interpreted as a compensatory reaction to the aggressive fears generated by the normal aggressive component of intercourse. Through the application of an "active" therapeutic technique involving enforced urethral, anal, and genital regulation, for example, Ferenczi would later discover that the "strong tendencies towards aggression" (chiefly in the form of lust-murder) exhibited by neurotics were frequently based on coitus anxiety:

Many neurotics unconsciously regard coitus as an activity which, either directly or subsequently, is calculated to injure life or limb, and in particular to damage the genital organ, i.e. an act in which are combined gratification and severe anxiety. Murder then at any rate partly subserves the purpose of avoiding anxiety by rendering the love-object incapable of inflicting injury; gratification can then be enjoyed undisturbed by castration anxiety [1925, p. 279].

At the same time that aggression as sadism became the earmark of a distinctly zonal phase of pregenital organization capable of exaggerated isolation, however, the third source of sexual excitement enabled it to gain expression as one component impulse independent of zonally directed sexual activity. "The history of human civilization shows beyond any doubt that there is an intimate connection between cruelty [*Grausamkeit*] and the sexual instinct," Freud had noted, "but nothing has been done towards explaining the connection, apart from laying emphasis on the aggressive factor [*aggressiven Moments*] in the libido" (1905a, p. 159; 1905b, p. 58). By his own admission, the analysis of sadism and the recognition of the normal admixture of aggression in adult sexuality were hardly revolutionary. Indeed, this latter fact, as we earlier noted, had been clearly recognized by Breuer in his contribution to the *Studies on Hysteria*. Rather, it was in conceptualizing the child's aggression not simply as sadism, i.e., a developmentally conditioned variant of sexual satisfaction with residual traces, but as the product of an innately gratifying "cruel component" (*Grausamkeitskomponente*) that Freud actually went beyond the present state of affairs. Thus, far more significant than the observation of potentially erogenous infantile zones, was the discovery that

> infantile sexual life, in spite of the preponderating dominance of erotogenic zones, exhibits components which from the very first involve other people as sexual objects. Such are the instincts of scopophilia, exhibitionism and cruelty [*Triebe der Schau- und Zeigelust und der Grausamkeit*], which appear in a sense independently of erotogenic zones; these instincts do not enter into intimate relations with genital life until later, but are already to be observed in childhood as independent impulses [*selbständige Strebungen*], distinct in the first instance from

erotogenic sexual activity [Freud, 1905a, pp. 191-192; 1905b, p. 92].

A little later he added: "The cruel component [*Grausamkeits-komponente*] of the sexual instinct develops in childhood even more independently of the sexual activities that are attached to erotogenic zones" (1905a, p. 192; 1905b, p. 93).

Admittedly, even such non-phase-specific cruelty is consigned to the status of a partial "sexual" instinct. The choice of label, however, does not alter the conceptual significance of the discovery. To call a zonally independent cruelty component a "sexual" component because, in the context of normal adult sexuality, it should never transcend a preliminary mode of forepleasure ultimately absorbed by the more profound quest for "genitality," is an attractive equation, but one that leaves a disturbing semantic aftertaste. Our perplexity is heightened once we realize that genital primacy is itself a sad misnomer, that we all retain our pregenital infantile heritage, and that the component impulse of "sadism" is, in fact, the most likely to resist accultural subordination. Thus, even in the face of societal outrage, it routinely persists as "the most common and most significant" perversion (Freud, 1905a, p. 157).

To understand fully why Freud elected to subsume these expressions of nonzonal cruelty under the category of component sexual instincts, it is necessary to return momentarily to Chapter 2 of our study and the "delayed-reaction" hypothesis of repression. Freud, we recall, initially used the mechanism of a delayed reaction to explain how hysteria-inducing childhood seductions could acquire sexual significance during adolescence. We further suggested that Freud was also implicitly utilizing this same mechanism when, in the explication of obsessional neurosis, he spoke of preadolescent "aggressions" which later gave rise to obsessional and sexually charged self-reproaches.

In the *Three Essays on the Theory of Sexuality* the notion of a delayed reaction can be appropriated to help unravel the problem of childhood cruelty as Freud probably construed it. Children are cruel in decidedly pregenital and non-phase-specific ways, but now, given our knowledge of the child's elastic polymorphously perverse sexual disposition, we are entitled to label such nonzonal cruelty a "component instinct," even though we are perfectly aware that this type of gratification does "not enter into intimate relations with genital life until later" (Freud, 1905a, pp. 191-192). It is only retrospective and retroactive insight acquired after adolescence that makes such cruelty "sexual."

Freud himself would say as much in later years. His twenty-first Introductory Lecture on the "Development of the Libido and Sexual Organization" delivered 12 years later would be a model of experimental open-mindedness. "At the moment," he confessed, "we are not in possession of any generally recognized criterion of the sexual nature of a process, apart, once again, from a connection with the reproductive function which we must reject as being too narrow-minded" (1916-1917, p. 320). He proceeded to label the infant's "originally indifferent bodily pleasure" sexual only because adult sexuality itself could not be defined as more than "organ pleasure" — usually, but not invariably, focusing on one pair of organs (1916-1917, pp. 323-325). Freud viewed the theoretical possibility of a variant of organ pleasure which was not "sexual" as abstruse and clinically unessential: "I know too little about organ-pleasure and its determinants." This much, however, he readily confessed: ". . . we call the dubious and indefinable pleasurable activities of earliest childhood sexual because, in the course of analysis, we arrive at them from the symptoms after passing through indisputably sexual material. They need not necessarily themselves be sexual on that account — agreed!" (1916-1917, p. 324). The delayed-reaction hypothesis can consequently be applied not only to the problem of childhood cruelty, but to all the other perverse component instincts as well. Indeed, the existence of infantile sexuality itself is not directly discovered, but retrospectively inferred from the "discovery" of partial pregenital components (of both a zonal and nonzonal type) in adult sexuality which have genetic links to infantile "organ pleasure." The existence of infantile sexuality cannot be demonstrated; it can only be definitionally deduced.

If there is, in fact, an initially nonerogenous inclination toward cruelty apart from the sadism biologically implicit in the activity of the anal zone, what is its source? To answer this question Freud returned to the child's primordially "egoistic" disposition, which he previously considered in the context of oneiric death wishes directed against siblings in *The Interpretation of Dreams*. The aggressive impulses generated by sibling rivalry were found to be natural correlates of this egoistic status, and could further be translated into actual "death wishes" because such egoism precluded the presence of "adult" restraints to temper the expression of hostility. Freud now applied this same level of analysis to the nonzonal cruelty he postulated as an independent partial impulse: "Cruelty [*Grausamkeit*] in general comes easily to the childish nature, since the obstacle that brings the instinct for mastery [*Bemächtigungstrieb*] to a halt at another person's pain—namely a capacity for pity [*Mitleiden*]—is developed relatively late" (1905a, pp. 192-193; 1905b, p. 93). Aggression, it now appears, can be linked not only to anal sadism, but to a nonsexual "mastery" impulse (*Bemächtigungstrieb*) which describes the immature ego's reflexive attempt to control and structure its environment. Such ego-directed mastery is not in itself explicitly (or definitionally) cruel. The "cruel" child is not one who has a positive interest in destruction, but rather one who does not care at all. His object interests relate only to potential sources of gratification and potential threats; his "aggressive" goal is only the end of uncomfortable situations (Fenichel, 1945, p. 86). Consequently, his actions acquire "cruel" overtones only by default, through the absence, that is, of socially cultivated pity. Thus,

> It may be assumed that the impulse of cruelty arises from the instinct for mastery [*die grausame Regung vom Bemächtigungstrieb herstammt*] and appears at a period of sexual life at which the genitals have not yet taken over their later role. It then dominates a phase of sexual life which we shall later describe as a pregenital organization [Freud, 1905a, p. 193; 1905b, pp. 93-94].

With this verdict, the tension between competing strands of aggression in the *Three Essays* dissipates. The "aggressive" dimension of anal sadism is confronted by a cruelty component instinct which, however independent of zonal functions, still acquires its aggressive dimension only as an inadvertent offshoot of childish egoism. Freud's 1905 verdict has been confirmed by later clinicians: the child is not aggressive so much as it is "childlike" (Fenichel, 1945, p. 86). Nineteen hundred and five proved an unusually productive year. While Freud found the nature of a non-phase-specific cruelty instinct severely circumscribed with reference to childhood sexuality, he would locate evidence for a more directively "adult" strain of aggression through a new medium —jokes. Initially, the misleading indirection of this work tends to obscure its theoretical impact. The problem of instinct is not tackled directly but through the intervening problem of the joke and the peculiar sources of satisfaction that are incumbent to it.

Theoretically, the role of aggression in *Jokes and Their Relation to the Unconscious* (1905d) hinges on the location of two distinct varieties of jokes. In addition to "harmless" jokes, in which gratification is intrinsic to the joke activity or "technique" of the joke itself, Freud posited a species of "tendentious jokes" (*tendenziösen Witze*) in which enjoyment is derived from the gratification of some latently animated tendency that the joke serves.

When appropriated by a tendency, Freud observed, jokes "make possible the satisfaction of an instinct (whether lustful or hostile) [*des lüsternen und feindseligen*] in the face of an obstacle that stands in its way. They circumvent this obstacle and in that way draw pleasure from a source which the obstacle had made inaccessible" (1905d, p. 101; 1905e, p. 110). What are these potentially satisfying tendencies? As Freud indicates, they are either "lustful" or "hostile," and they give rise both to the obscene joke (*obszöner Witz*) and the hostile joke (*feindseliger Witz*) (Freud, 1905d, p. 97; 1905e, p. 105). Obscene jokes constitute the disguised derivative of smutty jokes, serve as a sexual exhibition, and provide obvious libidinal gratification. Hostile jokes, conversely, are decidedly nonlibidinal, even though they derive from infantile impulses that "have been subject to the same restrictions, the same progressive repression, as our sexual urges" (1905d, p. 102). Such civilized mastery of our hostile emotions, Freud proceeds to tell us, is actually incomplete. We cannot obliterate the "powerful inherited disposition to hostility" (*mit kräftigen Anlagen zur Feindschaft*) of childhood; we can at best strive to displace. Consequently, "Brutal hostility [*gewalttätige Feindseligkeit*], forbidden by law, has been replaced by verbal invective" (Freud, 1905d, pp. 102-103; 1905e, p. 112).

As a specific strategy of invective, jokes serve such "hostile aggressiveness" (*feindseligen Aggression*) by soliciting the approval of a third person against a purported enemy and consequently by permitting indirect release of blatantly aggressive impulses:

> By making our enemy small, inferior, despicable or comic, we achieve in a roundabout way the enjoyment of overcoming him —to which the third person, who has made no efforts, bears witness by his laughter.... A joke will allow us to exploit something ridiculous in our enemy which we could not, on account of obstacles in the way, bring forward openly or consciously; once again, then, the joke *will evade restrictions and open sources of pleasure that have become inaccessible* [1905d, p. 103; 1905e, p. 113].[1]

The instinctual primacy of the obscene and aggressive tendencies appropriated by jokes is further illustrated through an examination of the "pleasure mechanism" which the expression of the joke utilizes. The governing principle, Freud discovered, was one of economy, specifically, economy in the psychic expenditure needed to maintain various ego-syntonic inhibitions and suppressions. Such an economy became a source of pleasure primarily because the psychic expenditure it permits us to avoid is one we are customarily prepared to make. In momentarily eluding it we experience "effortless" release from our adult suppressions that brings welcome relief precisely because the suppressing psychic expenditure has become ego-syntonic; it is one which is "expected and prepared for" (Freud, 1905d, p. 157).

---

[1] On the question of aggressive jokes, see also Freud (1927) and Ferenczi (1911).

In the case of harmless jokes, the inhibitions we momentarily bypass are directed against the generically appealing word-pleasure and pleasure in nonsense we inherit from childhood, before the "pressure" of critical reason stifles the mind's play and compels it to conform to "right," i.e., reality-tested, modalities of thought. The pleasure intrinsic to the technique of jokes is thus a regressive pleasure, testifying to both the developmental primacy and psychic relief implicit in unencumbered primary processes and to the unnatural and highly reversible expenditure of psychic energy needed to suppress them. Despite the effects of socialization, our resistance to the pressures of thinking and reality is "far-reaching and persistent," and our entire secondary structure of thought can be easily toppled once the existing store of psychic expenditure is alleviated. It is the momentary alleviation of such energy expenditures that ensues when the "technique" of jokes is successfully employed.

With tendentious jokes, on the other hand, the neutralized psychic expenditures are not those that suppress the play motive of the infantile state of mind, but those that ordinarily contain our underlying sexual and aggressive tendencies. This conceptualization is highly important: aggression is no longer viewed as the sadistic outgrowth of infantile sexuality, but as the embodiment of innately aggressive "tendencies" which are subject to their own quota of suppressing psychic expenditure, analogous with (but not subservient to) that exacted by the sexual instincts. The *instinctual* core of these tendencies is beyond doubt: tendentious jokes, as Freud repeatedly enjoins, act in behalf of "the major purposes and instincts of mental life" (1905d, p. 133) and have at their disposal sources of pleasure to which harmless jokes have no access (1905d, pp. 96, 102). As the substrate of one separate category of tendentious jokes, aggressive tendencies must now, perforce presuppose their own nonsexual category of repressed pleasure. In grasping the psychogenesis of jokes, we realize, with Freud, that

tendentious jokes exhibit the main characteristics of the joke-work — that of liberating pleasure by getting rid of inhibitions —

more clearly than any other of the developmental stages of jokes. Either they strengthen the purposes which they serve, by bringing assistance to them from impulses that are kept suppressed, or they put themselves entirely at the service of suppressed purposes [1905d, p. 134].

What we have previously learned, and what we must integrate with this observation, however, is the realization that the locus of such tendency-directed pleasure is unalterably dualistic: hostile aggressive jokes exist apart from obscene sexual jokes and can thus only "set free pleasure" and "remove inhibitions" which derive from uniquely "aggressive" tendencies. Hence, in elucidating both the potency and the depth of the latent reservoir of pleasure tapped by tendentious jokes, Freud, in effect, strengthens the viability of a dualism in which aggressive and sexual tendencies, if coexistent, still call into action their own particular sources of instinctual energy and appropriate, on separate but equal terms, the respective quotas of "psychic expenditure" needed to suppress them.

Freud further confirms the equation of tendentious jokes with "the major purposes and instincts of mental life" by appropriately situating them in the unconscious. To be sure, the unconscious must be implicated in joke formation even in its generically "harmless" state. This is because the joke-work, as Freud discovered, was itself the verbally expressed analogue of dream-work, relying on the forms and technical modalities of dream-work, i.e., condensation, displacement, and indirect representation which were, themselves, properly unconscious (1905d, pp. 88-89, 165). Joke-work was compelled to revert to the unconscious, Freud reasoned, simply because the pleasure-bringing "techniques" on which it depended "arise there easily" (1905d, p. 169). Insofar as this is true, Freud can with good reason submit that jokes ensue only if "*a preconscious thought is given over for a moment to unconscious revision and the outcome of this is at once grasped by conscious perception*" (1905d, p. 166).

Joke formation is facilitated, however, when it can draw on powerful instinctual tendencies which are, themselves, unconsciously situated. Thus, the joke-work receives its most powerful stimulus when strong purposes reaching down into the unconscious [*bis ins Unbewusste reichender Tendenzen*] are present, which represent a special aptitude for the production of jokes and which may explain to us how it is that the subjective determinants of jokes are so often fulfilled in neurotic people. Under the influence of strong purposes even those who otherwise have the least aptitude for it become capable of making jokes [1905d, p. 178; 1905e, p. 203].

The point to be drawn from this observation is the same point that emerged from our consideration of the "economy of psychic expenditure" which must be achieved for tendentious jokes to gain expression. The unconscious germination of tendentious jokes ultimately falls back on the dualistic locus of these tendencies. If tendentious jokes can be either obscene or "hostile aggressive," each of these two strains has equal right to an unconscious source in laying claim to its relative psychic import.

The following problem remains, however: How is the existence of instinctual aggressive tendencies operative in joke formation to be reconciled with anal sadism and a partial "cruelty" impulse, the theoretic underpinnings of aggression inherited from the *Three Essays on the Theory of Sexuality*? In that work, Freud clearly implied that the explanation of adult aggressive behavior could be subsumed by a patently infantile phenomenon: the "polymorphous perverse" nature of *sexual* pleasure. Now we learn that joke formation, relying on an intellectual and communicative sophistication which is normatively adult, can draw on independent aggressive tendencies. Seen in the light of its predecessor, the book on jokes generates a paradox: if adult aggressive tendencies are now believed to exist independently of sexual ones, how can the former be explained by recourse to the developmental vicissitudes of the latter? Clearly, they cannot. For the time being, it seems that aggression has become a "full" instinct.

The early bifurcation of impulse life into sexual and aggressive tendencies in the jokes book would not long lie dormant. In 1907, Freud returned to it in analyzing religious practices as a collectively held obsessional neurosis. Like the obsessional neurotic, the religiously observant was given to obsessive "ceremonial" acts which were compulsively carried out at the risk of neurotically volatile "pangs of conscience." In both cases Freud found the primary causative factor to be the repression of an unconscious impulse. While such renunciation stemmed exclusively from "components of the sexual instinct" in private neurosis, however, that operative in collective religious rites derived from "self-seeking, socially harmful" ones (*eigensüchtige, sozialschädliche Triebe*) (1907a, p. 125; 1907b, p. 137).

II.

This inclination to acknowledge and even rely on aggressive tendencies when confronted with the perturbing collectivity would receive its most profound sanction five years later in Freud's provocative ethnological excursion in *Totem and Taboo* (1913b). Admittedly, Freud's ethnological subject matter is severely circumscribed by his clinical orientation. As Ricoeur has observed, his first two essays amount to little more than an "applied psychoanalysis" —one that can be transposed from dreams and the neuroses to taboo because of the close "structural affinity" between taboo and obsessional neuroses (Ricoeur, 1970, pp. 198-204; cf. Rieff, 1961, p. 231). Freud's principal concern is with justifying the pathogenic role of the Oedipus complex in the neuroses from a new perspective. No longer content simply to call neurotics primitive, he draws on the literature on the irrationalities of primitives to illuminate the behavior of neurotics (Rieff, 1961, pp. 211-212). In the horror of incest and emotional ambivalence displayed by savages, he claims to locate new experimental verification for his clinical suppositions (Ricoeur, 1970, pp. 198-204).[2]

---

[2] As Rieff has pointed out, all these connections between sickness and the past depend on the idea of parallelism implicit in the "phylogenetic law." Freud employed a sociological version of this idea, contending that "the individual mind presents in its development a résumé of human history." For the significance and the history of this notion in the context of Romanticism and Enlightenment rationalism, see Rieff (1961, pp. 205-211).

Yet an important shift in emphasis occurs in these two essays. While the infant's own ontogenetic prehistory could be at least formalistically subsumed by its "polymorphous perverse" sexual disposition and its successive recourse to different sexual component impulses, the juridical and social landmarks bearing witness to mankind's "collective" prehistory warrant a radically different phraseology. In considering "Taboo and Emotional Ambivalence" we learn that

> Taboo is a primaeval prohibition forcibly imposed (by some authority) from outside, and directed against the most powerful longings to which human beings are subject. The desire to violate it persists in their unconscious ... The fact that the violation of a taboo can be atoned for by a renunciation shows that renunciation lies at the basis of obedience to taboo [1913b, pp. 34-35].

We are now told, however, that there are two "important taboo prohibitions," and that while one is to avoid sex with totem companions of the opposite sex, the other is to avoid killing the totem animal itself (1913b, pp. 31-32).

The significance of this latter prohibition becomes clear in considering the ancient "Taboo upon Rulers," and explains the puzzling situation of primitive kings who could be worshipped as gods one day and killed as criminals the next (1913b, p. 44). The veneration and respect with which the ancients regarded their "privileged persons," Freud tells us, is always ambivalent at its core, opposed "in the unconscious [by] an opposing current of intense hostility" (*eine intensive feindselige Strömung*). And however much such hostility may be "shouted down" by an excessive increase of tenderness and compulsively expressed "apprehensiveness," it tenaciously persists as an independent "unconscious current" (1913b, p. 49; 1913c, p. 63) and receives sublimated satisfaction in the "ceremonious etiquette" the ruler is compelled to obey. Such an imposed network of "prohibitions and observances" has the intention

> not to contribute to his dignity, much less to his comfort, but to restrain him from conduct which, by disturbing the harmony of nature, might involve himself, his people, and the universe in one common catastrophe. Far from adding to his comfort, these

observances, by trammelling his every act, annihilate his freedom and often render the very life, which it is their object to preserve, a burden and sorrow to him [1913b, p. 44].

Indeed, the very prerogative to make contact with the ruler is taboo because, in Freud's words, the act "may hint at aggressive impulses" (*sie an aggressive Tendenzen mahnen kann*) (1913b, p. 48; 1913c, p. 62).

Freud similarly found "latent hostility" at the root of the primitives' fear of the dead. Thus, the compulsive conviction that the soul of the deceased would return as a demon during the period of mourning was in reality a defensive projection of the victors' own latent hostility and unconscious satisfaction at the victims' death. In addition, such projection constituted an archaic precursor of the "obsessive self-reproaches" that plague contemporary neurotics who suffer the death of a loved one:

> It is impossible to escape the fact that the true determining factor is invariably *unconscious* hostility [*die unbewusste Feindseligkeit als das regelmässig wirkende und eigentlich treibende Motiv*].... Accordingly, there follow the repression of the unconscious hostility by the method of projection and the construction of the ceremonial which gives expression to the fear of being punished by the demons [1913b, p. 63; 1913c, p. 80].

The dominating role of aggressive tendencies in the development of primitive races becomes clear from these indicators. Psychoanalysis dictates that taboo prohibitions must unfailingly coincide with a *"positive* current of desire." Applied to the question of primitives, we can most plausibly conclude that the strongest temptations involved not only incest, but aggressive tendencies to kill rulers and abuse the dead (1913b, p. 69). And while neurosis invariably presupposes prohibitions of a sexual nature, "In the case of taboo the prohibited touching is obviously not to be understood in an exclusively sexual sense but in the more general sense of attacking, of getting control, and of asserting oneself" (1913b, p. 73).

It was not until the final essay of *Totem and Taboo,* however, that this aggressive substrate underlying the taboo prohibition was accorded clear phylogenetic precedence. Here

Freud resolved the problem of "institutionalization" which his earlier "applied" essays had raised but left unanswered by positing at the origin of mankind a real Oedipus complex (Ricoeur, 1970, pp. 204-205). The "realistic archeology" (Ricoeur, 1970, p. 208) into which the psychoanalytic interpretation of the Oedipus complex is extended, however, requires another dramatic shift of emphasis. The stress on harmless infantile desire recedes, to be replaced by an "aggressive" primal crime which leaves the development of both religion and morality as its collective residue while handily explaining the emergence of all subsequent totemic and psychic ambivalence (Freud, 1913b, p. 157). Through the immutable and universal "scar" it left, this original parricide can be appropriated to explain how the ego adopts the external prohibitions of its social organization (Ricoeur, 1970, pp. 204-211). More important, it is a clear illustration of Freud's propensity to defer to acts of violence as the "original repressed substrata" of all social action (Rieff, 1961, p. 212).

To these ends, however, the tale must be told as one of aggression. Disrupting the static primitivism of the Darwinian primal horde, we are now told of a group of expelled brothers who "came together, killed and devoured their father and so made an end of the patriarchal horde" (Freud, 1913b, p. 141). And even the ensuing sense of remorse and "deferred obedience" which arose in the wake of this crime could not wholly obliterate the complex of instinctuality that had been activated by this earliest aggression. Thus, if the sons' enduring sense of guilt would dictate the subsequent deification of the totemic substitute and the renunciation of the liberated women for whom they had rebelled, their enduring sense of aggressive defiance would resist extinction with an equally intractable perversity (1913b, pp. 151-152). While the totem religion issued from the need to conciliate the injured father, the annual totem feast which it prescribed would make it a duty "to repeat the crime of parricide again and again in the sacrifice of the totem animal whenever ... appropriation of the paternal attributes threatened to disappear." Moreover, even when the aftermath of bitter feeling had subsided and the totem-sacrificial animal was replaced by a new god of transcendent paternalism, symbolizing the fullness of power and freedom from restriction which had been the primal father's, the groundwork of "hostile impulses" would persist, and

> the first phases of the dominance of the two new father-surrogates—gods and kings—show the most energetic signs of the ambivalence that remains a characteristic of religion. . . .
> The memory of the first great act of sacrifice thus proved indestructible, in spite of every effort to forget it; and at the very point at which men sought to be at the farthest distance from the motives that led to it, its undistorted reproduction emerged in the form of the sacrifice of the god [1913b, pp. 151-152].

The ethnographic unraveling of the Oedipus complex is thus subverted to a new end: to provide the base from which aggression might qualify as a full instinct. In this sense, *Totem and Taboo* becomes the linear descendent of *Jokes and Their Relation to the Unconscious.* The formulation of autonomous aggressive tendencies initially made on an interpersonal level is now anchored (and hence justified) sociohistorically.

III.

While it is one thing to extract the clear references to aggressive tendencies from the works of this period, it would clearly be another to confront this early Freud with the overt reality of an aggressive "instinct." Insofar as he was a conscious instinct theorist, Freud was committed to the encompassing duality of sexual and ego instincts, and resisted the attempt to attribute to "aggressive tendencies" the motive power of an "instinct" with force and ultimately considerable bitterness. Despite his willingness to experiment with aggressive tendencies in the book on jokes and to transmute the Oedipus complex into a tale of aggression in *Totem and Taboo,* Freud could not consciously conceptualize aggression as more than a partial sexual instinct until 1915.

The reasons for this early disavowal of aggression's instinctual primacy are complex and have important roots not only in Freud's intellectual commitments of the time, but in the political and cultural imperatives dictated by the emergence of an organized psychoanalytic movement. In the remainder of this chapter, we shall consider Freud's early insensitivity to a "full" aggressive instinct in terms of the social and professional *situation* generated by the young psychoanalytic movement. In our next chapter, we shall analyze his more pointed rejection of an "aggressive instinct" from 1909-1914 in terms of the specific political role he felt compelled to play in it.

While the *Three Essays on the Theory of Sexuality, Jokes and Their Relation to the Unconscious,* and *Totem and Taboo* offer penetrating insight into the nature of aggression, psychoanalysis as both a professional and social movement was predicated on the developmental vicissitudes and repressed offshoots of the sexual instinct. This simple truth, the legacy of Freud's split with Breuer over the unquestioned supremacy of "defensive" hysterias, rapidly became the infallible gauge by which the psychoanalyst's therapeutic integrity and his critic's postoedipal maturity could be measured.

As a therapy for the neuroses, its claim to distinction and its revolutionary legacy revolved squarely on the newly found forces of the sexual instinct—"the only constant source of energy of the neurosis" (Freud, 1905a, p. 163). This supposition was formalized in the 1912 paper on "Types of Onset of Neurosis." Here the four variants of neurotic precipitate—object removal, zonal fixation, developmental inhibition, and spontaneous increase in libidinal quantity—were all subsumed by the single question of libidinal vicissitude and all predicated on the assumption that only "the vicissitudes of the libido are what decide in favour of nervous health or sickness" (Freud, 1912, p. 231). In the *Introductory Lectures* delivered five years later, Freud was slightly more cautious, but the bent of his assessment had not altered. Although only the continued "progress of scientific work" could provide verification, he should not be surprised if "the power to produce pathogenic effects was in fact a prerogative of the libidinal instincts, so that the libido theory could celebrate its triumph all along the line from the simplest actual neurosis to the most severe alienation of the personality." Conversely, it was equally probable that the ego instincts were only "carried along secondarily by the pathogenic instigation of the libido" (Freud, 1916-1917, pp. 429-430). It was subsequently through this etiological *reductionism* that psychoanalysis became clinically recognizable and through which any forthcoming professional endorsement was made contingent. Apart from the clinical presuppositions of psychoanalysis, the social reaction to its exclusive reliance on "sexual etiology" went far in determining the way the psychoanalytic movement could be conceptualized by both followers and critics.

The Viennese *haute bourgeoisie* which initially reacted to Freud's work were a conflicted lot. Preoccupied on the one hand with the absorption of aesthetic culture and the ensuing sensitivity to psychic states, it remained saturated with the moralistic-scientific culture of law on the other:

> Morally it was secure, righteous, and repressive; politically it was concerned for the rule of law, under which both individual rights and social order were subsumed. It was intellectually committed to the rule of the mind over the body and to a latter-day Voltairism: to social progress through science, education, and hard work [Schorske, 1961, p. 933].

In contending that the sexual factor was operative in all neuroses, psychoanalysis unquestionably threatened the values embodied in this latter strain. Freud's era, as Jones observes, was still one in which the *odium theologicum* had been replaced by the *odium sexicum* but not yet by the *odium politicum* (Jones, 1955, p. 108). The effects of this social mind-set were most acute in the years before World War I. At that time psychoanalytic preoccupation with sexuality and "sexualization" was frequently linked not merely with eccentricity, but with a conception of positive wickedness that inspired "moral loathing." "In those days," Jones notes,

> Freud and his followers were regarded not only as sexual perverts but as either obsessional or paranoic psychopaths as well, and the combination was felt to be a real danger to the community. Freud's theories were interpreted as direct incitements to surrendering all restraint, to reverting to a state of primitive license and savagery. No less than civilization itself was at stake [1955, pp. 108-109].

Subsequently, the movement's social credibility had to be sought within the coordinates imposed by an assaulting social value system. Concurrent with a clinical reductionism which dictated how psychoanalysis could *cure* went a culturally induced selectiveness which determined what psychoanalysis could *mean:* the sexual question became the only significant *institutional* question. To the extent that this is true, Szasz (1961) is right: Freud's orientation to the psychoanalytic movement, unlike his orientation to the subject matter of his discipline, was decidedly unscientific and directed to the ethics of institutional groups rather than to the ethics of the scientific community. Insofar as the success of the psychoanalytic movement hinged on its ability to cope with an uncritical and scientifically irrational imputation of "wickedness," however, it is hard to see how he could have "oriented" himself otherwise.

Although there is, to date, little research exploring the medical and social *conceptualization* of psychoanalysis in the pre-World War I years, Nathan Hale's recent study of Freud's reception in America does offer some preliminary support for this analysis in the one foreign country in which the fate of the psychoanalytic movement was of "special interest" to Freud (Jones, 1955, p. 115).

The early reception of Freud's sexual theories there was highly skeptical, with acceptance accruing in a halting and highly fragmentary way (Hale, 1971, pp. 189-194). Until 1908, Freud's professional reputation remained modest, and psychoanalysis itself was only vaguely equated with "catharsis, the discovery of suppressed complexes, and a not very explicit view of the importance of sexuality in the neuroses" (p. 199). Putnam became the first genuine American convert that year by appreciating that psychoanalysis was not simply "catharsis," but a minute exploration of symptoms and dreams that invariably led back to childhood conflicts about sexuality (p. 213). The ensuing debate over psychoanalysis was tightly wedded to this claim. The "scientific" status of psychoanalysis could not be considered apart from its sexual claims, insofar as the latter were almost entirely derived from the psychoanalytic method (p. 291). Indeed, the conclusion that most skeptical physicians balked at, and that converts relentlessly pressed, was that disturbed sexuality was the etiological factor in *every* case. It was the sexual issue which skeptics used to discredit psychoanalysis and which converts used to make their opponents seem "hidebound, obscene, and squeamish." To Putnam and most American analysts, prudery was the paramount, if not the only, recognized cause of opposition (pp. 291-307).

The public conceptualization of psychoanalysis similarly hinged on the implications of its sexual reductionism. Primed by the "purity" campaigns of the 1880's and 1890's and the impact of Havelock Ellis's New Sexual Hygiene, Americans quickly drew psychoanalysis into cultural battles revolving around the repeal of reticence. The issue here was not the technical efficacy of psychoanalysis as a new therapeutic method, but the inevitable ramifications of psychoanalysis on that precious but fragile nineteenth-century inheritance, "civilized" morality (Hale, 1971, pp. 267-273, 298-301). Psychoanalysis moved onto the American intellectual scene just as many Americans were rebelling against prevailing sexual mores, and it was because of the sexual orientation of "the new woman" in America that psychoanalysis won as easy a hearing as it did (Ruitenbeek, 1966, pp. 18-19).

Together, this early etiological monism and the social conceptualization of psychoanalysis it generated seem to have exerted an important "predisposing" effect when Freud turned to the problem of instinct. It initially subordinated the entire theoretical issue of instinctuality to the examination of a narrowly defined range of clinical subject matter on which the claim of therapeutic efficacy (and hence sexual etiology) rested. As Jones observes, "Freud did not ... regard the investigation of the instincts as his main task in life, which was the elucidation of particular mental phenomena that puzzled him and aroused his interest, notably those of neurotic suffering and of dream life. His study of the instincts was at first incidental to this task" (1935, p. 155).

The early notion of instinct is consequently illustrative less of an independent biopsychological problem than of the need to support the validity of a given genre of clinical interpretation. By ascribing all infantile pleasure to a "polymorphous perverse" disposition that was, a priori, "sexual," and reducing the problem of nonzonal "cruelty" to a partial sexual impulse at the same time that "sadism" was placed at the feet of a developmental erogenous zone, Freud made it unnecessary to confront directly the possibility of an aggressive "instinct." More important, however, the reduction of aggression to a "partial" component impulse provided Freud with a ready-made clinical linkage which could be appropriated to dissipate the significance of "aggressive tendencies" which might appear in different contexts.

This is clearly illustrated in the book on jokes. Here Freud outlined one type of tendentious joke relying on an independent stream of unconscious "aggression," but belittled the theoretic significance of this observation by informing us that the persons most successful with this kind of tendentious joke are those "in whose sexuality a powerful sadistic component is demonstrable" (1905d, p. 143). Similarly, in the 1910 study of Leonardo, Freud analyzed an "exaggerated sympathy" for animals as a reaction formation not of its true *affective* inverse — an intrinsically aggressive disposition — but of "strong sadistic traits" of childhood associated with "*crudely sensual* activity" (1910, p. 132).

The proclivity to sexualize aggressive manifestations culminated a year later in the Schreber case history: symptomatically "aggressive" fears were not merely interpreted, but analytically transfigured into "sexual" ones. Analytic unraveling yields a common core of conflict in male paranoics stemming from the following proposition: " 'I (a man) *love him* (a man)' " (Freud, 1911a, p. 63). Thus Schreber's fear of "persecution and injury" at the hands of his physician Flechsig becomes, in reality, a fear of sexual abuse which can be traced to an outburst of homosexual libido (1911a, pp. 43, 45, 47, 59, 62). Such fears of being violently "aggressed" consequently serve to justify the patient's own "hatred" for his alleged persecutor. Schreber's "hatred" for his physician can be no more intrinsically "aggressive" than the quality of his persecutory fear, however. Such "hatred" becomes, in itself, a defensive means to ward off the homosexual wish-fantasy which stems from libidinal fixation at the narcissistic stage (1911a, pp. 59-63). The whole matter, in other words, is blatantly "sexual."

The direction of these clinical interpretations prepares us for the final outcome of *Totem and Taboo*. Initially, we are confronted with the two equally influential laws of totemism: the injunction not to kill the totem animal and the injunction to avoid sex with totem companions. The reconstruction of the primal crime serves to emphasize the former law. The historically actualized Oedipus complex is a blatantly aggressive affair, and the substratum of ambivalence and obsessive ritual it generates does not stem from possession of the mother but from the "aggressive disposition" that had been activated to dispose of the father. While the symptomatic legacy of the primal crime stems from its aggressive elements, however, narrower clinical concerns impel Freud subtly to give psychoanalytic precedence to the aftermath of the event. He was, it seems, oblivious to the possibility that desire for the mother might, in itself, only serve to consolidate and channel and ultimately trigger an underlay of instinctual aggression which would be experienced in any case. (See Freud, 1926, p. 124, for direct recognition of this kind of distinction from the standpoint of the elicitation of ego defense at the ontogenetic level.) Though man rebelled against the father, he tells us, it is ultimately woman for whose sake he rebelled (Freud, 1913b, p. 144).

IV.

On this note, the conflicted input on "aggression" generated by Freud's early theoretical development achieves tentative equilibrium. While the "aggression" of oedipal rivalry may psychologically function as a "full" instinct, it must invariably be rationalized in terms of a strategy of desire. When clinical "aggression" cannot be explained as a strategy of desire, it must be analyzed as a component of desire: the "full" instinct ultimately falls back on the "partial," sexually charged variant.

We can now appreciate why this was the case. The early need to comprehend "aggression" only as an infantile "cruelty" impulse and the hallmark of a specific phase of pregenital sexual organization functioned as the inverted representation of the need to establish the invariably "sexual" etiology of the neuroses. This quest to celebrate the triumph of the libido theory "all along the line" constituted the predominant clinical concern of the period, on which the professional and social identity of the psychoanalytic movement itself depended. It was consequently this issue to which the entire problem of instinct theory itself was initially subordinated. Thus, while willing to experiment on different levels with jokes and collective prehistory, when pinned down in "Neurosis and Nosogenesis," Freud reverts to the ego and sexual instincts which serve his more delimited clinical ends and the organizational concerns which are imposed on them. It would not be until 1915, in the early essays on metapsychology, that the independent "aggressive tendencies" located in the study on jokes would be fully incorporated into his genetic psychology.

5

A LITTLE FLIESS RETURNED:
ADLER AND THE POLITICS
OF AGGRESSION

Although the early dissection of sexuality into component instincts and differentially pleasurable erogenous zones made the assumption of an independent aggressive "instinct" unnecessary, it did not render the issue of aggression antagonistic to psychoanalysis. Freud did not become consciously defiant about the existence of an aggressive instinct until a "morose and cantankerous" protégé (Jones, 1955, p. 130) attempted to appropriate the psychoanalytic banner for a new theoretic perspective, one allegedly focusing on an overlooked wellspring of aggressiveness.

In fact, this contention is a grossly distorted oversimplification. However open-ended the ramifications of Alfred Adler's 1908 paper on the aggressive drive, "Der Aggressionstrieb im Leben und in der Neurose," the contention (made by Jones, for instance) that he was entirely preoccupied with the "aggression" arising from a masculine protest amounts to uninformed reductionism. Even in this paper, aggression was not designated a delimited source of instinctual drive, but was considered the "superordinated dynamic force" that would direct the converging "confluence" of instincts with which he had been previously occupied. Adler presented in this paper a new concept of drive by assigning an instinct to each organ. In this context, aggression was not thought to be a drive proper, but belonged to the total superstructure which represented "a superordinated psychological field connecting the drives" (*ein*

übergeordnetes, die Triebe verbindendes psychisches Feld)
(Ansbacher and Ansbacher, 1956, p. 34; Adler, 1908, p. 28).
This conceptualization of aggression as a connective energy
net was not merely formulated apart from the issue of aggressive instinctuality qua instinctuality, but became antithetical
to the reality of instinctual aggression by virtue of the reactive,
secondary quality Adler assigned to aggressive manifestations
which went beyond the energic impetus normally imparted to
each organ. Thus, for Adler, an actual aggressive instinct
could be expressed directly only when a primary drive was
frustrated: aggression qua aggression represented the un-
finished excitation (*unerledigte Erregung*) that flowed in
(*einströmt*) when the primary drive was denied satisfaction
(*Befriedigung*). In this reactive sense, the strongest expressions
of aggression normally corresponded to the incomplete
activity of the strongest primary (organ) drives and, conversely, the primary drives themselves were directly served by
the excitation and discharge of the aggressive drive proper
(*dass der Primärtrieb durch Erregung und Entladung des
Aggressiontriebes zur Befriedigung gelangt*). In reality, then,
Adler in 1908 is much more willing to subsume aggression
under the pleasure principle than Freud had been in 1905 in
either *Three Essays on the Theory of Sexuality* or *Jokes and
Their Relation to the Unconscious*. Adler has no need to
invoke an innate cruelty impulse to explain the quality of the
child's polymorphous perverse satisfactions. Like Freud, Adler
sees the young child routinely expressing blatantly hostile
(*feindselig*) emotions, but unlike Freud, he finds that the
hostile dimension of the child's confrontation with the
external environment is from the very first a purely reactive
phenomenon conditioned by the difficulties placed in the way
of organ satisfaction. The *Aggressionstrieb* itself, then,
assumes its "aggressive" quality only as an environmentally
conditioned struggle for satisfaction. It is, in fact, *der Trieb
zur Erkämpfung einer Befriedigung* (Adler, 1908, pp. 28-29;
for a partial translation, see Ansbacher and Ansbacher, 1956,
pp. 34-35).

As a transcendent principle designed to deprive all the
"primary drives" of their autonomy, aggression was so broadly

construed as to become generically vacuous for clinical purposes. The aggression drive meant only "a sum of sensation, excitations, and their discharges (Freud's motor discharge in hysteria belongs here), the organic and functional substratum of which is innate" (Ansbacher and Ansbacher, 1956, p. 34). In the context of psychopathology, aggression was defined in a similarly nonfocused and almost symbolic way.[1]

The following year, in probably his most substantive contribution to the psychoanalytic literature, *Über neurotische Disposition: Zugleich ein Beitrag zur Ätiologie und zur Frage der Neurosenwahl* (1909), Adler invoked a new psychophysiological explanatory concept, oversensitivity (*Überempfindlichkeit*), in order to restate the same basic verdict about aggression. Aggressive release, Adler repeats, is associated with the normal activity of every organ. If an organ is inferior, however, the aggression associated with it is displaced to general behavior and released in (usually) antisocial, counterproductive ways. Unreleased organ aggression, in other words, becomes characterological aggression because, from the vantage point of Adler's new mediating schema, organic inferiority translates into a certain realm of organic oversensitivity (*organische Überempfindlichkeit*) which, in turn, reactively yields enough psychological vulnerability to constitute the foundation for neurosis. This kind of pathological vulnerability Adler designates psychic oversensitivity (*psychische Überempfindlichkeit*) (Adler, 1909, pp. 530-533).

A year later, Adler himself began to recognize the misleading semantic problems caused by his equation of a reactive state of aggression with an aggressive drive. As his "superordinated principle," the aggressive drive would be

---

[1] "All these manifestations of the aggression drive are found again in the neuroses and psychoses. We find pure expressions of the aggression drive in temper tantrums and attacks of hysteria, epilepsy, and paranoia. Phases of the turning round of the drive upon the self are hypochondria, neurasthenic and hysterical pain, the entire syndrome of complaints in neurasthenia, hysteria, accident neurosis, ideas of reference and persecution, self-mutilation, and suicide. Reversals into its opposite are the mild traits and Messianic ideas of hysterics and psychotics" (Ansbacher and Ansbacher, 1956, p. 36).

replaced with a more suitably labeled "masculine protest." Once again, Adler selected a new conceptual apparatus to recast his enduring clinical perceptions on the compensatory nature of child development. The young child is still seen as a hostile combatant on behalf of its own frustrated organ satisfactions, but the child's perceptions of this frustration and its resultant struggle are now associated with new cognitive categories: the masculine and feminine sex roles. Anchored in the existence of a "psychical hermaphrodism" in childhood, the "masculine protest" symbolized the inevitable rebellion against the irreducibly "feminine" submissiveness, dependence, and obedience into which the infant was born and which it initially welcomed. For the child, the cognitive dimension of all active striving—defiance, strength, violence, mastery, passion—is always "masculine" and always occasioned by the "feminine" weakness which it first experienced (Adler, 1910, 1912a). Later the "masculine protest" would be recast in terms of various formulations of striving, ultimately, the striving for perfection.[2]

I.

From these early ego-psychology formulations, Adler's system of "Individual Psychology" would later evolve.[3] As expounded in his most systematic work, *Understanding Human Nature* (1927), Individual Psychology was not concerned with the problem of instinctuality, aggressive or otherwise, but with the inevitable "compensatory" path ego development was destined to follow. Adler's principal concern was with the unified personality and the subjectively formulated goals of psychic movement which evolved in the context

[2] See Ansbacher and Ansbacher (1956, p. 34). In his 1931 essay on "Compulsion Neurosis," Adler explicitly acknowledged his earlier error in characterizing a social state of aggression as an aggressive drive: "In 1908 I came upon the idea that every individual really exists in a state of aggression, and, imprudently, I called this attitude the 'aggression drive.' But I soon realized that it is not a drive at all, but a partly conscious, partly not understood attitude toward tasks of life" (Adler, 1931, p. 114).

[3] In this paragraph we generally follow Ellenberger (1970, pp. 608-619).

of a "personal" life plan. While it fell to Freud to emphasize the cause of psychic movement, Adler stressed the aim and intentionality underlying psychic processes. Juxtaposed with movement toward personal goals, however, was a strong element of community feeling reflecting the general interdependence of the cosmos and manifesting itself as the spontaneous willingness to conform to the natural demands of community life. Having come under the influence of Vaihinger's *Philosophy of the As If* in 1911, Adler proceeded to present a conception of normality that utilized Vaihinger's concept of "fiction." Relying on the contention that things proceed *as if* an ideal norm was set to human activity, Adler postulated the law of absolute truth,

> a fictitious norm set for the conduct of the individual that consists of an optimal balance between the requirements of the community and those of the individual, in other words, between community feeling and legitimate self-assertion. The individual who conforms to that ideal stands in absolute truth, meaning that he conforms to the logic of life in society and, as it were, to the rule of the game. The occurrence of unhappiness, failure, neuroses, psychoses, perversions, and criminality gives a measure of the degree of deviation from this basic rule [Ellenberger, 1970, p. 610].

Adler's epistemological emphasis on the intentionality of psychic processes translated into a clinical emphasis on the educative function of therapy. Convinced that the child's earliest strivings for superiority radiated from a demand for security and contentment in the face of its natural inferior position (Adler, 1927, pp. 24, 69-71), he placed increasing faith in the clinical reality of *Gemeinschaftsgefühl*—the inborn potential for community feeling and selfless communal activity—as a therapeutic remedy for the pathogenic directions these strivings could easily assume in later life (Adler, 1927, 1933). By playing off personal psychic movement toward subjective life goals with the relatively untapped power of community feeling, Adler's psychology ultimately became a dynamics of interpersonal relationships premised on the dialectic competition between the individual's private goals and the adaptive pull of his social environment.

To Adler, the balance between community feeling and natural self-assertion was disturbed early in life and was unfailingly based on the "feeling of inferiority" (*Minderwertigkeitsgefühl*). Convinced that cultural opportunities for the development of community feeling in the child were relatively rare (1927, pp. 156-157), and further convinced that family education itself abetted rather than countered an antisocial striving for personal power via its own "pathological family egoism" (1927, pp. 64, 279-280), Adler increasingly equated mental health with a willful commitment to social adaptation. This in turn was proportional to the degree to which one could be "educated" to community feeling, both through the schools and (if necessary) through individual therapy. Despite the highly variable nature of the individual's imagined goals, such educative efforts invariably came back to the feeling of inferiority.

Such inferiority was initially felt to be organically determined. In his important monograph of 1907, Adler expounded a theory of organ inferiority that was well received by the Vienna analysts and that Freud himself considered a valuable addition to the knowledge of neurosis (see Freud, 1914b, p. 99, and Jones, 1955, p. 131). In this work, Adler invoked the concept of the inherited inferior organ (in terms of both morphology and function) to account for the fact that certain diseases were both inherited and confined to a particular organ, and thereby to provide a heuristic clinical device which could complete "the otherwise insufficient etiology" of certain syndromes (pp. 1-11). While this work was largely independent of psychoanalysis, it did address itself to the question of neurotic "predisposition" that Freud recognized. Adler attempted to make a contribution to psychopathology by postulating that organ inferiorities did not merely entail compensations at a corresponding organic level, but implicated the central nervous system in a way that made for psychical compensations as well.[4]

[4] Adler hoped to find an ordering concept that could make the symptomatic phenomena of psychoanalysis comprehensible within the framework of clinical medicine. Convinced that adequate organ functioning entailed the adequate directing activities of the "psychomotor superstructure of the organ," and con-

At the time of his separation from Freud in 1911, Adler formulated a far more encompassing theory of neurosis, which crystallized with the publication of *The Neurotic Constitution* in 1912. While his starting point was once again the compensation occasioned by inferior organs, Adler quickly branched into a broader social theory of neurosis which recognized not only the constitutionally inferior child as predisposed to neurosis, but the unattractive child, pampered child, and excessively disciplined child as well (Adler, 1912b, pp. 12-13). The neurotic child's "uncertainty of existence," we now learn, exists to a lesser degree among normal children (1912b, p. 14), and the "guiding fiction" of imagined superiority by which the child seeks to free itself from the feeling of inferiority, is common to the healthy and unhealthy alike (1912b, pp. 18, 29, 36, 54, 66-67). Although both normal and neurotic were invariably "ensnared in the wishes of [their] particular fiction," only the neurotic was unable to find his way back to reality (1912b, pp. 36-37): "The normal individual too may

vinced that inferior organs were those least able to meet the demands of culture, he basically attempted to buttress Freud's genetic perspective on childhood developmental defects with the medical observation that "The childish faults are only the externally perceptible phenomena arising from the disturbed psyche and mark the lack of an adequate compensation in the psychomotor superstructure of the organ" (Adler, 1907, p. 59). His notion of childish defects as "lines of direction from the psyche" and "signals which indicate the peripheral and central inferiority [that] has not yet been successfully overcome" was meant to subsume all neurotic symptoms (Adler, 1907, pp. 61-62). Adler, however, did not simply claim that all the phenomena of neuroses referred back to organ inferiority. He attempted to show, in considerable detail and with considerable clinical illustrative material, how specific neurotic symptoms could be reinterpreted as motor discharges arising from "the motor portion of the compensating superstructure" (1907, p. 64). Further convinced that inferior organs were routinely accompanied by inferior sexual organs, Adler indicated that the "sexual basis" of the neuroses resolved itself into the psychic overcompensation of a specific inferior organ and overcompensation of the correspondingly inferior sexual organs. Both pathogenic sources, he argued, produced infantile masturbation as the motor expression of a disproportionately heightened degree of psychic attention aimed at obtaining pleasure (1907, p. 65). It is thus not quite accurate to reduce Adler's theory, as Ellenberger (1970, pp. 603-606) does, to an attempt to offer "a plausible theory of the substratum of neurosis." Adler wrote his organ-inferiority monograph as a psychiatrically informed internist more interested in reinterpreting neurotic phenomena in line with a heuristic ordering device (the inferior organ) which would have wider clinical relevance for his medical colleagues than Freud's strictly psychoanalytic account of symptomatic childhood defects.

and does create his deity, feels drawn upward but never loses sight of reality, and always takes it into account as soon as he is called upon to act" (1912b, p. 67).

In all this, Adler came to give increasing recognition to that normative "inferiority" which was intrinsic to the infantile situation itself. The irresistibility of his scheme, he submits, owes to the perennial "uncertainty in childhood, the great distance which separates the child from the potency of man, from the distinctions and privileges of manhood, forebodings and knowledge of which the child possesses" (Adler, 1912b, p. 37). Two years later, in a summary paper on "Individual Psychology, Its Assumptions and Its Results," he would write:

> ... throughout the whole period of development, the child possesses a feeling of inferiority in its relations both to parents and the world at large. Because of the immaturity of his organs, his uncertainty and lack of independence, because of his need for dependence upon stronger natures and his frequent and painful feeling of subordination to others, a sensation of inadequacy develops that betrays itself throughout life. This feeling of inferiority is the cause of his continual restlessness as a child, his craving for action, his playing of roles, the pitting of his strength against that of others, his anticipatory pictures of the future and his physical as well as mental preparations. The whole potential educability of the child depends upon this feeling of insufficiency. In this way the future becomes transformed into the land that will bring him compensation [Adler, 1914, p. 14].

Despite the aggravating nature of organ inferiority, our earliest subjective evaluations all feed on this infantile substrate and generate "goals" which are always "compensatory." Such goals must invariably have as their objective "superiority" in one form or another:

> Whether a person desires to be an artist, the first in his profession, or a tyrant in his home, to hold converse with God or humiliate other people; whether he regards his suffering as the most important thing in the world to which everyone must show obeisance, whether he is chasing after unattainable ideals or old deities, over-stepping all limits and norms, at every part of his way he is guided and spurred on by his longing for superiority, the thought of his god-likeness, the belief in his special magical power [Adler, 1914, p. 7].

Within this context, Adler formalized the verdict he had reached in his initial explication of the aggression drive. The question of aggression was, in fact, a secondary consideration, arising from a substratum of compensatory dynamics and the conditioned inevitability of the quest for superiority. The neurotic "aggressive attitude in life," Adler wrote in 1912, developed out of an original sense of inferiority and aimed at "overcoming" the ensuing uncertainty (1912b, p. 19). Sadism and hate did not emanate from an innate instinct, but represented character traits which aimed at elevating a feeling of worth by degrading others (Adler, 1912b, p. 44). Aggression was not conceived as a willful "cruelty impulse" directed towards others, but as one coping response addressed to the feeling of inferiority. As such, it attained characterological pre-eminence only in conjunction with the quest to satisfy organic needs:

> One can scarcely evaluate this phenomenon in a more correct way than by assuming that the necessary denial of the gratification of certain organic functions forces the child from the first hour of his extrauterine life into assuming a combative attitude towards his environment. From this result tension and accentuations of certain organically acquired abilities — *c'est la guerre!* — as I have described them in my "Studie" and the "Aggressionstrieb" [Adler, 1912b, p. 15].

While the attitude of child to environment must initially be "aggressive" in this loose, organic sense, the generic quest for superiority in interpersonal relations remained multifaceted and capable of adopting different kinds of characterological masks. The child, Adler reminds us, may grope towards its masculine goal not only through obstinacy, but through obedience as well (1912b, pp. 15-16), not only through the exercise of "superior efforts," but in "a greater dependence, for the attainment of which, anxiety, a feeling of insignificance, weakness, awkwardness, incapacity, sense of guilt and remorse serve as strongholds" (1912b, pp. 57-58). While the feeling of inferiority might introduce into the child's life "a hostile and fighting tendency," it also teaches us to differentiate, "gives us poise and security, moulds and guides our deeds and activities and forces our spirit to look ahead and to perfect itself" (Adler, 1914, p. 8).

These apparent facts of childhood are equally true for neurotics: while the goal of "god-likeness" must, to a certain degree, transform the relation of the individual to his environment into hostility, the emergent struggle may follow not only a direct path of "aggressiveness" but also an indirect byway suggested by precaution (Adler, 1914, p. 13). Indeed, from the perspective of inhibiting neurosis, the still activated feeling of inferiority may actually exclude the direct expression of aggression as a means to the end state of superiority, promoting instead more circuitous routes possessing only "vaguely active, sometimes masochistic and always self-torturing characteristics" (Adler, 1913, p. 36). In reality, the neurotic could draw from two opposing strands to reach the situation of imagined dominance. Neurotic superiority hinged not only on activity but on caution as well, and juxtaposed with the control gained by direct affective expressions of rage, anger, and jealousy were conquests along the lines of "obedience, submissiveness, 'hysterical impressionability', in order to chain people down through [his] weakness, fear, passivity, need for tenderness" (Adler, 1913, p. 36). The masculine protest, in other words, could readily use the feminine role to attain its own ends (Adler, 1912b, pp. 32, 43, 58). Later, Adler would delineate an entire range of nonaggressive character traits which, if not openly hostile, conveyed a sense of hostile isolation wholly antithetical to community feeling. Such traits constituted avoidance responses masking undercurrents of ambition and vanity; they were, in fact, detours used to demonstrate personal power (Adler, 1927, pp. 233-251).

This brief sketch, however incomplete, is sufficient to reveal the reductionistic bias with which Adler's work has been dismissed by the Freudians. The incompleteness of Adler's system as a self-contained developmental psychology has caused analysts to dismiss him altogether. Adler was an ego psychologist who chose to occupy himself with the single issue of ego defense. And while one may readily accept the criticism that Adler "overstated" the importance of one kind of ego defense, i.e., overcompensation (Alexander and Selesnick,

1966, pp. 233-234), it is unreasonable to offer the blanket condemnation that Jones does: "Adler's view of the neuroses was seen from the side of the ego only and could be described as essentially a misinterpreted picture of the secondary defenses against the repressed and unconscious impulses" (1955, p. 131). The fact that Adler was largely preoccupied with the problem of defense indicates only that he had a limited type of concern with neuroses. It does not mean that his work constituted a "misinterpreted picture" or one that was clinically valueless.

Although one can argue the virtues and limitations of Adler's work in terms of the inherent shortcomings of any perspectivistic ego psychology, the accusation that he presented a "one-sided" view of neurosis hardly makes for the simplistic contention that Jones proceeds to make. Adler's "whole theory," he tells us, was based on "the aggression arising from 'masculine protest,' " and, in addition, the tendency to compensate for feelings of inferiority was reinforced by an "innate aggressivity" (Jones, 1955, p. 131). As we shall see, Jones's statement mimics Freud's own tendency to reduce all of Adler's work to an encompassing "aggressive instinct" and to dismiss him summarily on that basis alone. While we may attribute Jones's reduction of Adler to "aggression" to simple carelessness, however, we shall see that there may be more important, subjective reasons why Freud felt compelled to do so.

II.

More important than the real significance of Adler's work was the context in which it was received and judged by Freud himself. Adler was the earliest rebel, provoking the first scission in the psychoanalytic movement, and Freud was subsequently obliged to respond to the Adlerian "threat" in order to insure both the prerogative to equate psychoanalysis with his own theoretic presuppositions and to consolidate his personal control of the psychoanalytic movement itself. If, as Jones informs us, the response to Adler was, in fact, not one

of rancor or bitterness, it was clearly one of analytic conde-
scension: Adler was "a little Fliess come to life again," a degen-
erate child who was "rapidly developing backwards" and
would soon end up "denying the existence of the unconscious"
(Jones, 1955, p. 130). In the ensuing attempt to repudiate
Adler's improperly "psychoanalytic" pretensions, the issue of
aggression, removed from its descriptive role within the
context of defense, was to function as a convenient symbol of
divergence and a ready source of refutation.

There is considerable irony in this, because the two lengthy
presentations that epitomized Adler's divergence from Freud
and marked the effective termination of his participation in
the discussions of the Vienna Psychoanalytic Society not only
divorced the masculine protest from the issue of an innate
aggressive drive, but proceeded to question the clinical utility
of the concept of instinctual drives altogether. A brief review
of the two lectures that ended Adler's interaction with the
Freudians may help to explicate the seeming unfairness of
Freud's subsequent fixation on the Adlerian aggressive drive.

Adler enunciated in these presentations an ego psychology
reactively predicated on the growing child's need to "safeguard" itself characterologically against early experiences of
insecurity which stemmed from the normal helpless state of
infancy, but which were abetted by educational mistakes and
a lack of affective concern on the part of the adult environment. As such, there are striking similarities between Adler's
1911 presentations and the developmental systems of later
theorists like Horney (1939, 1950) and Sullivan (1953).

In the first part of his "Critique of the Freudian Sexual
Theory of Nervousness," Adler addressed himself to the role of
sexuality in the neuroses. His basic argument is that the libido
should not be taken at face value, but examined as one vehicle
for the expression of the masculine protest. According to
Adler, only the organ-inferior child becomes precociously
libidinal, and he becomes so only because his concomitant
anxiety and need to achieve some form of masculine security
yield a thirst for knowledge (*Wissbegierde*) as a compensatory
product. This thirst for knowledge leads to a strained fantasy
activity about birth and sex differences, which in turn

provides the stimulus (*Reiz*) for the emergence of the sex drive as a means to demonstrate masculine dominance. From the vantage point of this reconstructed sequence, Adler contends that the neurotic's preoccupation with sexual anxieties and fantasies must be traced back to the theme of masculine vindication that prompted the emergence of sexual precocity in the first place. The clinical observations remain the same, but the categories of interpretation are once again new. Neurotic birth fantasies and castration anxieties reflect neither sexual wishes nor repressed fantasies, but fears of "feminine" victimization. The incest fantasy, the alleged core problem of neurosis, functions to nourish the masculine belief in one's own overpowering libido while permitting the evasion of the threat to masculinity associated with a "real" sexual encounter (Adler, 1911, pp. 95-98; partial translation in Ansbacher and Ansbacher, 1956, pp. 57-60). In short, Adler argues that sexuality is not at the source of neurosis, but represents the mask adopted by the masculine protest for purposes of the neurosis. Sexuality, therefore, is awakened early only when an existing inferiority and a strong masculine protest are present and are subsequently exaggerated or devaluated to serve the safeguarding tendency of the patient. The sexual impulses themselves are never causes, but always worked-over material and a means of personal striving (*bearbeitetes Material und Mittel des persönlichen Strebens*) (Adler, 1911, p. 102; Ansbacher and Ansbacher, 1956, p. 60).

In the second part of his exposition, "Repression and the Masculine Protest," Adler dissociated his masculine protest from the notion of an aggressive drive in the clearest possible manner. He argues that, from the standpoint of drive life (*Triebleben*), culture is the constant factor, drive satisfaction depends on social institutions and economic conditions, and drives are consequently consigned to the status of mere direction-giving means (*richtunggebendes Mittel*) to initiate future satisfactions. In a spirit strikingly reminiscent of Marx's argument in Part I of *The German Ideology*, Adler intimates that we can never benefit from a discussion of instincts qua instincts, inasmuch as their expression, from earliest infancy, is shaped by the social and economic environment (Adler,

1911, pp. 105-106; partial translation in Ansbacher and Ansbacher, 1956, pp. 64-66). From the standpoint of this developmental premise, Adler never proceeds to consider the innately "aggressive" or "cruel" child, but only the child whose healthy drive endowment is pathologically shaped by defiance (*Trotz*) as a certain kind of direction-giving tendency. Such children receive insufficient affection and comfort in their early years, find themselves subject to insecurity and feelings of displeasure (*Unlustgefühlen*), and subsequently resort to a character style distinguished by defiance as a defensive attempt to achieve a degree of masculine mastery over the environment. The aggressive child, in other words, is only the child who uses aggression as an interpersonal safeguard (*Sicherung*). The acts of protest (*Protesterscheinungen*) which characterize this strategy are utilized not because they are intrinsically pleasurable (*lustvoll*), but because they are valuable (*wertvoll*) in the struggle with others (Adler, 1911, pp. 106-107; partial translation in Ansbacher and Ansbacher, 1956, pp. 66-67).

Adler delivered these two presentations to the Vienna Psychoanalytic Society in January and February, 1911. The third volume of the Society's minutes lays before us the ensuing vitriolic debate that preoccupied the members for four weeks and culminated in Adler's resignation of his chairmanship on February 22, 1911. For purposes of the present discussion, one salient feature emerges from this debate: Freud's rejection of Adler's theories at the time of their formal promulgation had nothing to do with the equation of the masculine protest with an aggressive drive. Freud's general resentment stemmed from his perception that Adler was, in fact, talking about the same things that he was, but without using the terms he had already designated. Freud proceeded to criticize the antisexual tendency in Adler's writings and his tendency to minimize the value of a detailed phenomenology of the different neuroses on behalf of his advocacy of the unity (*Einheit*) of neuroses. To these criticisms, he appended three general reservations: that Adler had contaminated psychoanalysis by subjecting it to biological viewpoints, that he had overestimated the intellectual sense in the child's early valuation of sex, and that he had represented neurosis only from the standpoint of the ego (Nunberg and Federn, 1974, pp. 145-147). These criticisms, however justified or unjustified, established the wide parameters that characterized the ensuing discussion. The resulting dissension crystallized around two broad issues implicit in Adler's developmental approach: the relative explanatory primacy of the libido and the masculine protest and the relative merits and deficiencies of a theory of neurosis that restricted its purview to the psychology of the ego (Nunberg and Federn, 1974, pp. 102-111, 140-158, 168-177).

Interestingly enough, however, Freud was unwilling to formulate his estimate of Adler's role in the history of psychoanalysis in accord with the broad referents that emerged in the Vienna Society discussions. Instead, Freud's published attempts to appraise critically the merits of Adler's ego-psychological approach invariably falter and yield to a distorted reductionism by which Adler symbolized only the "aggression" arising from the masculine protest. Seemingly unconcerned with what aggression actually meant to Adler, Freud ultimately assailed him by erroneously attacking the validity of aggression as a separate instinctual aim. In the process, he may well have consolidated his own somewhat uncertain commitment to an all-encompassing dichotomy of sexual and ego instincts.

The first medium for the repudiation of Adlerian "aggression" occurred in the "Little Hans" case history of 1909. Paradoxically, the analysis of this case constituted, in large measure, an extended discourse on both the manifest and latent aggressive dimensions of oedipal rivalry. Beginning with the boy's anxious need to be "coaxed" by the mother and a subsequent fear of being "bitten" by horses (the father), the analysis proceeds to unravel the constellation of intertwined "aggressions" underlying these anxieties. And while the resolution of this phobia ultimately hinges on the resolution of a broader problem, specifically, the confused childhood fantasies of birth and copulation, the emergent symptom still takes as both its starting point and nexus a complementary array of decidedly "aggressive" propensities.

Constant reference is made not only to the consciously articulated and unconscious substratum of "hostility" Little Hans directs toward his father (Freud, 1909b, pp. 82-83, 90, 111, 123, 131, 134-135, 137), but to the "sadistic" dimensions of his quest for his mother (Freud, 1909b, pp. 81, 83, 130, 135) and the hostile death wishes directed toward his infant sister Hanna (Freud, 1909b, pp. 68-69, 72-73, 113-114, 128). To be sure, such feelings do not emerge in an interpersonal vacuum. The Little Hans case history is not one of aggression alone, but of the neurotic conflict that inevitably ensues when suppressed aggressive tendencies are countered by strong emotions of love and affection. Thus, we learn that Hans "deeply loved the father against whom he cherished these death-wishes," and that his "aggressive tendencies" were almost immediately transformed into feelings of pity and compassion (Freud, 1909b, pp. 112, 134). Indeed, the very impasse of phobic inhibition which Little Hans experienced resulted because "his two active impulses—the hostile one towards his father and the sadistic-tender one towards his mother—could be put to no use, the first because of the love that existed side by side with the hatred, and the second because of the perplexity in which his infantile sexual theories left him" (1909b, p. 135).

At the time of this case history, Adler had not even formulated the "masculine protest" and Freud could only address himself to the earlier paper on the aggressive drive (1908). In this paper, Adler had hypothesized that anxiety itself could arise from the suppression of aggression. It was to this early contention of Adler's that Freud juxtaposed the path the Little Hans analysis had taken. At an initial glance, he submitted, the facts of the case history appeared to be remarkably congruent with Adler's theoretical position in that paper.

As we have come to the conclusion that in our present case of phobia the anxiety is to be explained as being due to the repression of Hans's aggressive propensities (the hostile ones against his father and the sadistic ones against his mother), we seem to have produced a most striking piece of confirmation of Adler's view [1909b, p. 140].

Such token agreement, however, stemmed from different conceptual premises. While Adler (as Freud understands him) spoke of a special "aggressive instinct," Freud believed that all instincts were, a priori, "aggressive" in obtaining their ends. In 1915 he would speak of every instinct as a form of activity and would use the word pressure (*Drang*) to label officially this motor element, "the amount of force or the measure of the demand for work which it represents" (Freud, 1915a, p. 122). If "aggression" was a universal attribute of all instincts, it consequently became semantic nonsense to isolate one conceptually self-contained "aggressive instinct."

In the Little Hans case history, Freud further added that the facts of the case simply did not require the assumption of a special aggressive instinct. This was basically because the libido theory itself posited an aggressive component impulse through which the etiology of this phobia could be comprehended. In one sweeping statement Freud thus believed he was rejecting Adler's interpretive position and reasserting his own control over the theoretic underpinnings of psychoanalysis:

> I cannot bring myself to assume the existence of a special aggressive instinct alongside of the familiar instincts of self-preservation and of sex, and on an equal footing with them. It appears to me that Adler has mistakenly promoted into a special and self-subsisting instinct what is in reality a universal and indispensable attribute of *all* instincts—their instinctual and 'pressing' character, what might be described as their capacity for initiating movement. Nothing would then remain of the other instincts but their relation to an aim, for their relation to the means of reaching that aim would have been taken over from them by the 'aggressive instinct.' In spite of all the uncertainty and obscurity of our theory of instincts I should prefer for the present to adhere to the usual view, which leaves each instinct its own power of becoming aggressive; and I should be inclined to recognize the two instincts which became repressed in Hans as familiar components of the sexual libido [1909b, pp. 140-141].

In this case history, Freud echoed the response he had made to Adler's paper when it was initially presented at the Viennese Psychoanalytic Society a year earlier. Adler's analysis is right, his conclusion wrong (or at the very least unnecessary); what he calls the aggressive drive "is our libido" (Nunberg and Federn, 1962, p. 408). Ironically, Freud's critical rebuttal— that all instincts possessed their own "pressing" aggressive character—captured more of the essential Adlerian position than the allegedly "Adlerian" aggressive instinct to which he juxtaposed it. What, after all, had Adler's 1908 aggressive instinct meant if not, in Adler's own words, "a superordinated psychological field connecting the drives" (Adler, 1908, p. 28; Ansbacher and Ansbacher, 1956, p. 34), and hence characterizing from the standpoint of "field theory" what was in reality "a universal and indispensable attribute of *all* instincts" (Freud, 1909b, pp. 140-141)? What the Freudians caricature as my "aggressive instinct," Adler might well have replied, is not Freud's "libido," but the pathological manifestations of a "defiant" resolution of the masculine protest.

Five years later in 1914, the renunciation of what Freud considered Adler's "misleading generalization" would warrant more than a laconic disavowal. In *On the History of the Psycho-Analytic Movement,* it would receive more extended and emotionally charged treatment.

By this time, of course, much had transpired since Freud's first tempered reaction to Adler in 1909. Adler's preliminary areas of divergence had crystallized into his own competing "system" with the two presentations before the Vienna Psychoanalytic Society in the winter of 1911, and his final "break" with Freud and the Vienna Society had occurred the following spring. Moreover, at the Munich Congress of 1913, the "break" with Jung had taken place.[5]

Both these events had shaken Freud in a way that transcended the empirical limitations of the competing Adlerian and Jungian systems. However sensitive to the fact of "deviation" in itself, Freud's annoyance was exacerbated by the stubborn persistence with which both Adler and Jung continued to call their work "psychoanalysis," causing, as Jones

---

[5] In addition to Freud's own account of the split with Jung in his *History of the Psycho-Analytic Movement* (1914a, pp. 58-66), see Jones (1955, pp. 137-151). Jung's retrospective account is contained in his autobiography (1961, pp. 146-169). For a recent re-evaluation of the Jung-Freud collaboration that attempts to make sense of these two diametrically opposed perspectives, see Stepansky (1976).

tells us, "endless confusion in the minds of those outside the whole field" (Jones, 1955, p. 362). It was primarily in response to this latter dilemma that Freud wrote *On the History of the Psycho-Analytic Movement,* hoping it would serve as both an explanation of these disturbing theoretic breeches and as a testimony to his continuing personal prerogative to direct the movement which his work alone had generated. Freud's stated reason for expounding the Adler and Jung episodes was thus limited and ostensibly justifiable:

> I am not concerned with the truth that may be contained in the theories which I am rejecting, nor shall I attempt to refute them.... I wish merely to show that these theories controvert the fundamental principles of analysis (and on what points they controvert them) and that for this reason they should not be known by the name of analysis [1914a, pp. 49-50].

During the interval between the Little Hans case history and the writing of the *History,* however, Freud's subjective appraisal of the Adlerian system as the embodiment of a special aggressive instinct had crystallized. As early as December 3, 1910, he had strongly protested to Jung that Adler tried "to force the wonderful diversity of psychology into the narrow bed of a single aggressive 'masculine' ego current" (Freud, 1906-1923, p. 376). On March 1, 1911, a week after the conclusion of the long debate on Adler's theories in the Vienna Psychoanalytic Society, Freud informed Jung of his personal resumption of the chairmanship of the Vienna group, adding: "I now feel that I must avenge the offended goddess Libido, and I mean to be more careful from now on that heresy does not occupy too much space in the *Zentralblatt"* (Freud, 1906-1923, p. 400). Two days later he reiterated to Karl Abraham that "Adler's behaviour was no longer reconcilable with our psycho-analytical interests, he denies the importance of the libido, and traces everything back to aggression. The damaging effects of his publications will not take long to make themselves felt" (1907a-1926a, p. 103). Even more telling than either of these professional communications, however, was the impressionistic rendering of the "split" Freud had sent several days earlier to a junior colleague, the psychoanalytically informed Swiss pastor Oskar Pfister. On February 26, 1911, only four days after Adler's resignation of his chairmanship, Freud informed Pfister that

> Adler's theories were departing too far from the right path, and it was time to make a stand against them. He forgets the saying of the apostle Paul the exact words of which you know better than I: "And I know that ye have not love in you." He has created for himself a world system without love, and I am in the process of carrying out on him the revenge of the offended goddess Libido. I have always made it my principle to be tolerant and not to exercise authority, but in practice it does not always work. It is like cars and pedestrians. When I began going about by car I got just as angry at the carelessness of pedestrians as I used to be at the recklessness of drivers [1909-1938, p. 48].

It was this subjective valuation of Adler as a monistic theorist elevating man's "aggressiveness" to a new place of primacy which nullified Freud's moderated intent and enabled the critique formulated in his *History of the Psycho-Analytic Movement* to branch into a sustained polemic. This polemic, in addition to demonstrating the irreconcilability of Adler's system with psychoanalysis, attempted to undermine the intellectual integrity from which his work had proceeded. Adler, we now learn, with his "particularly speculative disposition" and "striving for a place in the sun," had long resented standing in Freud's shadow, and had attacked him from motives of personal ambition (Freud, 1914a, pp. 50-51).

In reality, Freud's personal indictment of Adler was strongly colored by a depreciatory psychiatric assessment that had long since consigned Adler's ambition to the status of outright pathology. As early as November 25, 1910, he had complained to Jung that Adler was "always claiming priority, putting new names on everything, complaining that he is disappearing under my shadow, and forcing me into the unwelcome role of the aging despot who prevents young men from getting ahead." Here, however, he qualified this plaint with the following injunction: "Adler is a very decent and highly intelligent man, but he is paranoid" (Freud, 1906-1923, p. 373). In subsequent correspondence with Jung extending through June, 1911, Adler's alleged paranoia would function as a veritable leitmotif, and one which was decreasingly circumscribed by any allusion to Adler's decency or intelligence.[6] Shortly after Adler's resignation of the Vienna Society chairmanship, Freud also confided to Abraham his certainty about Adler's "fine paranoid traits" (Freud, 1907a-1926a, p. 105), and in the original draft of the *History of the Psycho-Analytic Movement* he made specific mention of Adler's complaints of "persecution." Abraham, who read the unpublished manuscript, made the following suggestion:

> There is only one expression which I would like to have changed. You say about Adler how much he complained of your persecution [*Verfolgungen*], and I am afraid this word might cause harm. Adler will protest against being called paranoid. An expression with less pathological implications, such as hostility [*Anfeindungen*], would be preferable [quoted in Freud, 1907a-1926a, pp. 169-170; 1907b-1926b, pp. 165-166].

Freud accepted the criticism, though with some misgivings:

> 'Persecution' is the term used by Adler himself. I shall replace it in accordance with your suggestion, and instead of the 'filthy' spirit [*'unsaubere' Geist*] of A. Hoche I shall insert 'evil' spirit [*'böse Geist'*] [Freud, 1907a-1926a, pp. 170-171; 1907b-1926b, pp. 166-167].

After his initial thrust at Adler's character, Freud proceeded in the *History* to make light of Adler's professional competence. We now hear that Adler had "never from the first shown any understanding of repression" (Freud, 1914a,

---

[6] On March 14, 1911, Freud characterized his two "deviant" Viennese disciples to Jung in the following way: "He [Stekel] represents the uncorrected perverse unconscious, Adler the paranoiac ego; the two of them together might add up to one human being as seen by psychoanalysis. Adler's ego behaves as the ego always behaves, like the clown in the circus who keeps grimacing to assure the audience that he has planned everything that is going on. The poor fool!" (Freud, 1906-1923, p. 403). On June 15, shortly after Adler resigned his editorship of the *Zentralblatt* and left the Vienna Society altogether, Freud penned Jung a postscript to the affair which again dwelt on the paranoid theme: "The damage is not very great. Paranoid intelligences are not rare and are more dangerous than useful. As a paranoiac of course he is right about many things, though wrong about everything. A few rather useless members will probably follow his example" (1906-1923, p. 428). For additional references to Adler's paranoia in this correspondence, see Freud (1906-1923, pp. 373, 376, 387, 422).

p. 56), and that his blanket denial of "libidinal trends" in favor of the "egoistic component" contained in them is nothing more than rationalization, resembling, in its un- witting concealment of unconscious motives, dream material which has undergone "secondary elaboration": "In Adler's case the place of dream-material is taken by the new material obtained through psychoanalytic studies; this is then viewed purely from the standpoint of the ego, reduced to the cate- gories with which the ego is familiar, translated, twisted, and—exactly as happens in dream-formation—is misunder- stood" (1914a, p. 52). In addition, Adler's now exalted masculine protest, the primary mode of expression of the individual's governing motive of self-preservation (as Freud perceived it), was in reality nothing "but repression detached from its psychological mechanism and, moreover, sexualized in addition" (1914a, p. 54). In the paper "On Narcissism" written that same year, Freud contended that psychoanalysis had always recognized the existence of a masculine protest, but, unlike Adler, had always viewed it "as narcissistic in nature and derived from the castration complex" (Freud, 1914b, p. 92).

More crucial for our purposes than the questionable validity of such criticisms is the reductionistic summary statement to which they led. Freud's last word on Adler followed the same law of condensation he discovered in the dream-work, and echoed his comments to Pfister and Jung three years earlier. From a condemnation of Adler's allegedly uncompromising belief that ultimately "everything alike is pressed into the service of the masculine protest, self-assertion and the ag- grandizement of the personality," we subsequently hear that "the Adlerian system is founded exclusively on the aggressive instinct; there is no room in it for love" (Freud, 1914a, pp. 57-58).

III.

From this cross-section of published material and personal correspondence, a fairly accurate reconstruction can be made of Freud's motives for rejecting Adler and the aggressive instinct he was made to represent.

The first explanatory strand, which has already been mentioned, relates to the political significance of Adler's rebellion in the context of the psychoanalytic movement itself. Despite Jones's strong protestations of Freud's receptiveness to intellectual independence (1955, pp. 127-128), subsequent research has clearly established the sense of urgency he attached to his personal leadership of the psychoanalytic movement (e.g., Stepansky, 1976). According to his earliest biographer Fritz Wittels, himself an early participant in the Wednesday evening discussions, Freud viewed his pupils as subjects owing "fealty" to him alone, and he sought able people who would merely systematize and amplify his own theoretic suppositions:

> Freud's design in the promotion of these [Wednesday evening] gatherings was to have his own thoughts passed through the filter of other trained intelligences. It did not matter if the intelligences were mediocre. Indeed, he had little desire that these associates should be persons of strong individuality, that they should be critical and ambitious collaborators. The realm of psychoanalysis was his idea and his will, and· he welcomed anyone who accepted his views. What he wanted was to look into a kaleidoscope lined with mirrors that would multiply the images he introduced into it [Wittels, 1924, p. 134].[7]

[7] The Wittels biography in general, and the passage I have quoted in particular, are, it should be noted, matters of controversy. Eissler (1971, pp. 135-137), in his long refutation of Roazen's (1969) study of Freud and Tausk, has challenged the accuracy of the "kaleidoscope" metaphor by referring to the retractions that Wittels himself subsequently published (Wittels, 1933). Though Wittels did come to regard the book as a "youthful indiscretion" (p. 362), his retractions centered on his earlier attribution to Freud of a despotic "Jehovah complex" (p. 362). This changed estimation of Freud is not, however, tantamount to a retraction of his characterization of the Wednesday evening discussion group, and in fact Wittels never made such a retraction. In modifying his assessment of Freud's personality and teaching following his readmission to Freud's circle, Wittels's basic point seems to have been that, as man and scientist, Freud was fully deserving of the supportive "mirroring" of his early disciples, not that such "mirroring" never occurred. Wittels never rescinded his initial characterization of the demands Freud placed upon his disciples; he sought instead to mitigate the authoritarian connotations of these demands by appealing to Freud's own personal modesty and modest expectations as to the fate of psychoanalysis. This seems to be the sense of claims like "Among all psychoanalysts, myself included, he [Freud] is perhaps the only one who is

The most basic element of Freud's leadership involved his prerogative to dictate those minimal prerequisites for what

---

not intoxicated with the method [of psychoanalysis] and its results," and "If one speaks of his world renown, he answers not only with the wisdom of Solomon that this is vanity, but he reminds us that many an 'immortal' together with his theories, has been forgotten in an incredibly short time" (p. 363). These claims in turn pave the way for Wittels's verdict that "Therefore it now seems to be that it is his disciples who bestow upon him a rank (*ipse dixit*) against which he does not defend himself because it is a matter of indifference to him" (p. 363). In a comparable way, Wittels does not claim that Freud openly tolerated deviation in the Wednesday evening discussions, but now submits that when "because he 'tolerates no deviation from his theory,' I called him a despot, I wronged him" (p. 364).

Moreover, there are other characterizations of the early Wednesday evening discussion group that substantiate Wittels's initial judgment and that come from reliable sources. Eissler (1971) does not mention these sources, and it is perhaps important to cite them here in support of my acceptance of the Wittels passage in question. I am referring to Helene Deutsch (1940), who wrote that "Freud's need for an assentient echo from the outer world expresses itself particularly in his relationship to his first small group of pupils. In the fervor of his work, in the overcoming of his own doubts which he expresses so often and with such humility in his writings, he had to have peace in his scientific house. His pupils were to be above all passive understanding listeners; no 'yes men' but projection objects through whom he reviewed—sometimes to correct or to retract them—his own ideas....

"As an inspired pathfinder he felt justified in regarding his co-workers as a means towards his own impersonal objective accomplishment; and with this end in mind, probably every impulse towards originality, when it subserved other than *objective* purposes, annoyed him and made him impatient. Freud was too far ahead of his time to leave much room for anything really new in his own generation. It seems to be characteristic of every discoverer of genius that his influence on contemporary thought is not only fructifying but inhibitory as well" (pp. 188-189, 191).

In addition to Deutsch's observations, we have the important reminiscences of Max Graf (1942), himself an early member of the Wednesday evening circle who subsequently left Freud but remained on good terms with him. Graf has recounted that at the early meetings "There was an atmosphere of the foundation of a religion in that room. Freud himself was its new prophet who made the theretofore prevailing methods of psychological investigation appear superficial. Freud's pupils—all inspired and convinced—were his apostles" (p. 471). Graf also felt that "Good-hearted and considerate though he was in private life, Freud was hard and relentless in the presentation of his ideas. When the question of his science came up, he would break with his most intimate and reliable friends. If we do consider him as a founder of a religion, we may think of him as a Moses full of wrath and unmoved by prayers, a Moses like the one Michael Angelo brought to life out of stone" (p. 472).

I quote the Wittels passage and these corroborative perceptions not to make any general claim about Freud's alleged "authoritarianism" or to comment on the alleged political character of the entire psychoanalytic movement as Fromm (1959) does, but merely to indicate that the institutional history of the psychoanalytic

could definitionally constitute psychoanalysis.[8] By presenting
a system of ego psychology that either minimized or ignored
several principal constituents of the theoretical structure of
psychoanalysis—the theory of repression, of the unconscious,
the etiological significance of sexual life—Adler had clearly
placed himself outside the boundary of even "healthy" dissent.
Lou Andreas-Salomé, that enigmatic newcomer who, for a
short time, was privileged to attend simultaneously Freud's
Wednesday evening and Adler's Thursday evening discussion
groups, accurately assessed Adler's situation in the fall of
1912. Between his "rationalisitc milieu therapy" and his
doctrine of organ inferiority based on physiology, she observed, "the Freudian Ucs. falls to the ground—as it were
between bodily defects and the formation of ideals" (Andreas-
Salomé, 1912-1913, p. 42).

In his *Autobiographical Study* of 1925, Freud would
(rightly or wrongly) relate the strength of both Adler's and
Jung's movements not to their content, but to the temptation

---

movement does provide an important basis for understanding Freud's unwilling-
ness to consider fully Adler's theories at the time they were formulated. In this
respect, I would supplement Waelder's (1963) formulation that the whole reality
behind the charge of Freud's authoritarianism actually boils down to the fact that
"Freud was *tolerant* of his disciple's opinions but *did not surrender his own views to
him*" (p. 636) by adding that Freud's "inner-directed" refusal to surrender to the
influence of others could in the case of Adler—and I would argue for Jung as well
(Stepansky, 1976)—obstruct full comprehension of what the deviating disciple was
actually saying. This perspective does not deny that Freud had every reason for
passing judgment on who could be a psychoanalyst, for, as Waelder observed, "it is
not outlandish for the man who invented and named a thing to request the right to
inspect the products offered by others under this name, and to judge whether they
are correctly so labeled" (1963, p. 633). It does suggest, however, that selective inattention to the complete theoretical grounds for deviance may be an unfortunate
byproduct of this justifiable prerogative, and it seems that just this kind of selective
inattention typifies Freud's cursory written refutation of Adler's theories.

[8] For the most explicit statement of this supposition, see Freud (1914a, p. 16): "It
may thus be said that the theory of psycho-analysis is an attempt to account for two
striking and unexpected facts of observation which emerge whenever an attempt is
made to trace the symptoms of a neurotic back to their sources in his past life: the
facts of transference and resistance. Any line of investigation which recognizes
these two facts and takes them as the starting-point of its work has a right to call
itself psycho-analysis, even though it arrives at results other than my own. But
anyone who takes up other sides of the problem while avoiding these two hypotheses
will hardly escape a charge of misappropriation of property by attempted imper-
sonation, if he persists in calling himself a psycho-analyst."

they presented of escaping the "repellent" findings of psycho-analysis without rejecting its "actual material" (Freud, 1925c, p. 52). This assumption, long the private *raison d'être* of un-flinching Freudians, is that the competing systems formulated by dissenting analysts cannot represent viable intellectual differences so much as "lost insight" to "repellent" findings generated by "the recurring wave of resistance" (Jones, 1955, pp. 126-128). By this time, Freud felt that Adler had

> entirely repudiated the importance of sexuality, traced back the formation both of character and of the neuroses solely to men's desire for power and to their need to compensate for their constitutional inferiorities, and threw all the psychological discoveries of psycho-analysis to the winds [Freud, 1925c, p. 53].

In the ensuing attempt to repudiate Adler, the issue of "aggression" was appropriated for several reasons. The first concerns its vulnerability to attack. The notion of "instinctual aggression" clearly existed outside the theoretical structure of psychoanalysis and, at the same time, could easily be subsumed by that structure. Freud, that is, could take clinical aggression when it was present and easily explain it in terms of the anal-sadistic organization and "aggressive" component instinct provided by the libido theory (as in Freud, 1911a, 1918). From this perspective, there simply was no *need* to speak of "aggression" apart from the "impulsive" energic quality intrinsic to all instincts. On the other hand, Freud's correspondence to Jung indicates a genuine concern that Adler's concentration on the "masculine" ego current and minimization of the sexual drive qua sexuality would provide the opponents of psychoanalysis with damaging leverage: ". . . our opponents will soon be able to speak of an experienced psychoanalyst whose conclusions are radically different from ours" (Freud, 1906-1923, p. 376). It is this auxiliary pre-occupation that caused Freud to reiterate to Jung on March 25, 1911, the pressing need of the psychoanalytic circle to reach a final decision about Adler "before he is held up to us by outsiders" (1906-1923, p. 409).

The second consideration relates to the convenience that was involved in reducing Adler's work to the question of aggression. Despite his hasty synopsis in *On the History of the Psycho-Analytic Movement*, Freud's published material never fully came to grips with the real inadequacies of Adler's system, and the analytic quality of his written critique does not confirm Jones's contention that he took Adler's ideas "very seriously and discussed their possibility at length" (Jones, 1955, p. 132). More telling, and certainly from the "Adlerian" perspective closer to the truth, was Adler's own plaint to Lou Andreas-Salomé during the summer of 1913:

> My position with respect to Freud's school has alas never had to reckon with its scientific arguments. All I ever see, all my friends ever see, is a busy-busy grabbing and pilfering and all the learned shenanigans of the kind Mach mentions in his *Analysis*. Why is it that the school attempts to treat our views as common property, whereas we have always insisted on the errors of their opinions? [quoted in Andreas-Salomé, 1912-1913, p. 160].

Given this context and given Freud's enormous emotional investment in his leadership of the Vienna Society, it seems possible that, at least for purposes of written refutation, his reading of Adler was highly inaccurate and his appreciation of Adler's findings purposefully rudimentary. It was through such an intentionally vague sense of what the masculine protest was and what part it played in a system of individual psychology that Freud could allow himself casually to associate Adler with nothing more than a mundane "aggressive instinct." As a clinician, Adler was not concerned with aggression, but with the whole question of neurotic superiority and the whole gamut of active and passive means through which interpersonal control could be achieved. For him, the psyche was simply "a name for the *life-potentiality of an inferior creature*," and the "aggressive drive" which it comprised was no more than "the tendency toward expansion, and a reaching out for that which is more highly valued culturally—the male" (quoted in Andreas-Salomé, 1912-1913, p. 161). It was simply not convenient for Freud consistently to underscore this distinction.

Yet, from the letters written to Jung, Abraham, and Pfister, it is clear that the political motives for attacking Adler

through aggression coalesced and interacted with a more subjective personal reaction to the very possibility of aggressive instinctuality. Sixteen years after the attack on Adler in his
History of the Psycho-Analytic Movement, Freud would admit
in *Civilization and Its Discontents* the emotional resistance he
originally displayed towards the existence of an aggressive
instinct: "I remember my own defensive attitude when the
idea of an instinct of destruction first emerged in psychoanalytic literature, and how long it took before I became receptive to it" (1930, p. 120). Clearly, this emotional resistance
is most dramatically exemplified in the reaction to Adler.
While receptive to the conception of sadism as one component
instinct of sexuality ultimately subordinated to genitality, to
a "cruelty impulse" that was harmlessly manifested in
childhood, and to the existence of fantasied death wishes
operative in dream-life, Freud was unable at this time to
accept emotionally the ramifications of an aggressive instinct
that was operationally "adult." This partly accounts for the
vituperation which colored his account of the Adler episode in
the *History*. Freud himself owned up to his own hostile intent
in a letter to Lou Andreas-Salomé,[9] and even so loyal a
defender as Jones admits that the last section of this essay
"contains a few personal expressions that had been aroused by
some painful experiences at the time" (Jones, 1955, p. 363).
What Freud's correspondence intimates, however, is that the
"painful experience" associated with this episode was directly
related to the *content* of Adler's system. In creating a world
system that was allegedly "without love," Adler had sinned
against "the offended goddess Libido" to which Freud
revealed a relationship that clearly went beyond the clinical.
    What was the source of this emotional reaction? Although
the question cannot be definitively answered, an important

---

[9] In a letter of June 29, 1914, Freud confided to Lou how distasteful it had been
to write the *History of the Psycho-Analytic Movement*: "I was only able to carry out
this inescapable task by writing as if I myself were the sole arbiter involved and by
concerning myself as little as possible with a jury to whose favour I might have been
appealing. Hence I intentionally gave everyone a good clobbering [*mit Absicht
jedem irgend eine Grobheit spendete*] and to my closest friends who needed no
winning over I paid as many compliments as I chose" (Freud, 1912a-1936a, pp.
17-18; 1912b-1936b, p. 19).

hint is embodied in Freud's own perception of the affair: Adler was "a little Fliess come to life again" and therefore probably evoked the same conflicted misgivings Freud felt toward Fliess. Indeed, Freud not only made the connection between Fliess and Adler explicit in two letters to Jung, but recognized the crucial affective analogy as well. "It is getting really bad with Adler," he confided to Jung on December 3, 1910. "You see a resemblance to Bleuler; in me he awakens the memory of Fliess, but an octave lower. The same paranoia" (Freud, 1906-1923, p. 376). Less than three weeks later he made a more pointed confession:

> I am very glad that you see Adler as I do. The only reason the affair upsets me so much is that it has opened up the wounds of the Fliess affair. It was the same feeling that disturbed the peace I otherwise enjoyed during my work on paranoia; this time I am not sure to what extent I have been able to exclude my own complexes, and shall be glad to accept criticism [1906-1923, p. 382].

A month later, in the midst of the Vienna Society debate on Adler's theories, Freud professed a fuller comprehension of Adler that had tempered the affective residue of the Fliess affair: "Now that I understand him fully, I have become master of my affects. I shall treat him gently and temporize, though without hope of success" (1906-1923, p. 387).

In the language used in these three letters, Freud underscores the importance of the Adler episode in the context of his own ongoing self-analysis, with particular reference to the recurring need to master the affects associated with the Fliess relationship.

What exactly were the recurring affects, the complexes, that disturbed Freud's equilibrium during this time and permitted things with Adler to "get really bad"? In *Freud: Living and Dying*, Max Schur analyzes Freud's own continual superstitious preoccupations as derivatives of the suppressed "hostile and cruel impulses" emanating from the Fliess episode. To do so, he borrows the analysis of superstition that Freud himself appended to the 1904 (second) edition of *The Psychopathology of Everyday Life:*

It can be recognized most clearly in neurotics suffering from obsessional thinking or obsessional states—people who are often of high intelligence—that superstition derives from suppressed hostile and cruel impulses. Superstition is in large part the expectation of trouble; and a person who has harboured frequent evil wishes against others, but has been brought up to be good and has therefore repressed such wishes into the unconscious, will be especially ready to expect punishment for his unconscious wickedness in the form of trouble threatening him from without [quoted in Schur, 1972, p. 234].

On the basis of close textual analysis and investigation of Freud's correspondence, Schur sees Freud's "guilt" over his hostile wishes towards Fliess and superstitious anticipation of punishment for this "aggression" as operative years after the episode had been formally concluded. While Freud's obsessive superstitions reached the intensity of a symptom in 1904, the year Fliess attacked him over the bisexuality question in Otto Weininger's *Sex and Character*, Schur argues that Freud's preoccupation with the traumatic Fliess affair and the guilt that his aggressive fantasies produced was still operative as late as 1913, in the analysis of "neurotic superstitions" in *Totem and Taboo* (Schur, 1972, p. 279, also pp. 237, 256-257).

As the first vivid reincarnation of Fliess, appearing at a time when the episode was still emotionally charged for Freud, Adler may well have aggravated the aggressive fantasies that Freud had not yet completely worked through.[10] Seen in this

---

[10] In this connection, it is important to note the extremely belligerent, depreciatory tone Freud adopted in July, 1914, after Lou Andreas-Salomé forwarded him Adler's letter to her of August 16, 1913 (quoted on page 138) in which he accused the Freudians of "a busy-busy grabbing and pilfering" of his ideas. Freud wrote Lou: "The letter shows his specific venomousness [*spezifische Giftigkeit*], and it is very characteristic of him. I don't believe that it belies the picture which I have given of him. Let us speak frankly (it will be easier than to continue): he is a loathsome individual [*ein ekelhafter Mensch*]" (Freud, 1912a-1936a, p. 19; 1912b-1936b, p. 21).

Three days later, he wrote Abraham: "Lou Salomé has sent me an exchange of letters with Adler that shows her insight and clarity in an excellent light and does the same for Adler's venom and meanness [*Giftigkeit und Gemeinheit*], and with such trash [*Gesindel*], etc. Sometimes even Casimiro loses heart" (Freud, 1907a-1926a, pp. 182-183; Freud, 1907b-1926b, p. 177). Three and a half months earlier, he had characterized Adler as "that pernicious creature [*Schädling*]" (Freud, 1907a-1926a, pp. 136-137; 1907b-1926b, p. 137).

light, Freud's need to disavow Adler's "aggressive drive" takes on a new dimension: to embrace the aggressive drive would compel him to acknowledge the instinctual primacy of his own aggressive fantasies and would, at the same time, exacerbate the guilty superstitious "dread" that accompanied them. To deny the aggressive drive, on the other hand, meant to minimize the aggressive residue of the Fliess episode and to deny the superstitious expectation of punishment that still plagued him.

IV.

In terms of a historical study of aggression in Freud's thought, the Adler episode is additionally important for the aftermath it generated. During the period 1909-1914, Freud felt compelled to reject the existence of what he perceived as an independent aggressive instinct for both personal and political reasons. In doing so, he could reassuringly fall back on an existing dichotomy of sexual and ego instincts and the generally suitable clinical alternative of an aggressive component instinct. He did so, however, to the neglect of the important substratum of independent "aggressive tendencies" which had already filtered into his work by this time. For the present, these tendencies, which figured so heavily in the book on jokes, would be consigned to the status of unincorporated analytic fragments pushed into the background by partly extraneous and partly personal considerations. This awkward situation, however, could be no more than a tenuous theoretic impasse. The aggressive impetus of World War I would change it.

6

THE IMPACT OF WAR: AGGRESSION AND THE METAPSYCHOLOGY

During the first 8 months of 1915, Freud composed the 12 essays that would constitute his metapsychology, that supreme mode of psychoanalytic presentation which viewed mental process in its dynamic, topographic, and economic totality (Freud, 1915b, p. 181). While Freud originally intended to publish them all in book form, the exigencies of war led him to conclude, in November, 1917, that the time was not ripe for it (Freud, 1907a-1926a, p. 261). Unfortunately, the book was destined to remain unpublished. Though Freud published the first five essays individually in journal form during the course of the war, none of the last seven ever reached print, and their manuscripts have not survived. The fate of these seven essays represents a sad story and one that is unlikely to be adequately resolved. It is unclear what Freud's attitude towards these essays was and why he felt obliged to destroy them, although Jones has offered one reasonable explanation.[1]

The first five essays, which we have been fortunate enough to inherit, were all written during a brief period of frenetic productivity lasting from mid-March to early July.[2] Of these

[1] See Jones (1955, p. 186): "My own supposition is that they represented the end of an epoch, the final summing up of his life's work. They were written at a time when there was no sign of the third great period in his life that was to begin in 1919. He probably kept them until the end of the war, and then when further revolutionary ideas began to dawn which would have meant completely re-casting them he simply tore them up."

[2] Freud's correspondence indicates he was thinking about the papers on metapsychology considerably longer than this, however. As early as November 25, 1914,

PAUL E. STEPANSKY

essays, which are clearly among the most profound and historically important of Freud's works, two announce the fundamental shift in his conceptualization of aggression that occurred during the war years, and it is to them that we consequently turn. Of the two, the more important is the first paper on metapsychology, "Instincts and Their Vicissitudes."

I.

Edward Bibring's 1934 paper on "The Development and Problems of the Theory of the Instincts" remains to this day perhaps the most authoritative account of the various phases of Freud's views upon the instincts. Both Jones and analytic aggression theorists like Heinz Hartmann (1948, p. 371; Hartmann, Kris, and Loewenstein, 1949, p. 10) and Robert Waelder (1956, p. 97) have cited it approvingly. It is consequently to Bibring that we initially turn in assessing the new role of aggression which appears in the metapsychology.

Bibring breaks down the evolution of Freud's theory of instincts into four steps, each based on the need to assimilate new clinical observations that could not be integrated within an existing theoretic framework. Thus, Freud's earliest formulation of sexual and ego instincts yielded to a concept of narcissism which, by postulating that the energy of the ego instincts was actually libidinal in origin and possessed aims "derived from the aims of narcissistic libido directed to the subject's own self and acting within and upon it," necessitated a revision of ideas about the ego instincts (Bibring, 1934, p. 108).[3]

he informed Lou Andreas-Salomé that he was "working in private at certain matters which are wide in scope and also perhaps rich in content" (Freud, 1912a-1936a, p. 21). Two weeks later, on December 11, he wrote Abraham that "After some good results, my own work has plunged into deep darkness; I go on because one cannot remain without 'something to do' . . . but often without enthusiasm and with only slight expectation of solving the very difficult problems" (Freud, 1907a-1926a, p. 204).

[3] Actually, in "On Narcissism: An Introduction," Freud had argued that in the primal narcissistic state, sexual and egoistic energy could not be discriminated. See Freud (1914b, pp. 76, 92).

It is in the third stage of instinct theory, one that Bibring associates with "Instincts and Their Vicissitudes," that aggression enters the picture, not as an instinct proper (the fourth stage), but as an independent, nonlibidinal "trend" ascribed to the ego instinct.

According to Bibring, this third reclassification was prompted by the lack of "a sound theoretic basis" for the sadistic component impulses. Although originally considered to be "erotogenically bound," subsequent observation increasingly revealed sadism as "an independent component instinct which permeated every level, was able to ally itself to any other component instinct, had its own vicissitudes and could be regarded, in accordance with the dominant criterion of that time, as linked to the striated muscular system as its 'source'" (1934, p. 110). In clinical practice, sadism could represent not only "sexual perversions," but nonerotic impulses of cruelty and harshness, as well as a separate "component" of the ego instincts—one concerned with control, assertion, and domination. It was in response to the "disparate" kinds of facts embraced by this term that, to Bibring, Freud modified his paradigm:

> Freud's next attempt to solve this point was to ascribe the characteristics of aggressiveness (or "sadism," to use the then current term for the last time) to the ego instincts and to assume that, side by side with an opposition between the sexual and ego (aggressive) instincts, which expresses itself, among other things, in conflict, certain states of fusion between them also occur [1934, p. 112].

By this analysis, sadism was actually removed from the category of sexual instincts: the sadism of the sexual instincts now represented an instinctual admixture, arising from the "aggressiveness" of the ego instincts. Furthermore, with this change, the nosological primacy of instinctual source yielded to that of instinctual aim; ego instincts were no longer typified by "hunger" but by "hatred," viz., aggression (Bibring, 1934, pp. 112-113).

In terms of a history of aggression, it is extremely important to recognize both the importance and the limits of the kind of "aggressive" disposition Freud enunciated in "Instincts and

Their Vicissitudes." While this was Freud's first attempt to write anything about the generic nature of instincts (Jones, 1955, p. 156), this essay still by and large resolved itself into "a conceptual scheme of libido"—a physicalistic attempt to organize the data of sexual life and neurosis in terms of bodily chemistry, biological needs and functions (Pleune, 1961, p. 480)—while arguing a conception of instinct according to the neurological model of the reflex arc. According to this scheme, the idea of biological need emanating from an internal stimulus was placed in opposition to the readily abolished external stimulus of the reflex. Because of its inescapable internal nature, biological need was seen as affording the basis for a constantly operating force, the instinct (Pratt, 1958, pp. 21-22; cf. Amacher, 1965, p. 66).

The reason Freud's conceptual scheme was to be limited to the development of libido was essentially empirical: while nominally recognizing two groups of primal instincts, Freud's comments still proceeded from the psychoanalytic investigation of mental disturbances which "has hitherto been able to give us information of a fairly satisfactory nature only about the *sexual* instincts; for it is precisely that group which alone can be observed in isolation, as it were, in the psychoneuroses" (1915a, p. 125). It is important to keep in mind that Freud's subsequent analysis of the transformation of love into hate is thus presented only as a vicissitude of the *sexual* instinct intended to illustrate how the "content" of an instinct may be changed into its opposite (1915a, p. 133).

Though initially intended as an explication of a sexual instinct, this task presented immediate problems. "Love" could not be reduced to a special component instinct of sexuality, and it was equally awkward to conceive it as "the expression of the *whole* sexual current of feeling" (1915a, p. 133). Thus, before he could even consider the problem of instinctual transformation, Freud was compelled to come to grips with the generic problem of "love" itself. Furthermore, because love and hate were ego-syntonic attitudes describing not the relation of "instincts" to objects, but the relations of "the total" ego to objects (1915a, p. 137), Freud could not resolve the definitional problem of "love" by simple recourse to polymorphous perverse sexual components. Rather, to understand the problem of love, he was forced to turn to the genetic history of the "loving" ego. It was only in the attempt to chart developmentally the evolution of "love," a preliminary digression given the initial problem of instinctual transformation, that Freud confronted the ego's independent disposition to "hate."

Such a hateful disposition, although developmentally inevitable, was not present at birth. At the very beginning of mental life, Freud tells us, the ego's instincts are directed wholly to itself. In this temporary and admittedly unrealistic condition of primal narcissism, the outside world is not "hated" but simply ignored; that is, it is "not cathected with interest (in a general sense) and is indifferent for purposes of satisfaction" (1915a, p. 135). The ego could be exclusively "loving," however, only so long as it indulged in narcissistic containment, a prerogative which was as ill-fated as it was infantile. Given both the needs and physiologic facts of self-preservation, the ego must almost immediately find objects and perceive certain "internal instinctual stimuli" as unpleasurable or painful. When this happened, an originally "functional" reality-ego (however predicated on the existence of "infantile" narcissism) yielded to a new creation—the purified pleasure-ego. Henceforth, reality testing would become the sole function of pleasure; the ego would absorb or "introject" into itself external objects that were a source of pleasure. At the same time, it would discard as ego-alien and external both pain-inducing objects in the environment and those sources of internal stimuli that were similarly associated with "unpleasure."

It was when primary narcissism had yielded to this affective bifurcation of both internal and external stimuli that "hate" developed. Whereas the earliest polarity of the ego and the external world made only for the antithesis of love and indifference, the emergent polarity of pleasure-unpleasure required the ego to undertake active efforts of repudiation. Such "aggressive" disavowal was directed to all "objects," but objects according to the pleasure-ego's unrealistic criteria of externality:

When the purely narcissistic stage has given place to the object-stage, pleasure and unpleasure signify relations of the ego to the object. If the object becomes a source of pleasurable feelings, a motor urge is set up which seeks to bring the object closer to the ego and to incorporate it into the ego. We then speak of the 'attraction' exercised by the pleasure-giving object, and say that we 'love' that object. Conversely, if the object is a source of unpleasurable feelings, there is an urge which endeavours to increase the distance between the object and the ego and to repeat in relation to the object the original attempt at flight from the external world with its emission of stimuli. We feel the 'repulsion' of the object, and hate it; this hate can afterwards be intensified to the point of an aggressive inclination against the object — an intention to destroy it [Freud, 1915a, pp. 136-137].

Such hate bore no relationship to the sexual function. Earlier in this paper, Freud has analyzed pain as a sexually bound primary masochistic aim: ". . . we have every reason to believe that sensations of pain, like other unpleasurable sensations, trench upon sexual excitation and produce a pleasurable condition, for the sake of which the subject will even willingly experience the unpleasure of pain" (1915a, p. 128). Now, however, he changes course, and presents pain as an encompassing category of physiologic discomfort that has nothing to do with libidinal "cruelty" aims. The attempts to escape all kinds of pain thus appear as a separate ego function existing apart from the quest for sexual gratification. Consequently,

The ego hates, abhors and pursues with intent to destroy all objects which are a source of unpleasurable feelings for it, without taking into account whether they mean a frustration of sexual satisfaction or of the satisfaction of self-preservative needs. Indeed, it may be asserted that the true prototypes of the relation of hate are derived not from sexual life, but from the ego's struggle to preserve and maintain itself [1915a, p. 138].

This was all in marked contrast to the decidedly "social" influences shaping our conception of love. Though initially applied to the pleasure-giving (and subsequently incorporated) object, "love" ultimately attached itself only to sexual objects "in the narrower sense" as well as to those "which satisfy the needs of sublimated sexual instincts." Moreover, insofar as the word conventionally described the relation of the "ego" to its sexual object, it became applicable only when all the component impulses had been synthesized and subordinated to genital primacy and further used only in the service of reproduction (1915a, pp. 137-138).

Ultimately, then, the ascription of "aggressive" trends to ego instincts in "Instincts and Their Vicissitudes" became the product of accident. The inquiry undertaken in this essay was to involve solely the "various vicissitudes which instincts undergo," and was to be further confined to the sexual instincts "which are the more familiar to us" (Freud, 1915a, p. 126). Freud's attempt to illustrate the transformation of instinctual "content" through the analysis of love and hate retrospectively appears as a conceptual mistake, not only because these two words represented "attitudes" rather than instincts, but because they did not even represent simple opposites pertaining to a similar instinctual source. By Freud's own admission, love and hate, though initially presenting themselves as "complete opposites" do not "stand in any simple relation to each other. They did not arise from the cleavage of any originally common entity, but sprang from different sources and had each its own development before the influence of the pleasure-unpleasure relation made them into opposites" (1915a, p. 138).

However wide of its initial mark, this excursion into the developmental history of love did permit the important theoretic reorientation that Bibring noted. In the process of tracing love, Freud stumbled across the genesis of the aggressively "hateful" ego. Moreover, the ego's "aggression" is no longer the concomitant of childish egoism; it is now ascribed a large dose of positive survival value. We no longer hate for want of "sympathy," but purposefully, in response to "unpleasurable stimuli." As an expression of the pain reaction induced by objects, Freud tells us, hate remains "in constant relation with instincts of self-preservation" (1915a, p. 139). Here, for the first time, we tentatively approach the equation of "aggression" with health.

The "hating" ego could also be appropriated for pathogenic ends, however, a problem to which Freud turned in "Mourn-

ing and Melancholia." The starting point here was the psychogenesis of melancholia, a perplexing syndrome in which the
conventional "mourning" reaction accompanying grief was
complicated by a dramatic fall in self-esteem "to a degree that
finds utterance in self-reproaches and self-revilings, and cul-
minates in a delusional expectation of punishment" (Freud,
1917, p. 244).

Analysis further reveals that such self-reproaches are not
fictional but betoken a compelling psychological reality:
under the pain of object loss, the melancholic regresses from
object cathexis to the narcissistic oral libidinal phase.[4] In line
with this regression, the melancholic "ego" incorporates its
lost object, setting up an identification which indeterminably
prolongs its existence. Through this mechanism of identification, the melancholic's self-reproaches and "dissatisfaction
with the self on moral grounds" can more accurately be seen as
"aggressions" directed towards the lost (but now introjected)
object. Object loss, in other words, has become "transformed"
into ego loss, and "the conflict between the ego and the loved
person [has become transformed] into a cleavage between the
critical activity of the ego and the ego as altered by identification" (1917, p. 249).

The discovery of an operative identification, however, only
serves to pose a second, more puzzling paradox. Why did the
melancholic direct reproaches toward the lost object he
mourned? Here we reach the core of Freud's analysis. Melancholia, we now learn, is conditioned by a "conflict of ambivalence," an ingrained component of love relationships
which is particularly likely to emerge in the wake of object
loss. At the same time that one component of the melancholic's object cathexis undergoes regressive identification,
another component, under the influence of an activated
ambivalence, is reduced to sadism. It does not reduce *solely* to
sadism, however. The ambivalence toward the abandoned
object is no longer reduced to one of competing levels of sexual
organization, i.e., "loving" genital versus anal-sadistic. Am-

---

[4] For amplification, see Abraham (1924, pp. 71-129).

bivalence is now taken to include the ego's nonlibidinal prerogative to hate. Thus, in the melancholic's predicament,

> hate comes into operation on this new substitutive object, abusing it, debasing it, making it suffer and deriving sadistic satisfaction from its suffering. The self-tormenting in melancholia, which is without doubt enjoyable, signifies, just like the corresponding phenomenon in obsessional neurosis, a satisfaction of trends of sadism and hate which relate to an object, and which have been turned round upon the subject's own self in the ways we have been discussing [1917, p. 251].

Of crucial import here is the conscious separation between sadism and hate; for an elucidation of this distinction, Freud refers his readers to "Instincts and Their Vicissitudes." In addition, not only does the "hating" ego exist apart from the question of anal-sadistic organization, it can actually function at the *expense* of libidinal investment. This is precisely what is represented by the melancholic's "aggression" toward its lost object: "Just as mourning impels the ego to give up the object by declaring the object to be dead and offering the ego the inducement of continuing to live, so does each single struggle of ambivalence loosen the fixation of the ego to the object by disparaging it, denigrating it and even as it were killing it" (1917, p. 257).

This level of analysis, we now see, runs in the same direction as that presented in "Instincts and Their Vicissitudes." Even in the context of pathology, aggression is now seen as a therapeutic *prerogative* of the ego. Just as the ego initially "hated" a hostile and pain-inducing environment for purposes of survival, so it now "hates" that it may reinstate health. Aggression has, in fact, become a higher, ego-syntonic function, and when its "disparagement" has actually succeeded in loosening the libidinal fixation, "The ego may enjoy in this the satisfaction of knowing itself as the better of the two, as superior to the object" (1917, p. 257).

Bibring, it will be remembered, credited the new ascription of aggressive trends to the ego to the "disparate" kinds of facts embraced by sadism. Seen in the light of "Mourning and Melancholia," however, it seems questionable whether Freud was actually addressing himself to a "sadism" of the ego instincts,

and highly unlikely that the result of this theoretic development was to take sadism out of the category of sexual instincts
and include it among the ego instincts. As we observed, Freud
consciously *distinguished* between the role of sadistic tendencies and "hate" in the self-torments of melancholics. Nonlibidinal "hate" did not amount to a redefinition of sadism, but
was injected alongside it.

In assuming that sadism came to embrace "facts of a disparate kind," Bibring further posits that clinical observation
could not be reconciled with an original view of the "sadistic
components" that was "erotogenically bound." This however,
represents a serious misreading of Freud's initial definition of
sadism. Dating from 1905 and the *Three Essays on the Theory
of Sexuality*, sadism was defined not only in terms of pregenital sexual organization, but as a non-phase-specific component instinct that persisted independently of the erogenous
zones (see Chapter 4, pp. 91-93). In the third set of Introductory Lectures delivered in 1917 (the year "Mourning and
Melancholia" was published, but two years after the reformu-
lation of "aggression" in "Instincts and Their Vicissitudes"),
Freud's conception of sadism remained essentially unaltered.
While he initially introduced sadism as a perversion of sexual
aim in which sexual desire centered on actions that were
normally preparatory to intercourse (1916-1917, pp. 305-
306), Freud *also* spoke of sadism as a nonzonal component instinct, an "impulse to mastery" which took an object from the
very beginning of life despite the simultaneous presence of an
autoerotic level of sexual organization (1916-1917, p. 328).
This was the same "cruelty impulse" he had spoken of 13 years
earlier.

It thus seems unlikely that an expanding recognition of
what sadism entailed compelled Freud to attribute an
aggressive component to the ego instincts. From its initial
formulation, sadism was a nonzonal ego attribute at the same
time as it was an "erotogenically bound" kind of sexual
organization.

Given this fact, however, the novelty of the two cited papers
on metapsychology remains. Although Freud had previously
described an encompassing "cruelty impulse," it had always

been broadly linked with gratification. Only in the metapsychology did he speak of "hate" as a purposeful ego-syntonic necessity. Clearly, a fundamental shift in his conceptualization of the potential for "healthy" aggression had occurred.[5] To understand the nature of this shift, however, it is insufficient to review the internal development of the first 20 years of psychoanalytic theory. Instead, it is necessary to review the historical circumstances in which the metapsychology was written, with special reference to the effect that the "aggression" of World War I had on Freud.

II.

Freud's immediate reaction to the outbreak of World War I represents a transitory but reassuringly human crack in the seeming impenetrability of his psychoanalytic armor. To state that his response to Austria's declaration of war was "unexpected" is an understatement. Jones writes:

> One would have supposed that a pacific *savant* of fifty-eight would have greeted it with simple horror, as so many did. On the contrary, his first response was rather one of youthful enthusiasm, apparently a re-awakening of the military ardors of his boyhood. . . . After Germany had handed round her declarations of war he wrote: "I should be with it with all my heart if only I could think England would not be on the wrong side." He was quite carried away, could not think of any work, and spent his time discussing the events of the day with his brother Alexander. As he put it: "All my libido is given to Austro-Hungary" [Jones, 1955, p. 171].

Such boyish and remarkably unanalytic enthusiasm found easy expression in his correspondence. "For the first time for

---

[5] Lou Andreas-Salomé was one who immediately appreciated this shift in conceptualization. Upon receipt of her offprint of the article in July, 1915, she wrote back to Freud: "In 'Instincts and their Vicissitudes' what seemed to me a new discovery, which struck me most forcibly, was the suggestion that love and hate did not arise 'from the cleavage of any originally common entity.' Hitherto hate as such, considered to be purely a kind of love in reverse and always presumed to be the result of repression, had always had pathological qualities ascribed to it, which would now appear to be the result of a regressive coalescence of ego-instinct and sexual function" (quoted in Freud, 1912a-1936a, p. 29).

thirty years," he wrote Abraham on July 26, 1914, "I feel myself to be an Austrian and feel like giving this not very hopeful Empire another chance" (Freud, 1907a-1926a, p. 186). This initial burst of euphoric expectancy persisted through the summer and early fall. On August 25, he told Abraham that "like everyone else, I live from one German victory to the next" (1907a-1926a, p. 193), and added in a letter dated September 3 that "The German victories have provided a firm basis for our morale" (1907a-1926a, p. 195).

This spurt of "infantile" patriotism, however, proved fatally short-lived. While Freud completely sympathized with the Central Powers for the first two or three years of the war (Jones, 1955, p. 170), his skepticism and cynicism reached "analytic" maturity in a matter of months. In Jones's (1955) words, "Freud came to himself" (p. 171). His initial loathing for the incompetence his "newly adopted" fatherland displayed in its campaign against the Serbians (Jones, 1955, p. 172) represented only a preliminary expression of his revulsion. By September 22, he was ready to inform Abraham that war was simply a time of "unleashed brutality" (Freud, 1907a-1926a, p. 197).

This judgment would not long remain the product of noetic detachment. As Jones convincingly documents, the war years quickly developed into a period of immediate deprivation and misery for Freud (along with the rest of Austria), in which considerable anxiety about his two soldier sons was compounded by the severe food shortage, a dearth of cigars, extemely limited access to his colleagues, and from 1917, the "reasonable" fear that he should end in bankruptcy (1955, pp. 168-206, passim). Freud has left us a record of his progressive demoralization in wartime correspondence to two contrasting adherents, one being the most orthodox of his followers, the other perhaps the most impressionistic and flamboyant. On November 25, 1914, he confided to Lou Andreas-Salomé that the admixture of psychoanalytic insight and the reality of war could only make for depressing fatalism. "I do not doubt that mankind will survive even this war," he wrote, "but I know for certain that for me and my contemporaries the world will never again be a happy place. It is too hideous. And the saddest thing about it is that it is exactly the way we should have expected people to behave from our knowledge of psycho-analysis" (Freud, 1912a-1936a, p. 21). By December 21, 1914, he admitted to Abraham that he "needed" someone to give him courage as he had "little left," and further confessed his occasional "horror of the meal to come" (Freud, 1907a-1926a, p. 205). Six months later, on July 30, 1915, he informed Lou that his eldest son Martin had recently been grazed by a bullet and that his youngest son Ernst had just received his "marching orders." "Since we don't dare to look into the future," he told her, "we just live for the day and try to get out of it what it is willing to yield" (Freud, 1912a-1936a, p. 32). He conveyed comparably despondent sentiments to her in the spring of 1916 (1912a-1936a, pp. 39, 43), and by October 10, 1916, he would tell Abraham: "It is a desolate world. There is no prospect of a pleasing, peaceful end, and there are all sorts of dark threats to the necessary victory" (1907a-1926a, p. 239).

By 1917, after two years of misery and anxiety, his outlook had taken a decided turn toward the morbid. He wrote Abraham:

> Life bears too heavily on me. I talk very little about this, because I know that others would take such statements as complaints and signs of depression, and not as objective descriptions, which would be unfair to me. I believe I have had my time, and I am not more depressed than usual, that is to say, I am very little depressed, and console myself with the assurance that my work lies in the good hands of men such as you and Ferenczi, and perhaps some others, who will carry it on [1907a-1926a, pp. 251-252].

In January, 1918, he was morbidly fatalistic: "If the war lasts long enough, it will kill off everybody anyway" (1907a-1926a, p. 269).

III.

It is, at first sight, difficult to see the effect of the war years on broad questions of psychoanalytic theory. In the important set of *Introductory Lectures* delivered during the winter of 1916-1917, those constituting the "General Theory of the Neuroses," the governing problem of neurosogenesis was delineated in "classic" terms basically similar to those adopted in the 1912 paper on "Types of Onset of Neurosis." Neurotic etiology was taken to be the governing clinical preoccupation of psychoanalysis, and its three causal components—the "frustration" resulting when the possibility of libidinal satisfaction was removed (Freud, 1916-1917, p. 344), the predisposing inclination toward libido fixation (1916-1917, p. 346), and the ensuing "conflict" occasioned by the condemnation directed towards the regressive paths the "frustrated" libido sought to follow (1916-1917, pp. 349-350)—were all adequately subsumed within a framework of sexual and ego instincts (1916-1917, pp. 350-352). Although Freud was as alert as ever to the possibility that "sexual gratifications" could, in fact, entail gratifications of lusts that are "cruel and horrible" (1916-1917, p. 302), the whole problem of aggression was still treated only in the context of sexual development: as a perversion of aim, a component instinct, the group of "sexual tendencies" precipitating obsessional symptoms (1916-1917, pp. 306-309), the hallmark of a particular "period" of pregenital organization (1916-1917, pp. 326-328).

Ironically, it was not in this series of lectures, but in the previous one on dreams given a year earlier (the winter of 1915-1916) that the "aggressive" drama of World War I first penetrated Freud's writing. Freud appealed to the present state of affairs to convince his readers of the "offensive" nature of the censored dream wishes:

> And now turn your eyes away from individuals and consider the Great War which is still laying Europe waste. Think of the vast amount of brutality, cruelty and lies which are able to spread over the civilized world. Do you really believe that a handful of ambitious and deluding men without conscience could have succeeded in unleashing all these evil spirits if their millions of followers did not share their guilt? Do you venture, in such circumstances, to break a lance on behalf of the exclusion of evil from the mental constitution of mankind? [1916-1917, p. 146].

Much more important for gauging Freud's reaction to the brutality of World War I than this lone interjection in the *Introductory Lectures*, however, was the essay "Thoughts for the Times on War and Death" which he had published earlier in 1915. Here, for the first time, Freud directly confronts the "disillusionment" of the war as a psychoanalytic problem in its own right, pointing to it as a "responsible" factor in the "mental distress" felt by noncombatants (1915c, p. 275). Such disillusionment initially appeared well founded. Having totally demolished the "unity among the civilized peoples" and interrupted the evolution of "ethical relations between the collective individuals of mankind," the Great War was not only

> more bloody and more destructive than any war of other days, because of the enormously increased perfection of weapons of attack and defence; it is at least as cruel, as embittered, as implacable as any that has preceded it.... it has brought to light an almost incredible phenomenon: the civilized nations know and understand one another so little that one can turn against the other with hate and loathing [1915c, pp. 278-279].

Yet, for all its rational appeal, Freud ultimately finds such disillusion predicated only on the destruction of an "illusion" and hence unjustified. Despite the constructive social possibilities entailed in the range of "instinctual vicissitudes" and the constructive potential of the "susceptibility to culture," man remained a creature of elementary impulses. In exaggerating the general susceptibility to civilization, Freud submits, we overlook the substantial portion of instinctual life that remains untransformed and primitive (1915c, p. 283). In compelling the individual to accept an increasingly greater estrangement from his instinctual dispositions, civilized society actually cultivated hypocrisy, for "Anyone thus compelled to act continually in accordance with precepts which are not the expression of his instinctual inclinations, is living, psychologically speaking, beyond his means, and may objectively be described as a hypocrite" (1915c, p. 284).

The peculiar nature of mental development, the special capacity for regression which allows earlier stages of development to persist alongside the later stages which evolve from them, insures the "imperishability" of the primitive mind (1915c, pp. 285-286). Hence,

> our mortification and our painful disillusionment on account of the uncivilized behaviour of our fellow-citizens of the world during this war were unjustified. They were based on an illusion to which we had given way. In reality our fellow-citizens have not sunk so low as we feared, because they had never risen so high as we believed [1915c, p. 285].

In the second section of his essay, that concerning "Our Attitude towards Death," Freud initially appears to regress to his preanalytic enchantment with the coming of war. Psychoanalytically, he reminds us, no one can conceive of his own death. Unconsciously we remain resolutely convinced of our immortality. Moreover, it is this unconscious substrate which generates our "civilized sensitivity" towards death; in social intercourse, we avoid considering the possibility of death, react deeply to death when it does occur, and adopt a special primitive attitude toward the dead themselves. When death strikes a loved one, our "conventional attitude" coalesces in "complete collapse." Yet, though dealing with a psychological inevitability, Freud goes out of his way to impress us with the social depletion that such an attitude generates. Given our strained sensitivity to death and continued attempts at denial,

> Life is impoverished, it loses in interest, when the highest stake in the game of living, life itself, may not be risked. It becomes as shallow and empty as, let us say, an American flirtation, in which it is understood from the first that nothing is to happen, as contrasted with a Continental love-affair in which both partners must constantly bear its serious consequences in mind [1915c, p. 290].

As a breath of refreshing realism, war "sweeps away" our conventional treatment of death:

> Death will no longer be denied; we are forced to believe in it. People really die; and no longer one by one, but many, often tens of thousands in a single day. And death is no longer a chance event. To be sure, it still seems a matter of chance whether a bullet hits this man or that; but a second bullet may well hit the survivor; and the accumulation of deaths puts an

end to the impression of chance. Life has, indeed, become interesting again; it has recovered its full content [1915c, p. 291].

Yet such invigorating social realism ultimately trails off into
a kind of fatalistic instinctual realism that can evoke neither
praise nor blame. We remain, Freud reminds us, rather hap-
less primeval men whose relation to that "first and most
important prohibition ... of the awakening conscience"—
Thou shalt not kill—has not evolved beyond that which
spurred our ancestors to devise it. Then as now, "so powerful a
prohibition can only be directed against an equally powerful
impulse," and "The very emphasis laid on the commandment
Thou shalt not kill makes it certain that we spring from an
endless series of generations of murderers, who had the lust for
killing in their blood, as, perhaps, we ourselves have to-day"
(1915c, p. 296). Moreover, while modern man no longer experiences the primal "final extension" of this impulse, the
"hate-gratification" lurking behind grief for the loved dead,
he has also forsaken the savage's awe of the spirits of his fallen
enemy, and in this way relinquished a "vein of ethical sensi-
tiveness" which was second nature to his "uncivilized" ancestors (1915c, p. 295). It would seem that in terms of social
precepts which honestly represent our "instinctual tendencies," we are consigned to a rather ineluctable status quo.

IV.

It is through appreciating the significance of "Thoughts for
the Times on War and Death" for Freud's own psychic equilibrium, I believe, that we can eventually return to the
"healthy hating ego" depicted in the metapsychology. When
this essay was written in early 1915, Freud's first patriotic
surge had subsided. Immediately before writing it, his eldest
son Martin had enlisted in the army and his daughter Anna
remained stranded in England (she eventually reached Vienna
through the staff of the Austrian Embassy in London).
Furthermore, in November, 1914, Freud learned that his
older half-brother, Emmanuel, with whom he had been close,
had died in a train accident in England. To crown this de-

pressing sequence, Freud's practice was minimal and he was already concerned with his lack of financial security (Schur, 1972, pp. 290-291). Thus, by the time he publicly summarized his "Thoughts" on the contemporary situation, Jones tells us, "Freud, like all highly civilized people, was not only greatly distressed, but also bewildered, by the frightful happenings at the onset of the First World War, when so many things took place of which no living person had any experience or any expectation" (1955, p. 368). Max Schur appraises Freud's state of mind when the essay on war and death was written in a similar fashion. However opposed to illusions and denial, and however realistic his understanding of the real "value of life," Freud remained something of an inveterate believer who could maintain that " 'Life is not all that wonderful, but still, it is all we have.' He hated destruction and he loved *logos*. Hence he hated war" (Schur, 1972, p. 294). On December 28, 1914, still laboring under the onus of his own emotional relapse at the outbreak of war, Freud communicated to the Dutch psychopathologist Van Eeden the distilled analytic essence of his perception of the war:

> Under the influence of this war I venture to remind you of two assertions psychoanalysis has put forward which have assuredly contributed to its unpopularity.
> Psychoanalysis has concluded from a study of the dreams and mental slips of normal people, as well as from the symptoms of neurotics, that the primitive, savage and evil impulses of mankind have not vanished in any individual, but continue their existence, although in a repressed state—in the unconscious, as we call it in our language—and that they wait for opportunities to display their activity.
> It has furthermore taught us that our intellect is a feeble and dependent thing, a plaything and tool of our impulses and emotions; that all of us are forced to behave cleverly or stupidly according as our attitudes and inner resistances ordain.
> And now just look at what is happening in this wartime, at the cruelties and injustices for which the most civilized nations are responsible, at the different way in which they judge of their own lies, their own wrong-doings, and those of their enemies, at the general loss of clear insight; then you must confess that psychoanalysis has been right with both its assertions [quoted in Jones, 1955, pp. 368-369].

Given this kind of reaction, it is easy to see how the essay on war and death came to constitute "an effort to clear his own mind about the most useful attitude to adopt to the current events" (Jones, 1955, p. 368). In it, Freud seeks to minimize and "bind" his revulsion at the suffering and brutality occasioned by war by *rationalizing* man's incapacity to avoid such pathogenic relapses. Given the fact that such potential barely existed, Freud might reassure himself and summon his resolve to see the war through with the quiet revelation that, after all, our "disillusion" is only based on "illusion." To be sure, the exposure of illusion, in itself, could provide no consolation. If this had been Freud's sole accomplishment, the only product could have been "hopeless pessimism." Rather, as Schur suggests, it was the fact that Freud had "subjected these illusions to an analytic appraisal in both a serene and scientific manner" (1972, p. 299) that forestalled pessimism. "I cannot be an optimist," he wrote to Lou Andreas-Salomé on July 30, 1915, "and I believe I differ from the pessimists only in that wicked, stupid, senseless things don't upset m e, because I have accepted them from the beginning" (Freud, 1912a-1936a, p. 33). Analytically speaking, one might say that Freud rationalized his horror at war's destruction by belittling the significance of war: given man's unrelenting "primaevalism," it remained a phylogenetic inevitability. The recognition of unconscious wishes led to one ineradicable conclusion: ". . . we ourselves are, like primaeval man, a gang of murderers" (Freud, 1915c, p. 297). He similarly rationalized the "death" war entailed by disparagingly appealing to the "primaevalism" of our conventional attitude toward death and the social impoverishment to which it led. Perhaps recalling the "boyish enthusiasm" he initially experienced in the summer of 1914 when all of his own "libido" had gone to Austro-Hungary, Freud now writes that only in war, when "death will no longer be denied," does life "indeed, become interesting again; it has recovered its full content." If war is inevitable on the one hand, and "invigorating" on the other, perhaps the tragic loss it ultimately brings can be partly mitigated.

In a comparable fashion, I believe the new aggressive trends ascribed to the ego in "Instincts and Their Vicissitudes" and

"Mourning and Melancholia" can be at least partially viewed as attempts to minimize the destructive impact of the aggression of the First World War. Oddly enough, there was no pressing *theoretical* reason for Freud to make this change. The omnipresent evidence of man's "primal, savage and evil impulses" generated by the war could be easily explained with reference to the same non-phase-specific "cruelty impulse" and urge to mastery that he had formulated in 1905.

What we are suggesting, to the contrary, is that Freud was *emotionally* unwilling to accept this level of analysis. While able to cope with the existence of fantasied "death wishes" in dream life, the petty "cruelties" of infancy and early childhood, and the murderous impulses of a hypothetical prehistorical man, Freud's aversion to the far-reaching social implications of "instinctual aggression" caused him to recoil from the ostensibly "primal" aggression of World War I with the same revulsion with which he had previously discarded Adler. Whereas Adler's formulation of an "aggressive instinct" could be dismissed as a misreading of select clinical evidence, however, the representation of manifest aggression provided by the war could not be summarily ignored. The wreckage and misery of war made it clear that man was irreducibly aggressive in some potent and elemental way. Yet, in what way? Repelled by the possibility of an operative aggressive instinct that could be intrinsically "destructive" and "cruel" on such a global and "adult" scale, Freud chose, instead, to reformulate his theory of the instincts so that the destructive aggression of World War I could be recast as a "perversion" of healthy and developmentally necessary aggression. Guilt-ridden and conflicted about his own aggressive propensities, from the infantile death wishes against his brother Julius and nephew John to the aggressive obliteration of a whole host of succeeding "revenants" (Schur, 1972, pp. 153-198, 225-272), Freud now takes an almost counterphobic "functional pleasure" (Fenichel, 1939, p. 166) in accepting the developmental primacy of the "hating" ego. In this sense, the "flight to developmental reality" in "Instincts and Their Vicissitudes" may really be regarded as Freud's belated attempt to master his own infantile anxiety about the expression of aggressive tendencies (Fenichel, 1939, p. 167).

The "developmental" reality of the hating ego which Freud discovers, however, is far removed from the aggressive social reality that war had produced. By situating aggression within the sphere of the ego's self-preservative functions, the "healthy hating ego" became part of Freud's strategy for rationalizing and hence reducing the aggressive/destructive impact of the war on him. War showed man to be unalterably aggressive, that is, but represented neither the intended nor developmentally natural outcome of aggression. Thus, while the war compelled aggression to assume a more fundamental role in instinct theory, Freud might still obtain peace of mind by assessing it as a constructive and self-preservative function only perversely linked to cruelty. Juxtaposed with the destructive aggression of war came the "healthy hating ego," rationally responding to the painful stimuli betokening a hostile, external world. Such "hate," at its natural and culturally consonant best, remained "in constant intimate relation with the instincts of self-preservation," and in the case of melancholia, promoted health by letting the suffering ego "disparage" its lost object and hence loosen the now pathogenic libidinal tie.

Support for this interpretation of the significance of "aggressive trends" comes from the circumstances in which the entire metapsychology was written. According to Jones, the great synthesis with which Freud had long been pregnant was facilitated by "the experiences of an indefinitely long war, the hardships of which he might well not survive" (Jones, 1955, p. 185). Analysis of the Abraham correspondence goes considerably further in demonstrating the redemptive personal significance that the writing of the five extant essays played. By the end of 1914, Freud's mood had become clearly depressed. His "lack of courage," "horror of the meal to come," and inability to summon morale he readily confessed to his senior pupil. In contrast to his own personal sense of "disillusion," he confided to Abraham,

> The only thing that is going well is my work, which at intervals produces respectable novelties and conclusions. . . .
> I might manage a theory of neuroses with chapters on the vicissitudes of the instincts, repression and the unconscious if my working energy does not finally succumb to my depressed mood [Freud, 1907a-1926a, p. 206].

From the moment of his commitment to produce the great synthesis, the actual writing of the essays on metapsychology became a struggle that was not easily won. On the last day of the year he subsequently complained:

> My own work is at a standstill. I have not got over certain difficulties, and as a consequence of my state of mind I no longer like my previous findings so much. Because of this estrangement I am often completely at a loss what to do with myself. The obvious remedies are of course those that are now generally recommended—patience and determination to see it through [1907a-1926a, pp. 208-209].

The inhibition that impeded Freud's progress gave way suddenly and dramatically. The two essays in which he recast his conceptual view of aggression were written in a spurt of cathartic creativity. By mid-February he had finished his new piece on melancholia (1907a-1926a, p. 211), by the beginning of March he had decided to publish three chapters of his "germinating summary" in successive numbers of the *Zeitschrift* (1907a-1926a, p. 213), and in mid-March he began his final draft of "Instincts and Their Vicissitudes" (1907a-1926a, p. 214). On May 4, he reported finishing the five papers that were eventually published (1907a-1926a, p. 221). By July 3, he had reached the middle of the eleventh of the proposed twelve papers (1907a-1926a, p. 225).

In all this, we clearly see a victorious struggle on behalf of productivity; Freud's "working energy" had not succumbed to his "depressed mood." Is it possible that the motive power for this victory can be at least partially found in the content of the metapsychology, specifically, the kind of ego-syntonic "aggression" to which he had recourse in "Instincts and Their Vicissitudes" and "Mourning and Melancholia"?

V.

Admittedly, this interpretation is speculative, and it can legitimately be asked whether it is justifiable to attribute such importance to thematic modifications found in only two of the papers on metapsychology. It is essential to keep in mind, however, that the kind of coping strategy we are describing is not confined to these two papers. It initially appeared in the important essay written early in 1915 which specifically addressed itself to the problem of "disillusion" in a time of war and death. Moreover, a basically compensatory "love of life" (Schur, 1972, p. 301) and "denial of pessimism" (Jones, 1955, p. 373) in the face of destructive war would again manifest itself soon after the completion of the metapsychology in the brief essay "On Transience" which Freud composed in the late fall of 1915 in response to an invitation from the Berlin Goethe Society.

In this small paper, Freud recounted "a summer walk through a smiling countryside" with a young poet the summer before war erupted. His concern was with the poetic in-justice of "transience," the "aching despondency" felt by the young poet because of the "proneness to decay" of all that is beautiful. Although sensitive to the artist's plight, the ma-turely artistic Freud rejects this "demand for immortality" as infantile, a product of wishes "too unmistakable to lay claim to reality" (1916, p. 305). While the poet's sensitivity to trans-ience prompts a kind of premature "mourning" that forestalls the present enjoyment of beauty, Freud allows his own appre-ciation of aesthetic mortality to heighten his responsiveness to beauty: "Transience value is scarcity value in time. Limitation in the possibility of an enjoyment raises the value of the enjoy-ment. It was incomprehensible, I declared, that the thought of the transience of beauty should interfere with our joy in it" (p. 305). Freud then jumped ahead to the war, which had "robbed the world of its beauties":

> It destroyed not only the beauty of the countrysides through which it passed and the works of art which it met with on its path but it also shattered our pride in the achievements of our civili-zation, our admiration for many philosophers and artists and our hopes of a final triumph over the differences between na-tions and races. It tarnished the lofty impartiality of our science, it revealed our instincts in all their nakedness and let loose the evil spirits within us which we thought had been tamed forever by centuries of continuous education by the noblest minds. . . .
> But have those other possessions, which we have now lost, really ceased to have any worth for us because they have proved so per-

ishable and so unresistant? To many of us this seems to be so, but once more wrongly, in my view. . . . When once the mourning is over, it will be found that our high opinion of the riches of civilization has lost nothing from our discovery of their fragility. We shall build up again all that war has destroyed, and perhaps on firmer ground and more lastingly than before [p. 307].

In this brief essay, it is clear that Freud anticipates, in descriptive language, the important theoretical conclusion he would reach a year later in "Mourning and Melancholia." There, we recall, he would assert that introjected "aggression" constituted a salubrious remedy for the pathogenic libidinal ties binding the melancholic to its lost object. In "On Transience" Freud intuits the healthy resolution of all "mourning" minus the technical understanding of object introjection and the "conflict of ambivalence" that would be required to explain the "healthy" resolution of pathogenic melancholia a year later:

Mourning, as we know, however painful it may be, comes to a spontaneous end. When it has renounced everything that has been lost, then it has consumed itself, and our libido is once more free (in so far as we are still young and active) to replace the lost objects by fresh ones equally or still more precious. It is to be hoped that the same will be true of the losses caused by this war [1916, p. 307].

The belittling of war's havoc in this essay is merely another variant of the same rationalizing intent that revealed itself so clearly in "Thoughts for the Times on War and Death." There Freud sought to escape from the destructive aggression of war by a calm, scientific assessment of man's potential for avoiding it. Unable to avoid war, he concluded that man had no right to despair when it occurred. In "On Transience" rationalization takes a dramatically different path, one in curious opposition to the previous analysis. It is no longer through a verdict of incurable "primaevalism" that Freud seeks solace. He now belittles the "aggressive" significance of war by appealing to an aesthetic potential which transcends time-bound conflict and is only heightened by the destruction of beauty that war entails. Limitation in the possibility of enjoyment only augments the value of enjoyment, and when the mourning for war is over, "our high opinion of the riches of civilization has lost nothing from our discovery of their fragility."

Years later, Freud's attempt to rationalize the destructive impact of the First World War would follow a still different path. In the concluding section of his letter to Einstein in 1932, he would skeptically probe the very possibility of pacific motive. There he raised the following question:

> Why do you and I and so many other people rebel so violently against war? Why do we not accept it as another of the many painful calamities of life? . . . The answer to my question will be that we react to war in this way because everyone has a right to his own life, because war puts an end to human lives that are full of hope, because it brings individual men into humiliating situations, because it compels them against their will to murder other men, and because it destroys precious material objects which have been produced by the labours of humanity. Other reasons besides might be given, such as that in its present-day form war is no longer an opportunity for achieving the old ideals of heroism and that owing to the perfection of instruments of destruction a future war might involve the extermination of one or perhaps both of the antagonists [1933b, p. 213].

Yet, while conceding that all this is "incontestably true," Freud opts for a different explanatory route: "It is my opinion that the main reason why we rebel against war is that we cannot help doing so. We are pacifists because we are obliged to be for organic reasons. And we then find no difficulty in producing arguments to justify our attitude" (p. 214). In reaching this verdict, he appealed to the "evolution of culture" and subsequent domestication to which man had been subjected:

> Of the psychological characteristics of civilization two appear to be the most important: a strengthening of the intellect, which is beginning to govern instinctual life, and an internalization of the aggressive impulses, with all its consequent advantages and perils. Now war is in the crassest opposition to the psychical attitude imposed on us by the process of civilization, and for that reason we are bound to rebel against it; we simply cannot any longer put up with it. This is not merely an intellectual and emotional repudiation; we pacifists have a *constitutional* intolerance of war, an idiosyncrasy magnified, as it were, to the highest de-

gree. It seems, indeed, as though the lowering of aesthetic standards in war plays a scarcely smaller part in our rebellion than do
its cruelties [pp. 214-215].

Here we locate a more profound and far-reaching demonstration of the same defensive strategy we saw at work in the
publications of World War I. Having belittled man's capacity
to avoid war, his primitive fear of death, and the cultural
finality of war's destructiveness, Freud now makes a more
scathing indictment of man's ability even to appreciate the full
horror of war. What do the aggression and death of war signify if man's attempts to preclude it do not even stem from conscious ethical dictates, but only an unyielding "constitutional
intolerance," the inevitable offshoot of his phylogenic accul-
turation? Freud here seems to rationalize war's destruction by
questioning man's innate capacity to be moved by it. Concerned men may be repelled by war, but as ethically sensitive
individuals or phylogenetically acculturated machines? By
throwing the issues in doubt, Freud attempted to soften the
intense, personal revulsion that, for him, was the aftermath of
World War I.

VI.

Once these ensuing attempts to mollify the impact of war
have been traced, the ulterior psychological rationale underlying the "hating" ego in "Instincts and Their Vicissitudes"
and "Mourning and Melancholia" becomes more readily
apparent. It was more than casual metaphor when Freud
described the papers on metapsychology as his "war-time"
atrocities (1907a-1926a, p. 228). At least with regard to the
two papers cited, this label masked a fundamental truth with
reference to the issue of "aggression." It was the impact of
wartime aggression that helped provide the motive power for a
basic reorientation toward the whole problem of instinct: ego
instincts were no longer defined in terms of some shadowy, irreducible notion of "self-preservative" interest. On behalf of
its survival, the ego was now endowed with the capacity to
"hate," not in a pathogenic or libidinally sadistic way, but in a

necessary, programmatic way. Moreover, such "aggression," while firmly anchored in the pleasure-pain principle, was to take its cue not from the quest for gratification, but from its necessary obverse, the reflexive recoiling from that which brings pain and discomfort (Freud, 1911b, p. 219). It was through recourse to the "healthy hating ego" which subsequently emerged that Freud was able to maintain his equilibrium in the face of the destructive antisocial violence that engulfed him during World War I.

7

FROM WAR TO QUIET THANATOS: *BEYOND THE PLEASURE PRINCIPLE* REVISITED

The final pages of *Beyond the Pleasure Principle* contain a suggestive passage of "critical reflection" in which Freud honestly inquires "whether and how far I am myself convinced of the truth of the hypotheses that have been set out in these pages" (1920, p. 59). He willingly admits his own lack of confidence in his findings and recognizes that the final development of instinct theory could be achieved only "by repeatedly combining factual material with what is purely speculative and thus diverging widely from empirical observation" (p. 59). Moreover, Freud adds that the "degree of uncertainty" involved in such speculation cannot be ascribed to simple intellectual impartiality:

> Unfortunately, however, people are seldom impartial where ultimate things, the great problems of science and life, are concerned. Each of us is governed in such cases by deep-rooted internal prejudices, into whose hands our speculation unwittingly plays. Since we have such good grounds for being distrustful, our attitude towards the results of our own deliberations cannot well be other than one of cool benevolence [p. 59].

This somber confession poses the crucial question around which our inquiry must culminate: What were Freud's own "deep-rooted internal prejudices" that prompted recourse to a vitalist theoretical biology and produced an empirically unnecessary death instinct? How is the death instinct organically linked to the history of Freud's comprehension of aggression?

170

I.

The misery and deprivation which Freud endured during World War I were exacerbated, rather than lessened, by the termination of hostilities. The economic and social stability of Austria was further undermined during 1919-1920, and Jones paints a bleak portrait of Freud's experience during those years:

> The years succeeding the world war were extremely hard. Everything had come to a standstill in Vienna and life there was scarcely bearable. The monotonous diet of thin vegetable soup was far from being adequately nourishing and the pangs of hunger were continuous. The winters of 1918-1919 and 1919-1920 were the worst of all, with their completely unheated rooms and feeble illumination.... To the inevitable hardships there were added many sources of anxiety. It was months before any news could be had of Freud's eldest son who was a prisoner of war in Italy.... The economic situation in Austria was as bleak as it could be, and the future prospects just as dark. Freud's own financial position was very serious and its future still more precarious. His earnings could not keep pace with the steady rise in prices, and he was forced to live on his savings. In October, 1919, he estimated that these would last another eighteen months, but that was on the optimistic assumption that the inflation would not increase [1957, pp. 3-4].

Indeed, without the two "paying customers" Jones sent to him, Freud would have been unable to make ends meet (Jones, 1957, p. 4). By May, 1919, economic misery, social isolation from his protégés, and the serious illness of his wife coalesced in another episode of depression. Several of the letters Jones cites from this period betoken more than the "mood of helpless but cheerful resignation" he is willing to infer. In a letter to Ferenczi of April 20, 1919, Freud bemoaned his current economic misery and unpromising prospects for the future:

> Thirty-three years ago today I was facing as a newly-qualified physician an unknown future with the resolve to go to America if the three months for which my reserves could last did not produce something very hopeful. Would it not have been better on the whole had fate not smiled so friendlily [sic] on me at that time? Whatever else I may have attained since then I have not attained security. Still I shall not be able to carry out much more

than another third of a century's hard work with human beings and demons [Jones, 1957, pp. 5-6].

In reply to Eitington's 1919 birthday congratulation, he was unable to reciprocate his student's hope for better times:

> I cannot deny that in the cheerful pessimism that was always characteristic of me the second element occasionally becomes the more prominent one.... I expect the next few months will be full of dramatic movement. We are no onlookers, however, nor actors or really even a chorus, but merely victims [Jones, 1957, p. 6].

Finally, on May 28, 1919, he wrote Jones:

> I can't remember a time of my life when my horizon was so dark or if so I was younger then and not vexed by the ailments of beginning old age. I know you had a bad time and bitter experiences yourself and feel extremely sorry that I have nothing better to report and no consolation to offer. When we meet, as I trust we shall in this year, you will find I am still unshaken and up to every emergency, but it is so only in sentiment, my judgement is on the side of pessimism [Jones, 1957; pp. 6-7].

Before these depressing circumstances would lift, they would be compounded by private tragedy. In March of 1919, Freud's close friend and Hungarian benefactor Anton von Freund developed suspicious signs of a recurring abdominal sarcoma. His death on January 20, 1920, following nine months of apprehension and uncertainty, was a severe personal blow to Freud. Three days later news arrived that Freud's daughter Sophie had contracted influenzal pneumonia. Her death on January 25 left him stunned and morbid. In a letter to Jones, he pondered when his "turn" would come (Jones, 1957, p. 19), while to Ferenczi he confessed the "bitter irreparable narcissistic hurt" his daughter's death produced, one which was "not to be healed" (Jones, 1957, p. 20).

Thus, the same circumstances that prompted Freud to intuit the "healthy hating ego" of the metapsychology to ward off the destructive aggression of World War I were still operative and immediate when he began to draft *Beyond the Pleasure Principle* in March, 1919. Furthermore, textual analysis suggests that the influence of a biological death instinct in this work actually serves the same ulterior psychological function as the inference of a "hating" ego in "Instincts and Their Vicissitudes"; it allows Freud to escape the really terrifying possibility of an innately "aggressive" instinct.

II.

By attributing phylogenetic priority to a repetition compulsion existing over and "beyond" the pleasure principle, Freud not only removed instinctual behavior from the modest realm of sublimation to which the pleasure principle could be subjected, but robbed man of the private prerogative to gratify his instincts in his own distinctly "antisocial" way. The supposition that all organic instincts are "conservative" and tend toward the restoration of an earlier "inorganic" state of things meant that organic life itself could be accountable only to "the pressure of external disturbing forces" (Freud, 1920, p. 36) operating against the tensionless inertia of inorganic matter. This contention that the state of life is no more than an aggravating diversion from nonexistence meant that the origins of life could be explained only in obscure vitalist terms:

> The attributes of life were at some time evoked in inanimate matter by the action of a force of whose nature we can form no conception. It may perhaps have been a process similar in type to that which later caused the development of consciousness in a particular stratum of living matter. The tension which then arose in what had hitherto been an inanimate substance endeavoured to cancel itself out. In this way the first instinct came into being: the instinct to return to the inanimate state [1920, p. 38].

This vitalist conception of life reduces death to an internal biological inevitability far removed from the particularly "destructive" road to death entailed in aggressive behavior. In terms of the intrinsic properties of life, "It was still an easy matter . . . for a living substance to die; the course of its life was probably only a brief one, whose direction was determined by the chemical structure of the young life" (p. 38). The potential for the "aggressive" destruction of life can be attributed only to the "disturbing and diverting" influences which interrupt the instinctual direction of life:

> For a long time, perhaps, living substance was thus being constantly created afresh and easily dying, till decisive external influences altered in such a way as to oblige the still surviving substance to diverge ever more widely from its original course of life and to make ever more complicated *détours* before reaching its aim of death. These circuitous paths to death, faithfully kept to by the conservative instincts, would thus present us to-day with the picture of the phenomena of life [pp. 38-39].

The path to death is hence an innocuous one, and aggression becomes an unnecessary bypath "destructively" subverting its peaceful biologic intent. The unhealthy "aggressive" route to death is not "instinctual" but rather the product of "decisive external influences." Here, perhaps harking back to his own initial reaction to the outbreak of hostilities in 1914, Freud seems to make definite allusion to World War I and the aggressive disposition it was able to foster. While war *makes* man "aggressive" and serves a larger instinctual "aim," he suggests, it does not tap a reservoir of innate "aggressiveness." Rather, it constitutes an unnecessarily tragic path to death. By arguing that aggression is not innate, but merely one route the organism might follow to death, Freud subsequently relieves "aggressive" man of responsibility for his own actions: the flight to death, however inevitable, need not be an intrinsically "aggressive" one, and the fact that it occasionally is testifies only to the "disturbing and diverting influences" that act upon it.

In reality, then, the death instinct signifies the final step in Freud's movement away from aggression. The recourse to theoretical biology provides the *rationalization* Freud needed to neutralize the aggressive destruction of World War I and removes once and for all the possibility of a naturally unhealthy "hating" ego that might purposefully induce such destruction.

Indeed, the postulation of the death instinct permits Freud to revoke his previous concessions to an "aggressive" instinct. In *Beyond the Pleasure Principle*, the dreams of patients suffering from traumatic neuroses were found to act in obedience to the repetition compulsion and could not be classified as wish-fulfilling dreams. They thus threw the whole wish-fulfillment theory of dreaming in doubt:

> Thus it would seem that the function of dreams, which consists in setting aside any motives that might interrupt sleep, by fulfilling the wishes of the disturbing impulses, is not their *original* function. It would not be possible for them to perform that function until the whole of mental life had accepted the dominance of the pleasure principle. If there is a 'beyond the pleasure principle', it is only consistent to grant that there was also a time before the purpose of dreams was the fulfilment of wishes [Freud, 1920, pp. 32-33].

If we recall the significant "aggressive" dimension of Freud's own dream specimens in *The Interpretation of Dreams*, we can readily perceive the enormous secondary gains this new position entailed. No longer would Freud have to confront his need to reduce competing colleagues and admired friends to expendable "revenants" in terms of his own aggressive propensities. The superimposition of the repetition compulsion served to reduce the ruthless revenant phenomena to a superordinate principle existing outside his control, and thus served to relieve him of the guilt associated with the aggressive death wishes he had at one time directed against Fleischl, Paneth, Breuer, Fliess—not to mention his bitter disavowal of Adler, Stekel, Jung, and Tausk.

Furthermore, the postulation of the death instinct enabled Freud to revoke the independent "aggressive" capacity he had attributed to ego instincts in 1915. Insofar as the ego instincts were under the jurisdiction of the conservative Nirvana principle,

> ... the theoretical importance of the instincts of self-preservation, of self-assertion and of mastery greatly diminishes. They are component instincts whose function it is to assure that the organism shall follow its own path to death, and to ward off any possible ways of returning to inorganic existence other than those which are immanent in the organism itself [1920, p. 39; also p. 44].

While on the level of *forces* the ego instincts were now absorbed by the death instinct to oppose the sexual life instincts, on the level of purposes, aims, and objects, the Eros-Thanatos dualism reinforced the topographical and economic distinction that resulted when "narcissism" was introduced into instinct theory in 1914 (Ricoeur, 1970, pp. 292-293). Seeing in the narcissistic libido of the ego a figure of life-preserving Eros, Freud later amended the identification of the ego instincts with the Nirvana principle and argued that these instincts were actually appropriated by Eros, "the preserver of all things," to oppose the death instinct. If this was the case, he circularly concluded, the ego instincts had to be of an entirely libidinal character:

> If the self-preservative instincts too are of a libidinal nature, are there perhaps no other instincts whatever but the libidinal ones? At all events there are none other visible.... We suspect that instincts other than those of self-preservation operate in the ego, and it ought to be possible for us to point to them. Unfortunately, however, the analysis of the ego has made so little headway that it is very difficult for us to do so.... The difficulty remains that psycho-analysis has not enabled us hitherto to point to any [ego] instincts other than the libidinal ones [1920, pp. 52-53].

In terms of the clinical insights that had been obtained by 1919, this position clearly represents a regressive retreat. In 1915, empirical observation and theoretical arguments led Freud to recognize the nonlibidinal portions of the ego instincts and to ascribe to them blatantly "aggressive" trends (Bibring, 1934, pp. 103, 110-113; and Chapter 6, pp. 144-153). Now, in 1919, choosing to ignore the substantial headway that had been made in the analysis of the nonlibidinal ego, Freud runs smack against his own mounting clinical documentation about aggressive trends operating both inside and outside the field of self-preservative functions, and completely subsumes the ego within the libidinal fold of a nonempirical vitalist life instinct. Analogously, the sadomasochistic phenomena that impelled Freud to consider the possibility of a "primary destructiveness" are denied the theoretical explanation that their empirical "primacy" warrants. Instead, "aggression" is only to be approached from the great vitalist opposition between life and death instincts (Freud, 1920, p.

53). Unable to stem from Eros, the preserver of life, sadism now becomes a displaced *example* of the innocuous biological death instinct: "Is it not plausible to suppose that this sadism is in fact a death instinct which, under the influence of the narcissistic libido, has been forced away from the ego and has consequently only emerged in relation to the object?" (1920, p. 54).

Masochism, on the other hand, formerly considered a turning inward of the sadistic impulse, now becomes "a return to an earlier phase of the instinct's history, a regression" (1920, p. 55). Such self-destructive behavior, however, is no longer destructive in and of itself, but now serves peaceful Thanatos, striving to abolish biological tensions in total accord with the internal life process of the individual.

III.

The psychological gains provided by the death instinct closely resemble those provided by the "healthy hating ego" of 1915. In his letter to Jones of May 28, 1919, which coincided with the completion of the initial draft of *Beyond the Pleasure Principle*, Freud's somber admission that his judgment is "on the side of pessimism" is followed by the following disclaimer: "We are living through a bad time, but science is a mighty power to stiffen one's neck" (Jones, 1957, p. 7). Freud's next important theoretical tract, *The Ego and the Id*, and his final cultural commentary, *Civilization and Its Discontents*, provide compelling testimony of the degree to which the formulation of a death instinct had "stiffened his neck." Once the flight to a vitalist theoretical biology was completed, the switch could be made from metabiological to metacultural considerations, and the death instinct could be used not only to account for clinical destructive and self-destructive phenomena, but to decipher aggression/destruction on the historical and cultural planes (Ricoeur, 1970, pp. 281-291, 294).

In *The Ego and the Id*, the switch from mere speculation to deciphering resulted from the integration of the dualistic instinct theory of *Beyond the Pleasure Principle* with the theory of the three psychic agencies—id, ego, superego. By elaborating the economic concepts of fusion and defusion to state in energy language what happened when an instinct placed its energy at the service of forces operating in different systems, Freud could use Thanatos to account for an entire sequence of "representatives," ranging from the biological erotogenic form of masochism to the culturally induced harshness of the superego (Ricoeur, 1970, pp. 296-300).

In this way, Freud is able to turn his attention once more to the clinical problem of aggression, but his recourse to the new economic language permits him to continue the implicit strategy of mediation adopted in *Beyond the Pleasure Principle*. The new formulation which permits the extension of this strategy along clinical lines becomes the equation of libidinal regression with a defusion of instincts (Freud, 1923a, p. 42). This utilization of instinctual defusion conveniently permits Freud to distill pure sadism out of a normally benign fused state and, in this way, to "defuse" the impact of primary aggressiveness as it appeared to manifest itself in sadism. Under normal circumstances, in other words, the sadistic component of the sexual instinct constituted "a serviceable instinctual fusion." When it appeared independently as a "perversion," however, it was "typical of a defusion" (1923a, p. 41), and hence to be considered a manifestation of regressive pathology.

When he turned to the "Dependent Relations of the Ego" (Chapter 5), Freud similarly invoked the concept of defusion to explain the debilitating unconscious sense of guilt that undercut the therapeutic progress of certain psychoanalytic patients. Freud took such guilt to be an indication of superego pathology, and he restated the clinical puzzle by asking why the superego should manifest itself "essentially as a sense of guilt" which furthermore "develops such extraordinary harshness and severity towards the ego" (Freud, 1923a, p. 53). He explained this eventuality by referring to the normal developmental circumstances of superego formation, with particular reference to the desexualization of object libido that proceeded from the identification with the father:

The super-ego arises, as we know, from an identification with the father taken as a model. Every such identification is in the nature of a desexualization or even of a sublimation. It now seems as though when a transformation of this kind takes place, an instinctual defusion occurs at the same time. After sublimation the erotic component no longer has the power to bind the whole of the destructiveness that was combined with it, and this is released in the form of an inclination to aggression and destruction. This defusion would be the source of the general character of harshness and cruelty exhibited by the ideal—its dictatorial 'Thou shalt' [1923a, pp. 54-55].

Here a further clinical elaboration of the biological death instinct is evident. While Thanatos represents an ultimate evasion of the problem of primary aggressiveness, its formulation as a theoretical covering law extends the range of non-erotic aggressive manifestations Freud is willing to isolate and explicate. Initially concerned with the clinical problem of sadism as a necessary externalization of the death instinct, he now refracts guilt as an internalized sadism of the superego which is a necessary accouterment of the healthy resolution of the Oedipus complex. By virtue of such oedipal resolution, the "dangerous death instincts" are permitted to "continue their internal work unhindered" (1923a, p. 44), but it is a continuance which serves the origin of conscience, provides the erection of a positive ego ideal, and reaches a pitch of pathogenic harshness only in clinical states such as obsessional neurosis and melancholia. Furthermore, as Freud would demonstrate three years later, the emergence of an intolerant superego in obsessional neurosis actually bolstered the ego's defenses against assaulting id demands that might otherwise have overwhelmed it. When the libido regressed to a harsh anal-sadistic level as part of the neurosis, that is, it yielded a commensurately "regressed" harsh superego whose strict standards assisted the threatened ego in rebuffing id impulses from a vantage point of relative strength. On the other hand, as the superego itself had to become "harsher, unkinder and more tormenting than where development has been normal" in order to effect this goal, it aggravated the obsessional conflict by rendering the defensive forces intolerant and producing neurotic reaction formations (Freud, 1926, pp. 115-117; for a less precise formulation see 1923a, pp. 53-54). Only in the condition of melancholia did Freud actually see the superego directed by "a pure culture of the death instinct" (1923a, p. 53). Here the superego persecuted the ego to such an extent that the patient complained of a fear of death and could actually be driven to suicide.[1]

Like "perverse" sadism, both obsessional neurosis and melancholia reveal that acts of aggression have become no more than pathogenic potentialities of a biological death instinct whose regressive biological intent is normally subverted in either a fused (sadism) or culturally elevating (healthy superego formation) way. By summarily associating the *condition* of defusion primarily with the release of defused aggression rather than defused Eros (Fenichel, 1935, p. 367), Freud's new economic concepts elaborate his conclusion about the derived quality of aggression reached in *Beyond the Pleasure Principle* for a wider range of clinical phenomena. Not only is aggression merely one route the organism might follow to death, but only in its regressed defused states does aggression even possess the potential to operate malignantly, whether externally or internally.

In *Civilization and Its Discontents*, the inference of the biological death instinct enabled Freud to present the new economic interpretation of culture which proceeded to assimilate, in its way, the aggressive/destructive insights obtained from the war:

[1] In one of his final essays, "Analysis Terminable and Interminable" (1937), Freud returned to the theme of superego guilt as a clinical roadblock to recovery, and proceeded to utilize the negative therapeutic reaction as a new form of evidence for the theory of primal instincts: "If we take into consideration the total picture made up of the phenomena of masochism immanent in so many people, the negative therapeutic reaction and the sense of guilt found in so many neurotics, we shall no longer be able to adhere to the belief that mental events are exclusively governed by the desire for pleasure. These phenomena are unmistakable indications of the presence of a power in mental life which we call the instinct of aggression or of destruction according to its aims, and which we trace back to the original death instinct of living matter. It is not a question of an antithesis between an optimistic and a pessimistic theory of life. Only by the concurrent or mutually opposing action of the two primal instincts—Eros and the death-instinct—never by one or the other alone, can we explain the rich multiplicity of the phenomena of life" (Freud, 1937, p. 243).

Prior to a theory of culture death is not yet manifested: culture is its sphere of manifestation; that is why a purely biological theory of the death instinct had to remain speculative; it is only in the interpretation of hate and war that speculation about the death instinct becomes a process of deciphering [Ricoeur, 1970, p. 306].

The heart of this reinterpretation, brilliantly summarized by Ricoeur (1970, pp. 303-304), is well enough known. Thanatos, that "silently operating" partner of "noisy" Eros, can indeed be heard in the external world, where a portion of it "comes to light as an instinct of aggressiveness and destructiveness." "In this way," Freud tells us, "the instinct itself could be pressed into the service of Eros, in that the organism was destroying some other thing . . . instead of destroying its own self" (1930, p. 119). Out of this "service," however, comes a sick culture saturated with deflected "death." Man's cultural dissatisfaction cannot be rationalized solely on the basis of general "erotics," and the impracticability of the injunction to love one's neighbors and enemies echoes the irrationality of the (now deflected) death instinct which lies outside a simple erotics:

> The element of truth behind all this, which people are so ready to disavow, is that men are not gentle creatures who want to be loved, and who at the most can defend themselves if they are attacked; they are, on the contrary, creatures among whose instinctual endowments is to be reckoned a powerful share of aggressiveness. As a result, their neighbour is for them not only a potential helper or sexual object, but also someone who tempts them to satisfy their aggressiveness on him, to exploit his capacity for work without compensation, to use him sexually without his consent, to seize his possessions, to humiliate him, to cause him pain, to torture and kill him [Freud, 1930, p. 111].

> . . . I adopt the standpoint, therefore, that the inclination to aggression is an original, self-subsisting instinctual disposition in man, and . . . it constitutes the greatest impediment to civilization. . . . This aggressive instinct is the derivative and the main representative of the death instinct which we have found alongside of Eros and which shares world-dominion with it [Freud, 1930, p. 122].

It is the death instinct, now identified with the primordial hostility of man toward man, which undermines cultural relations and requires society to rise as "the implacable dispenser of justice." This rebound of the cultural interpretation of Thanatos on the biological speculation has important effects: the "sense of guilt" previously viewed as the excessive severity of the superego now becomes the necessary instrument used by culture against man's aggressiveness.

Yet, if the economics of cultural suppression enable the superego to become the most dramatically defused and hence "instinctual" representative of the death instinct, it remains a representative with a built-in paradox: Thanatos can potentiate severe internal aggression only on behalf of the suppression of externalized aggression directed against the real world. Indeed, though the superego is initially the cause of instinctual renunciation, once the superego is established it is the subsequent renunciations of externalized instinct that provide it with the dynamic material which can increase its severity and intolerance (Freud, 1930, p. 128). Freud elaborates this unusual situation in the seventh section of *Civilization and Its Discontents* by suggesting that the original severity of the superego does not represent the severity experienced *from* the father figure so much as the child's aggressiveness *towards* the father figure. He accomplishes this by envisioning a certain mobility of identification within the child's psychic structure. Granted the fact that the child experiences considerable aggressive hostility towards the father which can never find expression, Freud submits,

> He finds his way out of this economically difficult situation with the help of familiar mechanisms. By means of identification he takes the unattackable authority into himself. The authority now turns into his super-ego and enters into possession of all the aggressiveness which a child would have liked to exercise against it. The child's ego has to content itself with the unhappy role of the authority—the father— who has been thus degraded.... The relationship between the super-ego and the ego is a return, distorted by a wish, of the real relationships between the ego, as yet undivided, and an external object [1930, p. 129].

Through the instrumentality of this kind of identification, Freud can conclude that the superego is subsequently reinforced by fresh suppressions of such "revengeful aggressiveness." The offshoot of his argument leads to a compelling convergence between the end product of the internalized enactment of the individual's "wishful" aggressive fantasies and culture's tremendous investment in the suppression of instinct: in both cases it is the potentially aggressive ego ready to direct its aggressive activities outward that is neutralized. From the perspective of culture this result is essential, and the concomitant severity of the superego becomes irreplaceable: it is only by employing internalized violence against externalized violence that culture can make life prevail against death (Freud, 1930, pp. 123-124; Ricoeur, 1970, pp. 306-309).

By 1930, then, Freud had not only tied man's aggressive potential to the biological death instinct that it served, but explained the need for cultural restraint and the resulting "guilty conscience" in terms of the potentially aggressive path the death instinct could follow. The movement away from aggression here comes full circle: the biological death instinct robs man of his capacity for innate aggressiveness, but posits the need for lasting social suppression insofar as displaced aggression can borrow the primal motive power of Thanatos. Inasmuch as the internal defusion of the death instinct culminated in a superego dedicated to the inhibition of external aggressive discharge, moreover, Freud could make this need for suppression converge with the ontogenetic requirements of normal child development. To be sure, this convergence represented an ideal balance between the superego's severity and society's needs. Whereas the superego would supplement social suppression by virtue of the energic dynamics underlying its very formation, any excessive harshness that transcended the threshold established by pragmatic social requirements would lead to excessive misery tantamount to pathology. As indicators of the ontogenetic potential for excessive superego severity, then, Freud's formulations in the final two sections of *Civilization and Its Discontents* not only embody deep pessimism about the fate of instinct in civilization, but complete the defensive retreat begun in *Beyond the Pleasure Principle*. Not only is aggressive instinctuality to be recast in terms of the biological death instinct, but the most important "defused" vicissitude of this instinct within the individual actually undercuts the very potential for any "derived" aggressive instinctuality to work its damage on the outside world.

8

EPILOGUE

On February 4, 1930, several months after the publication of *Civilization and Its Discontents,* the optimistic psychoanalytic religionist Oskar Pfister wrote Freud of his "difficulties" with the book:

> I regard the 'death instinct', not as a real instinct, but only as a slackening of the 'life force', and even the death of the individual cannot hold up the advance of the universal will, but only help it forward. I see civilisation as full of tensions. Just as in the individual with his free will there is a conflict between the present and the future to which he aspires, so is it with civilisation. Just as it would be mistaken to regard the actual, existing facts about an individual as the whole of him, ignoring his aspirations, it would be equally mistaken to identify with civilisation its existing horrors, to which its magnificent achievements stand out in contrast [quoted in Freud, 1909-1938, p. 131].

From Freud came the following pessimistic rejoinder:

> If I doubt man's destiny to climb by way of civilisation to a state of greater perfection, if I see in life a continual struggle between Eros and the death instinct, the outcome of which seems to me to be indeterminable, I do not believe that in coming to those conclusions I have been influenced by innate constitutional factors or acquired emotional attitudes. I am neither a self-tormenter nor am I cussed [*Bosnickel*] and, if I could, I should gladly do as others do and bestow upon mankind a rosy future, and I should find it much more beautiful and consoling if we could count on such a thing. But this seems to me to be yet another instance of illusion (wish fulfillment) in conflict with truth. The question is not what belief is more pleasing or more comfortable or more advantageous to life, but of what may approximate more closely to the puzzling reality that lies outside us. The death instinct is not a requirement of my heart; it seems to me to

be only an inevitable assumption on both biological and psychological grounds. The rest follows from that. Thus to me my pessimism seems a conclusion, while the optimism of my opponents seems an *a priori* assumption. I might also say that I have concluded a marriage of reason with my gloomy theories, while others live with theirs in a love-match. I hope they will gain greater happiness from this than I [Freud, 1909-1938, pp. 132-133].

Here, disclaiming personal motive, Freud attempts to subsume the cultural ramifications of the biological death instinct within the scientific *Weltanschauung* that still remained his methodological *raison d'être* (Freud, 1933a, pp. 158-160, 181-182). That the entire Eros-Thanatos dualism itself stems from mystical vitalist premises in which an excess of speculative hypothesis produces only "fragmentary and partial verifications" (Ricoeur, 1970, p. 282)—and from which observable "aggression" does not even logically derive—causes us to attribute more weight to the following paragraph of Freud's letter. Immediately after denying the "constitutional factors" or "acquired emotional atttitudes" that may have influenced the form of his final instinct theory, he confesses,

Of course it is very possible that I may be mistaken on all three points, the independence of my theories from my disposition, the validity of my arguments on their behalf, and their content. You know that the more magnificent the prospect the lesser the certainty and the greater the passion—in which we do not wish to be involved—with which men take sides [Freud, 1909-1938, p. 133].

If the analysis presented in this study is valid, there were indeed "emotional attitudes" of critical importance in the inference of a death instinct, attitudes which necessitate substantial modification of the conclusions reached about the history of instinct theory in Freud. The "theoretical unavoidability" of a death instinct in order to "fill in and gather together" the theoretical issues generated by the inevitable assumption of a primary aggressive/destructive instinct (Bibring, 1934, pp. 117-118, 120-122) is both compounded and confounded by the psychological motives which led to this conclusion. The theoretical and nosological problems raised by the presence of ego-dystonic "aggression" occurring in nonerotic sadomasochistic phenomena, self-destructive melancholic depressions, and self-destructive superego trends, became cathected with the social reality in which Freud theorized—and from which he recoiled with horror. Preoccupied with the awesome material, moral, and intellectual collapse wrought by World War I, Freud "solved" the problem of primary aggression by retreating to a vitalist biological model which could defuse it; confronted with the need to locate the original model of clinical self-destructive trends and reconcile it with his aversion for the aggressive destruction of the war, he retorts that death is a necessary component of life, and that the death instinct is no more than a tendency moving towards absolute rest, towards zero potential.

The flight to theoretical biology in *Beyond the Pleasure Principle*, rather than subserving a commitment to reduce psychoanalytic phenomena to a biological substrate, actually underscores Freud's chronic inability to explicate the problems presented by aggression within the methodological confines of the Helmholtz Program. This verdict does not seriously diminish the important ramifications of Freud's early status as a Helmholtzian. Bernfeld has convincingly established that Freud's early commitment to Brücke's "physicalistic" physiology was destined long to outlive his student years at the Physiological Institute, and that the revolutionary discoveries of psychoanalysis were, at their core, "a continuation of the work that Freud did for Brücke" (Bernfeld, 1944, p. 356). This conclusion is reasonable, and when Bernfeld emphasizes the continuity between Freud's invention of the psychoanalytic method and the innovative histological methods he discovered at Brücke's Institute (Bernfeld, 1949, p. 183) and traces the genetic theme of psychoanalytic research to Freud's early use of the genetic method in his cerebral anatomical research (Bernfeld, 1951, pp. 212-213), he provides important evidence for his contention that Freud conceptualized his activity as a cathartic psychoanalyst in the mid-1890's as a return to science according to viable Helmholtzian dictums (Bernfeld, 1949, p. 184).

The present study has attempted only to earmark the issue of aggression as one problem whose rich personal, social, and institutional connotations substantially undermined Freud's conscious efforts to deal with it within this scientific framework. In relation to the theoretical underpinnings of the death instinct, it was Bernfeld himself who originally questioned Freud's claim that biology was at the source of his drive theory. From the standpoint of his selective inattention to the entire teleological discussion which preoccupied biologists from the turn of the century on—the biological concern with the amazing agreement between the needs of the species and the individual's means for satisfying these needs; the consideration of purposefulness (*Zweckhaftigkeit*) as a dimension of instinctuality—Freud's final drive theory in no sense originates from biological considerations (*Danach kann keine Rede davon sein, dass Freuds Trieblehre der Biologie entstamme*) (Bernfeld, 1935, pp. 135-137). It has been the express purpose of this study, however, to broaden this critique by documenting the nonbiological considerations that affected Freud's treatment of aggression long before the final recourse to a biologically fallacious death instinct. From the very outset of his clinical postneurological work, Freud's perspective on aggression was seriously influenced by his socially conditioned perception of aggression as an expression of normative masculine activity (Chapter 2).[1] By the time he formulated the theory of unconscious wish fulfillment in *The Interpretation of Dreams*, he was actively wrestling with his personal relation to his own aggressive impulses (Chapter 3). In the aftermath of this episode, the historical development of aggression became successively intermingled with the institutional imperatives of the psychoanalytic movement (Chapter 4), Freud's personal imperative of maintaining unambiguous control over the theoretical development of psychoanalysis with special reference to the question of discipleship (Chapter 5), and Freud's

---

[1] In this respect, it would prove interesting to compare the presuppositions embodied in Freud's early work on hysteria and obsessional neurosis (Chapter 2) with the more explicit formulations of Otto Weininger, Karl Kraus, and, of course, Alfred Adler, who were also writing about the constitutional basis of male aggressiveness in *fin-de-siècle* Vienna.

ultimate need to retain his psychic equilibrium from the outbreak of World War I (Chapters 6 and 7).

As the final step in Freud's theoretical attempt to subsume
man's aggressive *potentialities* within a model that simultaneously mitigated man's responsibility for his aggressive
actions, the death instinct was the culmination of Freud's
defensive antipathy to the cultural implications of a primal
aggressive instinct. By reducing aggressive behavior to a displaced derivative of a superordinate biological force, Freud
could resist the pessimistic conclusion to which the experience
of the war naturally led, and deduce the need for enduring
social restraints that could forestall war in the future. With
the postulation of the biological death instinct, man was no
longer the repository of an "aggressive instinct," but an obedi-
ent biological organism occasionally driven to be aggressive,
and the massive spectacle of aggression, brutality, and cruelty
provided by the Great War merely constituted one "detectable
sign" of the "silently working" death instinct (Jones, 1957, pp.
273-274).

REFERENCES

Abraham, K. (1924), A Short Study of the Development of the Libido, Viewed in the Light of Mental Disorders. In: *On Character and Libido Development*, ed. B. Lewin. New York: Norton, 1966, pp. 67-150.

Adler, A. (1907), *Study of Organ Inferiority and Its Psychical Compensation*, trans. S. Jelliffe. New York: Nervous and Mental Disease Publishing Co., 1917.

———— (1908), Der Aggressionstrieb im Leben und in der Neurose. In: *Heilen und Bilden: Artzlich-pädagogische Arbeiten des Vereins für Individualpsychologie*, ed. A. Adler & C. Furtmüller. Munich: Ernst Reinhardt, 1914, pp. 23-32.

———— (1909), Über neurotische Disposition: Zugleich ein Beitrag zur Ätiologie und zur Frage der Neurosenwahl. *Jahrb. Psychoanal. Forsch.*, 1:526-545.

———— (1910), Der psychische Hermaphroditismus im Leben und in der Neurose. In: *Heilen und Bilden*, ed. A. Adler & C. Furtmüller. Munich: Ernst Reinhardt, 1914, pp. 74-83.

———— (1911), Zur Kritik der Freudschen Sexualtheorie der Nervosität. In: *Heilen und Bilden*, ed. A. Adler & C. Furtmüller. Munich: Ernst Reinhardt, 1914, pp. 94-114.

———— (1912a), Psychical Hermaphrodism and the Masculine Protest—The Cardinal Problem of Nervous Diseases. In: *The Practice and Theory of Individual Psychology*, trans. P. Radin. Patterson: Littlefield, Adams, 1963, pp. 16-22.

———— (1912b), *The Neurotic Constitution: Outline of a Comparative Individualistic Psychology and Psychotherapy*, trans. B. Glueck & J. Lind. New York: Moffat, Yard, 1916.

———— (1913), Individual-Psychological Treatment of Neuroses. In: *The Practice and Theory of Individual Psychology*, trans. P. Radin. Patterson: Littlefield, Adams, 1963, pp. 32-50.

———— (1914), Individual Psychology, Its Assumptions and Its Results. In: *The Practice and Theory of Individual Psychology*, trans. P. Radin. Patterson: Littlefield, Adams, 1963, pp. 1-15.

———— (1927), *Understanding Human Nature*, trans. W. Wolfe. New York: Greenberg, 1946.

———— (1931), Compulsion Neurosis. In: *Superiority and Social Interest*, ed. H. Ansbacher & R. Ansbacher. New York: Viking, 1964, pp. 112-138.

———— (1933), *Social Interest: A Challenge to Mankind*, trans. J. Linton & R. Vaughan. New York: Putnam, 1939.

Alexander, F., & Selesnick, S. (1966), *The History of Psychiatry: An Evaluation of Psychiatric Thought and Practice from Prehistoric Times to the Present*. New York: Harper & Row.

Amacher, P. (1965), Freud's Neurological Education and Its Influence on Psycho-analytic Theory. *Psychol. Issues*, Monogr. 16. New York: International Universities Press.

Andersson, O. (1962), *Studies in the Prehistory of Psychoanalysis*. Sweden: Bokforlaget/Norstedts.

Andreas-Salomé, L. (1912-1913), *The Freud Journal*, trans. S. Leavy. New York: Basic Books, 1964.

Ansbacher, H., & Ansbacher, R. (1956), *The Individual Psychology of Alfred Adler*. New York: Harper Torchbooks.

Bernfeld, S. (1935), Über die Einteilung der Triebe. *Imago*, 21:125-142.

———— (1944), Freud's Earliest Theories and the School of Helmholtz. *Psychoanal. Quart.*, 13:341-362.

———— (1949), Freud's Scientific Beginnings. *Amer. Imago*, 6:163-196.

———— (1951), Sigmund Freud, M.D., 1882-1885. *Internat. J. Psycho-Anal.*, 32: 204-217.

———— & Feitelberg, S. (1931), The Principle of Entropy and the Death Instinct. *Internat. J. Psycho-Anal.*, 12:61-81.

Bertalanffy, L. von (1950), The Theory of Open Systems in Physics and Biology. *Science*, 111:23-29.

Bibring, E. (1934), The Development and Problems of the Theory of the Instincts. *Internat. J. Psycho-Anal.*, 22:102-131, 1941.

———— (1943), The Conception of the Repetition Compulsion. *Psychoanal. Quart.*, 12:486-519.

Bonaparte, M. (1935), Passivity, Masochism, and Femininity. *Internat. J. Psycho-Anal.*, 16:325-333.

Brenner, C. (1957), *An Elementary Textbook of Psychoanalysis*. New York: International Universities Press.

Breuer, J. (1895), Studes on Hysteria. III: Theoretical. *Standard Edition*, 2:185-251. London: Hogarth Press, 1955.

———— & Freud, S. (1893), Studies on Hysteria. I: On the Psychical Mechanism of Hysterical Phenomena: Preliminary ·Communication. *Standard Edition*, 2:1-17. London: Hogarth Press, 1955.

Brown, N. (1959), *Life Against Death: The Psychoanalytical Meaning of History*. New York: Vintage.

Deutsch, H. (1930), The Significance of Masochism in the Mental Life of Women (Part I, "Feminine Masochism in Its Relation to Frigidity"). *Internat. J. Psycho-Anal.*, 11:48-60.

———— (1940), Freud and His Pupils: A Footnote to the History of the Psychoanalytic Movement. *Psychoanal. Quart.*, 9:184-194.

Eissler, K. (1971), *Talent and Genius: The Fictitious Case of Tausk contra Freud*. New York: Quadrangle.

Ellenberger, H. (1970), *The Discovery of the Unconscious*. New York: Basic Books.

Erikson, E. (1950), *Childhood and Society*, rev. ed. New York: Norton, 1963.

———— (1954), The Dream Specimen of Psychoanalysis. *J. Amer. Psychoanal. Assn.*, 2:5-56.

———— (1964), *Insight and Responsibility*. New York: Norton.

Fenichel, O. (1935), A Critique of the Death Instinct. In: *Collected Papers*, first series. New York: Norton, 1953, pp. 363-372.

———— (1939), The Counter-Phobic Attitude. In: *Collected Papers*, second series. New York: Norton, 1954, pp. 163-173.

_____ (1945), *The Psychoanalytic Theory of Neurosis*. New York: Norton.

Ferenczi, S. (1911), The Psycho-Analysis of Wit and the Comical. In: *Further Contributions to the Theory and Technique of Psycho-Analysis*, trans. J. Suttie. London: Hogarth Press, 1950, pp. 332-344.

_____ (1925), Psycho-Analysis of Sexual Habits. In: *Further Contributions to the Theory and Technique of Psycho-Analysis*, trans. J. Suttie. London: Hogarth Press, 1950, pp. 259-297.

Freud, A. (1936), *The Ego and the Mechanisms of Defense*. New York: International Universities Press, 1946.

Freud, S. (1887-1902), *The Origins of Psychoanalysis; Letters, Drafts and Notes to Wilhelm Fliess, 1887-1902*, trans. E. Mosbacher & J. Strachey. New York: Basic Books, 1954.

_____ (1894), The Neuro-Psychoses of Defence. *Standard Edition*, 3:45-61. London: Hogarth Press, 1962.

_____ (1895a), Studies on Hysteria. IV: The Psychotherapy of Hysteria. *Standard Edition*, 2:253-305. London: Hogarth Press, 1955.

_____ (1895b), Studies on Hysteria. II: Case Histories. *Standard Edition*, 2:19-81. London: Hogarth Press, 1955.

_____ (1895c), On the Grounds for Detaching a Particular Syndrome from Neurasthenia under the Description "Anxiety Neurosis." *Standard Edition*, 3:90-115. London: Hogarth Press, 1962.

_____ (1895d), A Reply to Criticisms of My Paper on Anxiety Neurosis. *Standard Edition*, 3:123-139. London: Hogarth Press, 1962.

_____ (1895e), Project for a Scientific Psychology. In: Freud (1887-1902), pp. 347-445.

_____ (1896a), Further Remarks on the Neuro-Psychoses of Defence. *Standard Edition*, 3:162-185. London: Hogarth Press, 1962.

_____ (1896b), Weitere Bemerkungen über die Abwehr-Neuropsychosen. *Gesammelte Werke*, 1:379-403. London: Imago, 1952.

_____ (1896c), Heredity and the Aetiology of the Neuroses. *Standard Edition*, 3:143-156. London: Hogarth Press, 1962.

_____ (1896d), L'Hérédité et l'Étiologie des Névroses. *Gesammelte Werke*, 1:407-422. London: Imago, 1952.

_____ (1896e), The Aetiology of Hysteria. *Standard Edition*, 3:191-221. London: Hogarth Press, 1962.

_____ (1896f), Zur Ätiologie der Hysterie. *Gesammelte Werke*, 1:425-459. London: Imago, 1952.

_____ (1898), Sexuality in the Aetiology of the Neuroses. *Standard Edition*, 3:263-285. London: Hogarth Press, 1962.

_____ (1900), The Interpretation of Dreams. *Standard Edition*, 4 & 5. London: Hogarth Press, 1953.

_____ (1905a), Three Essays on the Theory of Sexuality. *Standard Edition*, 7:135-243. London: Hogarth Press, 1953.

_____ (1905b), Drei Abhandlungen zur Sexualtheorie. *Gesammelte Werke*, 5:29-145. London: Imago, 1942.

_____ (1905c), Fragment of an Analysis of a Case of Hysteria. *Standard Edition*, 7:7-122. London: Hogarth Press, 1953.

_____ (1905d), Jokes and Their Relation to the Unconscious. *Standard Edition*, 8. London: Hogarth Press, 1960.

_____ (1905e), Der Witz und seine Beziehung zum Unbewussten. *Gesammelte Werke*, 6. London: Imago, 1940.

_____ (1906), My Views on the Part Played by Sexuality in the Aetiology of the Neuroses. *Standard Edition*, 7:271-279. London: Hogarth Press, 1953.

_____ (1906-1923), *The Freud-Jung Letters: The Correspondence between Sigmund Freud and C. J. Jung*, ed. W. McGuire, trans. R. Manheim & R. Hull. Princeton: Princeton University Press, 1974.

_____ (1907a), Obsessive Actions and Religious Practices. *Standard Edition*, 9:117-127. London: Hogarth Press, 1959.

_____ (1907b), Zwangshandlungen und Religionsübungen. *Gesammelte Werke*, 7:129-139. London: Imago, 1941.

_____ (1907a-1926a), *A Psycho-Analytic Dialogue: The Letters of Sigmund Freud and Karl Abraham*, trans. B. Marsh & H. Abraham. New York: Basic Books, 1965.

_____ (1907b-1926b), *Sigmund Freud-Karl Abraham: Briefe*. Frankfurt: S. Fischer, 1965.

_____ (1908), On the Sexual Theories of Children. *Standard Edition*, 9:209-226. London: Hogarth Press, 1959.

_____ (1909a), Notes upon a Case of Obsessional Neurosis. *Standard Edition*, 10:155-318. London: Hogarth Press, 1955.

_____ (1909b), Analysis of a Phobia in a Five-Year-Old Boy. *Standard Edition*, 10:5-149. London: Hogarth Press, 1955.

_____ (1909-1938), *Psychoanalysis and Faith: The Letters of Sigmund Freud and Oskar Pfister*, ed. H. Meng & E. Freud, trans. E. Mosbacher. London: Hogarth Press, 1963.

_____ (1910), Leonardo da Vinci and a Memory of His Childhood. *Standard Edition*, 11:63-137. London: Hogarth Press, 1957.

_____ (1911a), Psycho-Analytic Notes on an Autobiographical Account of a Case of Paranoia (Dementia Paranoides). *Standard Edition*, 12:9-82. London: Hogarth Press, 1958.

_____ (1911b), Formulations on the Two Principles of Mental Functioning. *Standard Edition*, 12:218-226. London: Hogarth Press, 1958.

_____ (1912), Types of Onset of Neurosis. *Standard Edition*, 12:231-238. London: Hogarth Press, 1958.

_____ (1912a-1936a), *Sigmund Freud and Lou Andreas-Salomé Letters,* trans. W. & E. Robson-Scott. London: Hogarth Press, 1972.

_____ (1912b-1936b), *Sigmund Freud-Lou Andreas-Salomé: Briefwechsel.* Frankfurt: S. Fischer, 1966.

_____ (1913a), The Disposition to Obsessional Neurosis. *Standard Edition*, 12:317-326. London: Hogarth Press, 1958.

_____ (1913b), Totem and Taboo. *Standard Edition*, 13:1-161. London: Hogarth Press, 1953.

_____ (1913c), Totem und Tabu. *Gesammelte Werke*, 9. London: Imago, 1940.

_____ (1914a), On the History of the Psycho-Analytic Movement. *Standard Edition*, 14:7-66. London: Hogarth Press, 1957.

_____ (1914b), On Narcissism: An Introduction. *Standard Edition*, 14:73-102. London: Hogarth Press, 1957.

_____ (1915a), Instincts and Their Vicissitudes. *Standard Edition*, 14:117-140. London: Hogarth Press, 1957.

_____ (1915b), The Unconscious. *Standard Edition*, 14:166-204. London: Hogarth Press, 1957.

_____ (1915c), Thoughts for the Times on War and Death. *Standard Edition*, 14:275-300. London: Hogarth Press, 1957.

_____ (1916), On Transience. *Standard Edition*, 14:305-307. London: Hogarth Press, 1957.

_____ (1916-1917), Introductory Lectures on Psycho-Analysis. *Standard Edition*, 15 & 16. London: Hogarth Press, 1963.

_____ (1917), Mourning and Melancholia. *Standard Edition,* 14:243-258. London: Hogarth Press, 1957.

_____ (1918), From the History of an Infantile Neurosis. *Standard Edition*, 17:7-122. London: Hogarth Press, 1955.

_____ (1920), Beyond the Pleasure Principle. *Standard Edition*, 18:7-64. London: Hogarth Press, 1955.

_____ (1923a), The Ego and the Id. *Standard Edition*, 19:12-59. London: Hogarth Press, 1961.

_____ (1923b), Remarks on the Theory and Practice of Dream-Interpretation. *Standard Edition*, 19:109-121. London: Hogarth Press, 1961.

_____ (1924), The Economic Problem of Masochism. *Standard Edition*, 19:159-170. London: Hogarth Press, 1961.

_____ (1925a), Some Psychical Consequences of the Anatomical Distinction between the Sexes. *Standard Edition*, 19:248-258. London: Hogarth Press, 1961.

_____ (1925b), Some Additional Notes on Dream-Interpretation as a Whole. *Standard Edition*, 19:127-138. London: Hogarth Press, 1961.

_____ (1925c), An Autobiographical Study. *Standard Edition*, 20:7-74. London: Hogarth Press, 1959.

_____ (1926), Inhibitions, Symptoms and Anxiety. *Standard Edition*, 20:87-172. London: Hogarth Press, 1959.

_____ (1927), Humour. *Standard Edition*, 21:161-166. London: Hogarth Press, 1961.

_____ (1930), Civilization and Its Discontents. *Standard Edition*, 21:64-145. London: Hogarth Press, 1961.

_____ (1931), Female Sexuality. *Standard Edition*, 21:225-243. London: Hogarth Press, 1961.

_____ (1933a), New Introductory Lectures on Psycho-Analysis. *Standard Edition*, 22:5-182. London: Hogarth Press, 1964.

_____ (1933b), Why War? *Standard Edition*, 22:199-215. London: Hogarth Press, 1964.

_____ (1937), Analysis Terminable and Interminable. *Standard Edition*, 23:216-253. London: Hogarth Press, 1964.

_____ (1940), An Outline of Psycho-Analysis, *Standard Edition*, 23:144-207. London: Hogarth Press, 1964.

Fried, E. (1970), *Active/Passive: The Crucial Psychological Dimension*. New York & London: Grune & Stratton.

Fromm, E. (1959), *Sigmund Freud's Mission: An Analysis of His Personality and Influence*. New York: Harper.

_____ (1973), *The Anatomy of Human Destructiveness*. New York: Holt, Rinehart & Winston.

Fromm-Reichmann, F. (1950), *Principles of Intensive Psychotherapy*. Chicago: University of Chicago Press.

Graf, M. (1942), Reminiscences of Professor Sigmund Freud. *Psychoanal. Quart.*, 11:465-476.

Grinstein, A. (1968), *On Sigmund Freud's Dreams*. Detroit: Wayne State University Press.

Hale, N. (1971), *Freud and the Americans: The Beginnings of Psychoanalysis in the United States, 1876-1917*. New York: Oxford University Press.

Hartmann, H. (1948), Comments on the Psychoanalytic Theory of Instinctual Drives. *Psychoanal. Quart.*, 17:368-388.

———, Kris, E., & Loewenstein, R. (1949), Notes on the Theory of Aggression. *The Psychoanalytic Study of the Child*, 3/4:9-36. New York: International Universities Press.

Holt, R. (1965), A Review of Some of Freud's Biological Assumptions and Their Influence on His Theories. In: *Psychoanalysis and Current Biological Thought*, ed. N. S. Greenfield & W. C. Lewis. Madison: University of Wisconsin Press, pp. 93-124.

Horney, K. (1939), *New Ways in Psychoanalysis*. New York: Norton.

——— (1950), *Neurosis and Human Growth*. New York: Norton.

Jones, E. (1935), Psycho-Analysis and the Instincts. In: *Papers on Psycho-Analysis*. London: Ballière, Tindall & Cox, 1950, pp. 153-169.

——— (1953), *The Life and Work of Sigmund Freud*, Vol. 1. New York: Basic Books.

——— (1955), *The Life and Work of Sigmund Freud*, Vol. 2. New York: Basic Books.

——— (1957), *The Life and Work of Sigmund Freud*, Vol. 3. New York: Basic Books.

Jung, C. (1932), Sigmund Freud in His Historical Setting. In: *The Spirit in Man, Art, and Literature*, trans. R. F. C. Hull. Princeton: Princeton University Press, 1966, pp. 33-40.

——— (1961), *Memories, Dreams, Reflections*, trans. R. & C. Winston. New York: Vintage.

Kapp, R. (1931), Comments on Bernfeld and Feitelberg's "The Principle of Entropy and the Death Instinct." *Internat. J. Psycho-Anal.*, 12:82-86.

Karpman, B. (1950), Aggression, *Amer. J. Orthopsychiat.*, 20:694-719.

Kubie, L. (1939), A Critical Analysis of the Concept of a Repetition-Compulsion. *Internat. J. Psycho-Anal.*, 20:390-402.

Leavitt, H. (1956), A Biographical and Teleological Study of "Irma's Injection" Dream. *Psychoanal. Rev.*, 43:440-447.

Loewald, H. (1971), Some Considerations on Repetition and Repetition-Compulsion. *Internat. J. Psycho-Anal.*, 52:59-66.

Madison, P. (1961), *Freud's Concept of Repression and Defense, Its Theoretical and Observational Language*. Minneapolis: University of Minnesota Press.

Marcuse, H. (1955), *Eros and Civilization: A Philosophical Inquiry into Freud*. New York: Vintage.

Menninger, K. (1942), *Love Against Hate*. New York: Harcourt, Brace.

Miller, J., et al. (1969), Some Aspects of Charcot's Influence on Freud. *J. Amer. Psychoanal. Assn.*, 17:608-623.

Nunberg, H., & Federn, E., eds. & trans. (1962), *Minutes of the Vienna Psychoanalytic Society, Vol. I: 1906-1908*. New York: International Universities Press.

——— ———, eds. & trans. (1967), *Minutes of the Vienna Psychoanalytic Society, Vol. II: 1908-1910*. New York: International Universities Press.

——— ———, eds. (1974), *Minutes of the Vienna Psychoanalytic Society, Vol. III: 1910-1911*, trans. M. Nunberg. New York: International Universities Press

Penrose, L. (1931), Freud's Theory of Instinct and Other Psycho-Biological Theories. *Internat. J. Psycho-Anal.*, 12:87-97.
Pleune, F. (1961), Aggression and the Concept of Aim in Psycho-Analytic Drive Theory. *Internat. J. Psycho-Anal.*, 42:479-485.
Pratt, J. (1958), Epilegomena to the Study of Freudian Instinct Theory. *Internat. J. Psycho-Anal.*, 39:17-24.
Rado, S. (1933), Fear of Castration in Women. *Psychoanal. Quart.*, 2:425-475.
Rangell, L. (1972), Aggression, Oedipus, and Historical Perspective. *Internat. J. Psycho-Anal.*, 53:3-11.
Ricoeur, P. (1970), *Freud and Philosophy: An Essay on Interpretation*, trans. D. Savage. New Haven & London: Yale University Press.
Rieff, P. (1961), *Freud: The Mind of the Moralist*. New York: Anchor Books.
Roazen, P. (1968), *Freud: Political and Social Thought*. New York: Vintage.
_____ (1969), *Brother Animal: The Story of Freud and Tausk*. New York: Vintage.
Rochlin, G. (1973), *Man's Aggression: The Defense of the Self*. Boston: Gambit.
Ruitenbeck, H. (1966), *Freud in America*. New York: Macmillan.
Sadow, L., et al. (1968), The Process of Hypothesis Change in Three Early Psychoanalytic Concepts. *J. Amer. Psychoanal. Assn.*, 16:245-273.
Schlessinger, N., et al. (1967), The Scientific Style of Breuer and Freud in the Origins of Psychoanalysis. *J. Amer. Psychoanal. Assn.*, 15:404-422.
Schorske, C. (1961), Politics and Psyche in fin de siècle Vienna: Schnitzler and Hofmannsthal. *American Historical Review*, 66:930-946.
_____ (1973), Politics and Patricide in Freud's Interpretation of Dreams. *American Historical Review*, 78:328-347.
Schur, M. (1960), Phylogenesis and Ontogenesis of Affect- and Structural-Formation and the Phenomenon of Repetition-Compulsion. *Internat. J. Psycho-Anal.*, 41:275-287.
_____ (1966), Some Additional "Day Residues" of "The Specimen Dream of Psychoanalysis." In: *Psychoanalysis—A General Psychology*, ed. R. Loewenstein et al. New York: International Universities Press, pp. 45-85.
_____ (1972), *Freud: Living and Dying*. New York: International Universities Press.
Stepansky, P. (1976), The Empiricist as Rebel: Jung, Freud, and the Burdens of Discipleship. *J. Hist. Behav. Sci.*, 12:216-239.
Stewart, W. (1967), *Psychoanalysis: The First Ten Years*. New York: Macmillan.
Sullivan, H. (1953), *The Interpersonal Theory of Psychiatry*. New York: Norton.
Szasz, T. (1952), On the Psychoanalytic Theory of Instincts. *Psychoanal. Quart.*, 21:25-48.
_____ (1961), *The Myth of Mental Illness*. New York: Dell.
Thompson, C. (1950), *Psychoanalysis: Evolution and Development*. New York: Grove Press.
Toman, W. (1956), Repetition and Repetition-Compulsion. *Internat. J. Psycho-Anal.*, 37:347-350.
Waelder, R. (1956), Critical Discussion of the Concept of an Instinct of Destruction. *Bull. Phila. Assn. Psychoanal.*, 6:97-109.
_____ (1963), Historical Fiction. *J. Amer. Psychoanal. Assn.*, 11:628-651.
Wittels, F. (1924), *Sigmund Freud: His Personality, His Teaching, and His School*, trans. E. & C. Paul. New York: Dodd, Mead.
_____ (1933), Revision of a Biography. *Psychoanal. Rev.*, 20:361-374.

INDEX

197

ABOUT THE AUTHORS

ROY SCHAFER, PH.D., a training and supervising psychoanalyst, rose to the rank of Clinical Professor of Psychology in Psychiatry at Yale University, where he taught from 1953 to 1975. In 1975 he was appointed the first Sigmund Freud Memorial Visiting Professor, University College London. Since 1976 he has been Professor of Psychology in Psychiatry, Cornell University Medical College, New York, N.Y. In addition to numerous articles, he has published *The Clinical Application of Psychological Tests, Psychoanalytic Interpretation in Rorschach Testing, Projective Testing in Psychoanalysis, Aspects of Internalization,* and *A New Language for Psychoanalysis.*

PAUL E. STEPANSKY received his M.A. and M.Phil. in history from Yale University (1975, 1976), where he is at present writing a doctoral dissertation on the thought of Alfred Adler. In 1976, following the establishment of Yale's Kanzer Fund for Psychoanalytic Studies in the Humanities by Dr. Mark Kanzer, he was named one of the first Kanzer Fellows.

PSYCHOLOGICAL ISSUES